Globalization of Economies and Globalization of Cultures:

Thinking and Proof-seeking from History

经济全球化与文化全球化

——历史的思考与求证

Wang Shuzu / 王述祖 著
Gu Ming / 顾明 译

南开大学出版社

天 津

图书在版编目(CIP)数据

经济全球化与文化全球化：历史的思考与求证：英文 / 王述祖著；顾明译. —天津：南开大学出版社，2019.4
 ISBN 978-7-310-05772-6

Ⅰ. ①经… Ⅱ. ①王… ②顾… Ⅲ. ①经济全球化—研究—英文②文化—全球化—研究—英文 Ⅳ. ①F114.41②G112

中国版本图书馆 CIP 数据核字(2019)第 053567 号

版权所有　侵权必究

南开大学出版社出版发行
出版人：刘运峰
地址：天津市南开区卫津路 94 号　邮政编码：300071
营销部电话：(022)23508339　23500755
营销部传真：(022)23508542　邮购部电话：(022)23502200

*

北京建宏印刷有限公司印刷
全国各地新华书店经销

*

2019 年 4 月第 1 版　2019 年 4 月第 1 次印刷
230×170 毫米　16 开本　17.75 印张　3 插页　311 千字
定价：66.00 元

如遇图书印装质量问题，请与本社营销部联系调换，电话：(022)23507125

作者近照

全球化與全球化文化全球化經

丁述祖書

作者手迹

作者简介

王述祖，男，1942 年 11 月生，汉族，天津市人。天津建筑工程业余大学工业与民用建筑专业毕业，在职大专学历，高级工程师；1978 年 10 月加入中国共产党，1961 年 9 月参加工作。历任天津市二建公司车间副主任、技术科副科长、工区主任、副经理、经理，天津经济技术开发区筹备组成员。1985 年至 1988 年，先后任天津经济技术开发区总公司副总经理、开发区管委会副主任。1988 年任天津市外经贸委、市政府外事办公室副主任，市外商投资服务中心主任。1993 年 4 月任天津市外经贸委主任、市委外经外事工委（市委外经贸工委）副书记。1998 年 5 月至 2003 年 1 月，任天津市副市长。2003 年 1 月至 2008 年 1 月，任天津市第十四届人大常委会副主任。1986 年天津市劳动模范；1987 年全国外经贸系统劳动模范。

Mr. Wang Shuzu was born in November, 1942 and is a native of Tianjin. He is a senior engineer and obtained his associate degree from Civil Construction Program at Tianjin Construction Engineering Part-time College. He joined the Communist Party of China in October, 1978. He was first employed in September, 1969 and held positions successively as Deputy Workshop Director, Deputy Chief at Technical Section, Work District Chief, Vice President, and President at Tianjin No. 2 Construction Corporation, and Member of Tianjin Economic and Technological Development Area (TEDA) Preparation Group. From 1985 to 1988, he was Deputy General Manager of TEDA General Corporation, and Vice Chairman of TEDA Administrative Committee. In 1988, he held the position of Vice Chairman of Tianjin Municipal Commission of Foreign Economic Relations and Trade and Tianjin Municipal People's Government Foreign Affairs Office, and Chairman of Tianjin Municipal Foreign Investment Service Center. In April, 1993, he was appointed Chairman of Tianjin Municipal Commission of Foreign Economic Relations and Trade, and Deputy Party Secretary of Tianjin CPC Committee Foreign Economic Relations and Trade and Foreign Affairs Working Committee. From May, 1998 to January, 2003, he was Vice Mayor of Tianjin. From January, 2003 to January, 2008, he was Vice Chairman of the Standing Committee of the 14th Tianjin Municipal People's Congress. Mr. Wang was a Model Worker of Tianjin in 1986 and a Model Worker in China's national foreign economic relations and trade industry in 1987.

译者简介

顾明，天津市人。美国法律博士，美国工商管理学硕士。曾在国内任英语教师和经济师。现为美国执业律师。主要译著有《1900年：西方人的叙述——义和团运动亲历者的书信、日记和照片》（［美］弗雷德里克·A.沙夫和［英］彼德·哈林顿编著，天津人民出版社2010年1月出版）和《法律写作简明指南》（［美］凯蒂·罗丝·格斯特·普瑞尔著，北京联合出版公司2018年7月出版）。作为义和团历史研究学者，他曾接受凤凰卫视采访，并在由凤凰大视野制作、2011年5月23日首播的10集纪录片《国难1900：义和团事件始末》中播出。

Mr. Gu Ming is a native of Tianjin. He obtained his Master of Business Administration and Juris Doctor degree from the United States and has been an attorney at law in the US since 2002. Mr. Gu was an English language teacher and economist in China. He translated from English into Chinese and researched on and annotated *China 1900: The Eyewitnesses Speak: The Experience of Westerners in China* by Frederic Sharf and Peter Harrington, and published his translation by Tianjin People's Publishing House, Tianjin, China, in January, 2010. Moreover, he translated from English into Chinese *A Short Guide to Writing about Law* by Katie Rose Guest Pryal, and published his translation by Beijing United Publishing Co., Ltd., Beijing, China, in July, 2018. Furthermore, as a result of his translation and annotation/research in *China 1900: The Eyewitnesses Speak: The Experience of Westerners in China*, he was invited for a three-hour-long interview in Beijing by Mr. Tian Chuan on the history of the Boxer Rebellion, and his interview was featured in eight episodes of a 10-episode documentary on the Boxer Rebellion produced by Phoenix Satellite Television Holdings Ltd. or Phoenix Television. This documentary,

Phoenix Television Panoramic Eyeshot of Phoenix: *China's National Crisis 1900, The History of the Boxer Rebellion*, was aired nationally in China by China Central Television Station, Beijing, China since May 23, 2011.

译者的话

在本书英文版即将出版之际，作为译者，我想谈一下我对该书中文版的一些想法。

本书虽然出版于2006年6月，但对于当今世界的形势和我国与世界其他国家的经济和文化交往仍有借鉴和启示。作为历史和经济学科的爱好者，我认为本书选题精准且极具前瞻性。这源于作者长期从事对外经济和文化交流工作，能够充分和透彻理解国内外形势，并以此为依据客观预测经济和文化事务的发展趋势。

20世纪90年代中期，我曾在天津经济技术开发区从事招商引资工作，了解并亲身参与了几家著名跨国公司在天津市内和天津经济技术开发区进行的前期考察、谈判、投资设厂以及后期运营和管理的具体工作。而且，我也是国家40年改革开放事业取得巨大成就的亲历者和受益者。再者，90年代后期来美国求学和工作的经历让我有机会直接而深入地了解和体验了西方国家经济和文化的实质。

习近平主席曾讲过："中华民族具有5000多年连绵不断的文明历史，创造了博大精深的中华文化，为人类文明作出了不可磨灭的贡献。""独特的文化传统，独特的历史使命，独特的国情，注定了中国必然走适合自己特点的发展道路。我们走出了这样一条道路，并且取得了成功。""中华民族是一个兼容并蓄、海纳百川的民族，在漫长的历史进程中，不断学习他人的好东西，把他人的好东西化成自己的东西，这才形成了我们的民族特色。"

中国的自信，本质上是文化自信。文化自信，是继道路自信、制度自信、理论自信之后，中国极为重视的第四个自信。

林毅夫先生曾说："几十年的实践证明，发展中国家尚无依靠'西天取经'实现现代化成功的先例，用西方国家的理论也不能解释中国改革开放以来所创造的经济奇迹。"

一个民族的复兴需要强大的物质力量，也需要强大的精神力量。文化是民族生存和发展的重要力量。习近平主席曾说过："实现中国梦，是物质文明和精神文明比翼双飞的发展过程。"

清代龚自珍《定庵续集》里说："欲知大道，必先为史。灭人之国，必先去其史。"了解历史，就了解了世间大道；把握史学，才把握住社会规律。而要一个民族灭亡，首要方法是让它的史观消亡——践踏民族历史，解构民族文化，涤荡民族自信，破坏民族认同。

现今的世界并非一个祥和的世界，而是一个各国经济和文化相互挑战、碰撞并相互融合的世界，这一过程有时会是异常激烈和残酷的。所幸我生在了一个具有悠久历史和优良文化传统而又和平且强大的国家。

我的中国，我祝你不断走向富强；我的同胞，我愿你心中充满对祖国文化和经济的自信。

顾明

2018 年 12 月 26 日

Translator's Note

At the time when my English translation of this book is on its way to the printers, as the translator, I would like to share my thoughts on the Chinese version of this book as follows.

Although this book was first published in June, 2006, it still holds its place as a good book on drawing lessons and enlightenment in the subject of today's world situation and China's economic and cultural exchanges with other nations. As an amateur of history and economics, I believe that this book has an excellent and precise choice of topic and is quite forward-looking. This is no surprise because the author has been long engaging in foreign economic relations and cultural exchanges between China and other nations. This book also reflects his comprehensive and thorough understanding of Chinese and overseas situations and his objective prediction based on the development trends in economy and culture.

In the mid-1990s, I worked in Tianjin Economic and Technological Development Area (TEDA) to invite and promote overseas investment in Tianjin. In this capacity, I was able to understand and get personally involved in the feasibility study, negotiations, investment in and construction of manufacturing facilities as well as operations and management of several world-famous multinational corporations in Tianjin city proper and/or TEDA. Moreover, I am a witness and beneficiary of China's reform and opening up for the past four decades. Furthermore, my studies and employment in the United States since the late 1990s have allowed me to understand and experience the substance of economy and culture in the Western world first hand and in a relatively in-depth manner.

Mr. Xi Jinping, President of China, said, "The Chinese nation enjoys a continuous civilization history of more than 5,000 years. It has created the Chinese culture of extensive knowledge and profound scholarship and made an indelible contribution to the civilization of mankind." "China's unique cultural heritage, China's unique historical mission and China's unique basic conditions have predestinated that China must embark upon a developmental path that suits China's own characteristics. We have blazed such a path and achieved our success." "The Chinese nation is one that is fully inclusive and equitable and embraces various schools of thoughts. In its long historical development, it has continuously learned good things from others and assimilated those good things into its own to form our national characters."

China's self-confidence, in essence, is the confidence in its culture. Self-confidence in culture is the fourth self-confidence that China emphasizes in addition to China's self-confidence in its chosen developmental path, political system, and guiding theories.

Mr. Lin Yifu said, "Practice of several decades has proven that developing nations have not yet created a precedent by exclusively relying on 'copying from the Western world's model' to achieve their own success of modernization. Theories in the Western world also fail to explain why China has accomplished its economic miracle since its reform and opening up."

Rejuvenation of a nation requires not only powerful material strength but also strong mental power. Culture is an important force in a nation's survival and development. President Xi Jinping said, "The realization of the China Dream is a hand-in-hand development process of both material progress and cultural and ideological progress."

Mr. Gong Zizhen, a scholar in the Qing Dynasty, stated in his *Ding'an Supplemental Collection* that "If one needs to understand the great universal way, one must understand the history first. If one needs to destroy a nation, one must eliminate the nation's history first." Once history is understood, the great universal way is comprehended. Once you have a firm grasp of history, you have mastered the social laws. In order to destroy a nation, the primary method is to make its historical viewpoints disappear, namely, stamp out its national history, decompose its national culture, wipe out its national self-confidence and erase its national recognition.

The world nowadays is not a peaceful one. Instead it is a world where economies and cultures of various nations are challenging, colliding with and integrating with one another. At times, this process can be extremely intense and cruel. Fortunately, I was born in China that enjoys a long history and profound cultural heritage and my motherland is a peace-loving and strong nation.

My dear motherland, I hope you will become increasingly rich and powerful. My country fellows, I hope you will become increasingly self-confident in our own culture and economy.

Gu Ming
December 26, 2018

Preface

From a historical perspective, globalization of cultures is not a subject that requires special proof-seeking because the development, imparting and inheriting of world cultures have been promoted on the basis of its continuance in being globalized, appreciated and accepted together by the human being. Without such a globalization of cultures, there is no continued enrichment of world civilization, to say nothing of a cumulative brilliant civilization. This civilization includes both material civilization and spiritual civilization.

However, things will be more complex if we connect globalization of cultures with globalization of economies. Economies are always associated with effective distribution of resources and gaining maximum benefits. This is especially true when the economic benefits among nations have differences and conflicts and globalization of cultures puts the nations on guard and causes some concerns about conflicts over economic benefits. When globalization of cultures influences the changes of economic systems and even the adjustments of political systems, such globalization is a matter that requires a conditional selection.

It is somewhat challenging for intellectuals to clearly understand the relationship between globalization of economies and globalization of cultures. The reason is that the complexity of such relationship does not result from cultures themselves; instead, it is closely related to the differences in economic benefits or economic benefits among nations. As a result, economists can only make a correct judgment of the pros and cons of globalization of cultures on the basis of weighing the economic benefits. Fortunately, globalization of cultures is beneficial to both the distributor and the recipient. The key to such benefits is that globalization or integration of cultures is helpful to the economic development and the realization and promotion of economic benefits to the participants. Meanwhile, when we seek proof of such a question, this is by no means a theoretical reasoning, instead it is more of a verification in history because human civilization development and evolution is a process of changes in thinking and recognition in concepts while material civilization is being accepted. On such a basis, technologies, systems and methods of economic operation are introduced to realize constant material civilization. This is exactly what Mr. Wang Shuzu has been trying to pursue, an analysis of such an integration between history and logics.

Moreover, this book puts a special emphasis on history and reality, namely, using history in the mutual promotion between globalization of economies and globalization of cultures in the world to prove that "closing the country to the rest of the world" is denial of globalization of cultures including advanced manufacturing techniques and advanced economic operation systems with the result that the economy at issue is deteriorating and the country is being attacked. Since China has been implementing reform and opening up its door to the outside world, we have accepted globalization of economies out of the perspective of pursuing speedy development of our economy, advancing our economic progress and improving the living standards of our people. However, the question is whether we can withstand the impact or integration of globalization of cultures. All this makes the research inside this book more appealing both in scholarship and practice.

Of course, our acceptance of globalization of cultures is by no means a denial of our Chinese domestic characteristics. The world is always a diverse one. The greatness of Chinese culture relies on the fact that it has the capability and potential of integrating inside its cultures; what is more important is that it can unite with other cultures and enhance its own cultures and promote Chinese economy while inheriting the Chinese traditional culture. The speedy development and rise of China's economy makes it possible for the advantages of Chinese culture constantly reveal itself to form an important part of world cultures that draws the attention of other nations. As far as I can see, the Chinese people will definitely enjoy greater development of both material civilization and spiritual civilization as we are actively embracing globalization of economies and at the same time rationally welcoming globalization of cultures.

Wu Chengming
March 5, 2006

Table of Contents

Chapter One   Introduction ··· 1
   Section One   A Summary of Globalization of Economies and
                Globalization of Cultures ··································· 1
   Section Two   China's Opening up to the Outside World and Impact of
                Outside Cultures ·· 14
   Section Three   Various Subjects of Globalization of Cultures ················ 24
**Chapter Two   Formation of Globalization of Cultures and Its Influence
             on Economies** ·· 31
   Section One   Globalization of Economies Goes Hand in Hand with
               Globalization of Cultures ··································· 31
   Section Two   Influence of Globalization of Cultures on the Economy
               of a Nation ··· 34
   Section Three   Influence of Globalization of Cultures on Globalization
                of Economies ··· 45
Chapter Three   The Renaissance and the Rise of Modern Europe ············ 51
   Section One   The Renaissance and the Technological Advances
               in Europe ··· 51
   Section Two   The Renaissance and European Economy ······················ 59
   Section Three   The Renaissance and Globalization of Economies ············ 71
   Section Four   The Renaissance and Globalization of Cultures ················ 77
**Chapter Four   Globalization of Cultures and Industrialization
             in Modern Japan** ·· 86
   Section One   Meiji Restoration in Japan and Outside Culture ················ 87
   Section Two   Meiji Restoration and Industrialization in Japan ·············· 101
   Section Three   Globalization of Cultures and Rise of Japan ················ 125

Chapter Five　Globalization of Cultures and Opening up to the Outside World in Modern China ·· 133
　　Section One　China's Traditional Society and Its Closed Culture ············ 133
　　Section Two　Outside Impact on Modern China ································ 146
　　Section Three　Slow Development of Industrialization in Modern China ··· 171
　　Section Four　Ideology of Political Independence and Economic
　　　　　　　　　Self-reliance ·· 186
**Chapter Six　Globalization of Cultures Moving toward Globalization
　　　　　　　of Economies** ·· 194
　　Section One　Influence of Cultural Dissemination and Globalization
　　　　　　　　　of Cultures on China ·· 194
　　Section Two　Empirical Analysis of Reform and Opening up to the
　　　　　　　　　Outside World and Influence of Globalization of Cultures ···· 208
　　Section Three　Relationship between Chinese Culture and Globalization
　　　　　　　　　of Cultures ·· 234
Conclusion ·· 251
References ·· 254

Chapter One   Introduction

Globalization of economies has drawn more and more attention in the world since the 1980s. However, globalization of cultures which goes hand in hand with globalization of economies has received much less attention. Cultures, as reflection of economies, have exerted an important influence on economies. From this perspective, study of globalization of cultures is important both in theory and practice. This is especially true for a developing country like China that is in its transforming stage and with a history as long as five thousand years.

Section One   A Summary of Globalization of Economies and Globalization of Cultures

Since the 1980s globalization of economies has been recognized by more and more international organizations, governments of various nations, academia and the common people. However, a lot of disputes exist in globalization of cultures that coexists with globalization of economies. Whether you agree with it or not, globalization of cultures has its influence felt in various aspects in real life. Therefore, it is necessary to make a basic analysis of globalization of economies and globalization of cultures.

I. Definition and form of globalization of economies

Since the 1980s globalization has received increasing attention of the world. Discussions of this subject appear frequently in newspapers, journals and other media. Scholars and international organizations have various opinions on this subject.

According to historical research, economies of a global nature started in Europe.

Jacques Ada, a French scholar, pointed out that "We may say that globalization is a continuation of an event that started in the Mediterranean Sea nearly 1,000 years ago and achieved a decisive development with the Great Geographical Discovery during the 15th and 16th centuries".[①] Formation of the world market in the 1870s is an indication of formation of the world economy. After the Second World War, internationalization of capital and manufacturing enjoyed a rapid development and achieved an astonishing scale by the 1980s. Some scholars began to use the concept of globalization of economies to describe the world economy that was characterized with internationalization of capital and manufacturing.

Exactly owing to the rapid development of internationalization of capital and manufacturing after the Second World War, international organizations emphasized the degree and scope of interdependence of the economies of nations in the definition of globalization of economies. In the late 1980s the European Parliament called several nations to form the Lisbon Group to concentrate on discussions of globalization subject. This group published *The Limit of Competition: Globalization of Economies and Future of the Human Being* in 1995. They thought the core meaning of globalization of economies was the inter-influencing among nations and regions in the world. Meanwhile, this inter-influencing had to reach a degree, namely, such inter-influencing had to occur among a great majority of nations and regions in the world instead of only a few nations and regions. In addition, this inter-influencing had to reach such a broad scope as to fundamentally constrain and influence economies and social development among the nations.[②] IMF's definition of globalization of economies is more representative: "globalization is increase in interdependence of world economy as a result of increase in the scope and form of transnational commodities and services exchange, and international capital as well as the wide distribution of technologies."

In accordance with the differences in transnational economic practices, forms of globalization of economies can be divided into the following: globalization of manufacturing, trade, investment, finance, technologies and information, and human

---

[①] Jacques Ada. *Economic Globalization*. Beijing: Central Compilation and Translation Press, 2000: 74.

[②] Lei Da, Yu Chunhai. *Into Globalization of Economies*. Beijing: China Financial and Economic Publishing House, 2001: 4-5.

resources. Globalization of manufacturing, investment, finance, technologies and information, and human resources is the optimal distribution of various essential production factors directly over the globe. Globalization of trade indirectly achieves optimal distribution of resources by moving commodities and services internationally. Globalization of market rules and integration of transnational systems and policy coordination provide a favorable environment for globalization of economies in the sense of transnational economic practices so as to achieve the optimal distribution of resources in the world. Therefore, Dr. Sylvia Ostry, former Chief Economist of OECD, thought that globalization of economies primarily meant the process of extensive movement of essential production factors globally to achieve optimal distribution of resources.[①]

The fundamental driving force for globalization of economies is scientific and technological advancement and improvement of productivity, especially the development of information technology and the establishment of the Internet that provide a broader horizon for globalization of economies. On this basis, manufacturing, distribution, exchange, consumption and market economy, with their intrinsic law, extensively cross national borders and distribute globally, thus connecting nations' economies in an increasingly connected manner. According to UNCTAD statistics, in 2003, the world export amount (USD 7,443.692 billion) and world FDI inflow stock (USD 8,245.074 billion) accounted for 20.55% and 22.93% of the world GDP respectively. For developing countries, these two indicators accounted for 33.42% and 32.42%, respectively. From the perspective of productivity category, globalization of economies is a process of continued expansion and deepening of both material civilization and spiritual civilization collectively created by the human being and modernization achievements under global space, which is an objective law and an inexorable trend that is independent of man's will, thus without doubt putting an increasingly important influence on nations' economies, politics and even cultures.

[①] Liu Li, Zhang Zhang. *Globalization of Economies: Good Fortune or Disaster?*. Beijing: China Society Press, 1999: 1.

II. Connotation of Globalization of Cultures

Understanding of "globalization of cultures" has several different views. One view is that globalization of cultures refers to one common or individual cultural formation; another view is that it is a process that both homogenization and heterogenization are in progress at the same time; and still another view is to deny the existence of globalization of cultures, for instance, Samuel P. Huntington's well-known "The Clash of Civilizations" that said the world history's development would strengthen the differences and conflicts between various civilizations. The reason that differences occurred in views on globalization of cultures is primarily twofold: One is the understanding of "globalization" and the other is the definition of "culture". In order to understand the connotation of globalization of cultures, the connotation of "culture" needs to be defined first.

Anthropologists have more than 160 definitions of culture. In summary, culture "in a broad sense means the sum of the material and spiritual production capability gained and the material and spiritual property created from the experiments of human society. In a narrow sense, it means the spiritual production capability and the spiritual products including all the natural science, technology science and social consciousness shapes in the form of social consciousness".[①] The broad sense definition of culture covers all the fields of social life and all of human being's social activities, all the activities that human beings do to the nature and human society conscientiously all belong to the categories of culture, human beings reform themselves while reforming the nature, and this process of reforming and being reformed forms the culture's connotation during the same period. The narrow sense definition of culture includes: (1) intellectual culture, i.e., science and technology, education, knowledge, languages and so on; (2) arts culture, i.e., literature, movie, fine arts, music and so on; and (3) social culture, also called as basic culture, is composed of normative culture and ideology culture. Normative culture can then be divided into restrictive and non-restrictive normative culture. The former covers social organizations, political systems, legal forms and so on. The latter covers

---

[①] Xia Zhengnong. *Cihai*. Shanghai: Shanghai Dictionaries Publishing House, 2002: 1765.

ethics and so on. Ideology culture is also known as core culture which centrally reflects people's ideology, belief and values and is an ideological culture. The culture that affects people's behaviors is primarily social culture, especially ideology culture. Normative culture is connected with ideology and is a system culture that changes with changes in the economic foundation and it needs to be coordinated with the economic and political development. Ideology culture is the basic idiosyncrasy that distinguishes different cultures and a matter that exists in various cultural groups to reflect different cultural characteristics and is a mode of thinking and behaviors to show value orientation. This characteristic in common of ideology cultures makes it analyzed as an economic capital, "social capital" in the discussions on cultures and development questions in the 1980s and 1990s. Normative culture acts as a safeguard in the cultural changes. But ideology culture, as the core culture, has relative stability and it will react actively to the impacts by the outside cultures.

When culture parallels with economy and politics as a definition, it obviously refers to the non-restrictive culture and ideology culture in the narrow sense of culture. This is because intellectual culture is one of the economic production's input factors, and arts culture is an important component in the economic output. Restrictive norms are the environment that supports economy and political activities and can be categorized into economy and politics. Despite this, owing to the differences in research emphases, scholars' definitions have different preferences and representations. However, most scholars have included ideology culture into the definition of culture. For instance, Francis Fukuyama thinks that culture refers to unofficial and common values, codes of behaviors, connotation and behaviors that represent human society's characteristics. Mark Casson (2003) defines culture as common values, beliefs and their representations that are related to the fundamental questions. Rene M. Stulz and Rohan Williamson define culture as the belief system that forms individual behaviors in the society. In addition, Douglass North's so-called key factor in economic growth and development, "institution", refers to the normative system that standardizes people's behaviors and is composed of the state official restraint, the socially recognized unofficial restraint and the corresponding implementation mechanism. The core of the unofficial restraint in it is ideology factor.

As a result, the culture in the globalization of cultures we need to discuss is the non-restrictive and normative culture and ideology culture, and the psychological quality, mode of thinking, aesthetic consciousness and ethics of the reactions that are gradually internalized in response to the outside world.

We know from the IMF's definition of globalization that globalization of economies mainly refers to a situation that products and production factors break through national territorial barriers to flow to other countries in the world and the expansion of such flows. Correspondingly, globalization of cultures should be defined at least as follows: the process of cultures of various peoples constantly breaking through limitations on their respective territorial boundaries and the modes and expanding to the other parts of the world. The academic circles have little differences on this definition of globalization of cultures.

Just as the increased interdependence of the world economy leading to the cross-country flow of commodities, services and capital and the extensive distribution of technology is the meaning of globalization of economies, to what extent of the influence to the world cultural structure and cultures of various peoples constantly breaking through limitations on their respective territorial boundaries and the modes and expanding to the other parts of the world should also be a necessary component of the meaning of globalization of cultures. The differences in the emphases and views of this outcome are exactly what the academic circles bitterly disagree as to the understanding of globalization of cultures. The disagreement centers on: do the cultures of various peoples expanding in the world cause the world cultures to tend to be identical or the diversity of the world cultures will be maintained?

From the development process of cultures of various peoples, there are contradictions and conflicts among different cultures, but there are also integration and complementation. This is an important rule of the cultural development of various peoples. Between them, the latter has always been the mainstream in the world cultural development. Prior to globalization of economies, interactions and exchanges among different peoples' cultures were both limited and slow. With globalization of economies, especially information network that provides material conditions for such exchanges, the width and depth of various peoples' cultures expanding in the world increased and their exchanges were quicker. This intensifies the degree of contradictions and conflicts, integration and complementation among different cultures. As a result, the outcome of various peoples' cultures expanding in the world can be analyzed from the property that caused such conflicts and integration.

First of all, cultures have the global property (or called common character). The global property of cultures shows human being's surpassing of the nature, which is personal, and is a matter that is deposited from the vicissitudes of history and that is relatively stable, and it is the culture's significance and value. Although cultures of various peoples are all rooted in their soil and possess the time and space condition and scope that they rely on for their survival, they all have their own individuality. However, individuality of national cultures has only relative significance. No matter how unique the national cultures are, they are all generalization and summary of people's practice modes, survival modes, behavior modes and modes of thinking, which in a certain sense reflect the common character of people's practices. As a result, the individualities of national cultures must have their common character. Then, the essence of genuine national cultures must contain the global elements. This is the so-called "national character is also global". The presence of common character in the national cultures is exactly the foundation of national cultures expanding and being recognized in the world.

Through extensive exchanges, mutual penetration and complementation and mutual blending, cultures of various peoples have surpassed the original territories of national cultures and are recognized culturally in the course of evaluation and judgment by the cultural values of other peoples and accepting or rejecting, and then the cultural ingredients of the common character in the cultures of various peoples are being constantly transformed to global cultural ingredients.[①] For instance, human

---

[①] The reason that "global cultural ingredients" is used instead of "global culture" is that these global cultural ingredients cannot constitute a culture system by themselves, and they are contained in the cultures of various peoples. After all, cultures are of the people. Before the world forms one unity, global culture cannot be formed. Moreover, it needs to surpass cultures' diversity to form some kind of global ideology, but it cannot escape from the outside boundary of the various diversity of the culture tradition, it can only seek some kind of "overlapped consensus" among the cultural tradition with diversity, namely, the global cultural ingredients. This "overlapped consensus" can only be in some degree and cannot be complete.

beings' recollections on some major issues in today's world which threaten their survival and development, which decide their fate, and which can only be solved relying on all human beings' concerted efforts so as to promote the formation of human beings' values; recommendation and advocacy of civilized, healthy and scientific ways of life so as to promote reforms and improvement in ways of life; and recognition of the significance of being integrated into globalization of economies so as to promote conscientious following by different countries norms and customs of cross-country economies and accepting the corresponding cultures. For example, the cross-country economic system formed a set of homogeneous operation rules in the global arena so as to gradually affect people's mode of thinking and value orientation and to form the so-called "modern enterprising spirit". With the global development, the most obvious global cultural ingredients are such universal ideas as liberty, democracy, equality, rule of law, science and technology, contract, and free market and so on. These ideas are being accepted by most countries in the world. The global cultural interaction then accelerates this process. We can see that national cultures expanding to the world makes the global ingredients in the national cultures transform to global cultural ingredients.

In addition, cultures also have national characters (or called individualities). Culture's national character refers to the very local contents formed on the basis of the difference in geographical environment, mode of experiment, cognitive form, and affective experience and so on, which are indications of some people's survival and development and some people and its culture's root of growth. This is because any national culture is the result of people's blending and creation of their natural condition and social condition in the course of their survival and development process. Once it is formed and established, it will form their common values, ideology and belief, code of behaviors and mode of activities that are different from other peoples', which hold together their survival and development. A famous British historian Arnold Joseph Toynbee believes that every people's culture is their response to the challenges caused by their growth environment.[①] Owing to the differences in various peoples' specific survival and development conditions

---

[①] Refer to Arnold Joseph Toynbee. *A Study of History I*. Shanghai: Shanghai People's Publishing House, 1997: 304.

(including natural condition, economical condition and political condition and so on), the cultures formed have their individualities that are different from others, and in turn the diversity in the world cultures is shown. National cultures are long deposited and have super stable ingredients. Their development shows a stable and prudent trend. Because of this feature, individualities of national cultures and the super stable property have caused contradictions and conflicts with other national cultures in their course of expanding in the world.

Finally, culture's global property and national property are symbiotic and interdependent. Elevation and expansion in the culture's global property are conditional on the individual and national culture's development. It exists in the culture's national property. Without the carrier of individuality and national property, the culture's global property will not exist. Meanwhile, national cultures contain the common property of human beings' survival and development. Objectively, it will definitely provide references to development of other national cultures. Moreover, cultures of various peoples are not a system that is self-isolated and unable to exchange and communicate with the outside world. Instead they are able to keep improving and developing themselves in their exchanges with other peoples. National cultures cannot be improved without human beings' common property and without timely drawing and referencing from the advanced ingredients of other national cultures.

The course of various national cultures marching to the world provides a cultural mode of constantly improving their own cultures and an opportunity of new blending. This improvement and blending make the national cultures in the new cultural experiments elevate their nationality and present their global property. With the direct and frequent cultural exchanges as a result of the globalization of economies, people's ways of life and values will undergo subconsciously more or less changes. These changes are based on the deposits of the national cultures. Then some ingredients in the foreign culture and the home culture will gradually be blended so as to make the home culture optimize and develop based on the absorption of the quintessence of the foreign culture. In the 1990s, France 2 and *Le Figaro* conducted an opinion poll. Those who were polled came from all walks of life. One of the questions was to provide a list of values and the pollees were asked to complete three beliefs that they treasured most. The result was freedom 58%, tolerance 48%, work 45%, mutual assistance 40%, and equality 35%. Among the slogan of "freedom, equality and fraternity" that the French people had advocated for 200 years, equality and fraternity devalued substantially and tolerance rose to the second place in these values.[①]

The process of the national cultures' absorption and blending of some ingredients from the foreign cultures is localization of the foreign cultures. After the national cultures' optimization as a result of confrontation and blending with the advanced factors in the foreign cultures, a complete set of cognizance system that is rooted in their own history of traditions, habits, ways of life, symbols and values again earns its homage. This phenomenon is the so-called localization of the national cultures. Localization of the national cultures also enhances the diversity of the world cultures. As a result, localization of the foreign cultures and the national cultures is the inevitable outcome of the national cultures marching to the world.

Under the grand background of globalization of economies and globalization of cultures, localization of cultures has its inevitability. First, the national cultures, after history's panning and depositing, formed an interconnected organic system. This system cannot be broken and smashed within a short period of time, and especially the core component in the cultures has relative stability. Moreover, in the course of mutual actions between economy and culture, evolution of cultures is a progressional and uninterrupted process. Although the traditional national cultures contain certain ingredients that are not suitable to globalization of economies, they also contain many ingredients that are excellent and beneficial to a country's economic development. Second, existence of one country and nationality has its cultural basis that is different from those of other cultures. Globalization of economies does not remove the political barriers among the countries. Every country conducts its international exchanges with other countries in its own interests. Presence of these national interests inevitably makes every country to start with maintaining its national independence to promote and foster its national culture. Third, in their collisions, conflicts and blending between foreign cultures and the

---

[①] Huang Jianyuan, Cai Qinyu. *Modern French Popular Culture*. Beijing: China Economy Publishing House, 2000.

national cultures, foreign cultures cannot completely escape the national cultures and entirely take root in the host land. Foreign cultures must respect the excellent ingredients in the national cultures. While foreign cultures are impacting the national cultures, they must adapt themselves to the large picture of the national cultures. In the attrition between foreign cultures and the national cultures, the passive ingredients in the foreign cultures that are not beneficial to the national economic development are discarded and the active ingredients are maintained. Finally, collection of information has its cost. This means everyone forms his beliefs based on the limited information he has. Sources of information are typically localized. This means that the sources of their respective information people rely on come from different crowds, which results in differences in their beliefs and cultures.

From the above, we think that globalization of cultures means the various national cultures, in their process of constantly breaking their respective territorial boundaries and limitations on the modes to march to the world, under the interaction of conflicts and mutual blending at the same time, result in the process or outcome of dynamic evolution to produce the global cultural ingredients and to create localization of the foreign cultures and the national cultures.

III. Relationship between globalization of economies and globalization of cultures

Economy is the material basis of human beings' survival and social development, and after culture is created on its basis, it penetrates into and serves the economic development. As economy is for the people and culture is for the people, the two are intrinsically integrated in people's experiments. Economy and culture are mutually existent, constrained and promoted. Economy is the basis of culture and also an important carrier of culture. Culture leads economy and also achieves its value in economic activities.

In its ancient history of changes, human culture formed the economic development standards and development mode that are suitable to the human being. These economic development standards and development mode in turn lead the cultural development. Then among cultures and economic modes during different periods in different regions, there are features of the periodic changes of "scientific and technological advancement—cultural improvements—economic prosperity". In summary, there are four productivity development upsurges in the human history. The first productivity development upsurge happened in the feudal society between the 3rd century B.C. and the 13th century A.D. and lasted more than 1,600 years. This upsurge was featured by "ancient civilization" as its representative science and technology achievement. With Confucianism as the leading cultural thought and natural economy as its economic development, its influence scope was only limited to a certain land region. The second productivity development upsurge occurred in the capitalism rise between the 17th century and 18th century and lasted about 200 years. This upsurge was featured by astrology and Newton's mechanics as the representative subject revolution, invention of the steam engine as the representative technology achievement, humanism and scientific methodology as the leading cultural thought and rise of market economy as its economic development. Its influence scope broke the regional barrier, and expanded from land to sea. The third productivity development upsurge appeared in the establishment and consolidation of the capitalist system and rise of the proletariat revolution between the mid-19th century and the early 20th century and lasted about 100 years. This upsurge was featured by chemistry, biology and physics as the representative subject revolution, chemical engineering, microorganism synthesis technology, and telecommunications technology as the representative technology achievement, capitalist democracy, liberty, individual liberation and Marxism's establishment and its dissemination as the leading cultural thought, and market economy's establishment and development as its economic development. Its influence scope was from regions to the globe, from the earth to the space, from macrobiology to microorganism, and surpassed the time and space concept. The fourth productivity development upsurge started in the 1960s and so far it has lasted 50 years. This upsurge is featured by system science as the representative subject revolution, information technology as the representative technology achievement, and fully developed market economy as its economic development. Its influence scope expands further from the globe to the outer space.

From a simple retrospect of the productivity development history, we can find that each productivity upsurge has intrinsically presented the interaction between culture and economy. Moreover, with the development of science and technology advancement and innovation, this interaction relationship is becoming more and more obvious.

At the turn of the century, globalization has become an unstoppable historical current. The cross-country flow of commodities, services and capital shown by globalization of economies promotes the national cultures that are contained in them to break their respective territorial boundaries and limitations on mode and to march in the world. Marx and Engels had made a very penetrating and thorough statement in *Capital*: "capitalists, because they had explored the world market, had made all countries' production and consumption as global in nature ... the local and national self-sufficiency and closed-country status in the past were replaced by interchange among the various nationalities and in all sides and mutual reliance by all sides. Material production is the same, and spiritual production is the same too. Spiritual products of various peoples became the public properties. National partiality and limitation became increasingly impossible. Then many peoples' and places' literature forms a global literature."[①] With his profound world outlook, Marx discerned the deep influence of "globalization of economies" on all walks of life, and profoundly elaborated the basic function of "globalization of economies" for "globalization of cultures". Globalization of economies accelerates the collisions, conflicts and blending of the diverse cultures in the world. The increasingly extensive and frequent cooperation and exchanges in the cultural field make the common property of civilization surpass with each passing day the individuality of the various national cultures, and become an important representation of global concept. Development in information, telecommunications, communications, computers, satellites, networks and other technologies shrinks the distance among the countries. Contacts between economies and cultures increase greatly.

In the course of the national cultures breaking their respective territorial boundaries and limitations on mode and marching in the world, the global cultural ingredients that are formed under the simultaneous impact of conflicts and mutual blending and that are blended into the various national cultures are beneficial to the further development of globalization of economies and also beneficial to solving the

---

[①] *Selected Works of Marx and Engels (Volume I)*. Beijing: People's Publishing House, 1972: 254-255.

major issues that are challenging the human beings nowadays (such as wars, racial conflicts, ecological environment, population, energy, drugs, gap between poverty and wealth, corruption and so on). As a result, the global cultural ingredients that are formed by globalization of cultures are both a result of globalization of economies and the necessary condition to the smooth boosting of globalization of economies.

Localization of the Chinese national culture in the globalization of cultures should be dialectically recognized. Although localization of the national cultures means highlighting of the individuality of the national cultures, the cross-country flow that is not beneficial to standardized commodity and service is obtained in the framework that globalization of cultures is beneficial in its entirety to globalization of economies. Moreover, from another perspective, the difference in market as shown by the individuality of the national cultures provides a prerequisite to the differentiation development of commodities, which is an important basis to boost the development of globalization of economies.

As a result, globalization of economies is the basis of globalization of cultures, and globalization of cultures is the objective request and necessary outcome. Reversely, globalization of cultures is also helpful to the further in-depth development of globalization of economies.

Section Two   China's Opening up to the Outside World and Impact of Outside Cultures

The opening up to the outside world caused the interactions between China and the outside world. This means the Chinese culture is no longer a closed system, but a national culture in the global network that is open and interactive. In globalization of economies and cultures, foreign cultures will definitely have an important influence on the Chinese culture. On the basis of criticism and inheritance, the traditional Chinese culture needs to blend with the excellent ingredients in the foreign cultures and be innovative in the great experiments of reform, opening up, and modernization.

I. Choice of China's strategy of opening up to the outside world

The across-the-board opening up to the outside world is connected with the full development of commodity economy. A society with the traditional thoughts that lay stress on agriculture, restrain trade and advocate the dominant viewpoint of "righteousness prior to benefits" and a feudal society with a small peasant economy combined with handicraft industry are hostile to commodity economy. As a result, in China's feudal society, the opening up to the outside world that featured commodity economy was simply like commodity economy itself and would not gain full development and would not be carried out from the start to the end. From the time that Ming Dynasty Emperor Zhu Di issued the closed-door order to "prohibit folk sea-going vessels" to the time that Qing Dynasty's implementation of the severe closed-door policy "no sailing to the sea at all", China adopted a closed-door policy for almost 300 years. The long-term closed-door policy prevented the introduction of foreign capital, advanced technology, production methods and the advanced thoughts and cultures from serving our country's economic construction, and China's entry to the international market to participate in the international circulation. All this obstructed development in our country's social productivity and resulted in a decline of an ancient civilization.

After the founding of the People's Republic of China, China obtained some funds and technologies from the Soviet Union that were necessary to restore and develop our national economy. Since the 1950s, the Western countries adopted a policy of hostilities, blockade and embargo against China. However, with China's efforts, some Western countries gradually changed their stand of isolating China and directly or indirectly traded with China. At one time, China's trade volume with Western Europe and Japan was 46% of the total import and export.

In the 1960s, owing to the deterioration of Sino-Soviet Union relationship, the Soviet Union withdrew its experts and revoked its loans. The Sino-Soviet Union trade volume nosedived. China's gate toward the Soviet Union and Eastern Europe's market was forced to close and the scope of foreign economic exchanges and technological cooperation further shrank. Meanwhile, Chinese Communist Party's (the CPC) "leftist" thoughts gained popularity, which made us move closer to a self-closed country. Especially during the "Ten-year Turmoil", self-reliance and development in foreign economic and technological exchanges were mutually opposed, which made China's economic construction suffer severely, stay out of line with the global market, and miss the best opportunity that the ever-deepening new technology revolution would have brought. When the "turmoil" ended, China's national economy reached the brink of collapse, the economic and scientific and technological development lagged far behind and its gap with the developed countries and world leading science and technology level was widening and China's international political and economic environment became very grave, and China's peaceful image in the international arena and international economic position suffered grossly.

Deng Xiaoping used his historical vision to examine China and the world, took the time's pulse and expressly pointed out that "today's world is an open one. China lagged behind after the Industrial Revolution in the West. One major reason for this is our closed-door policy. The 30-year experience shows us that construction behind closed doors does not work and there is no way for development".[1] "Opening up to the outside world is very significant. It is impossible for any country to isolate itself, adopt a closed-door policy and then develop."[2]

The Third Plenary Session of the 13th National Conference of the CPC's Central Committee was a congress that has a great historical significance. The Congress formed the CPC's second-generation leadership with Deng Xiaoping as the core and decisively made a policy of shifting the entire CPC's key work and adopting reform and opening up to the outside world. The Congress communique pointed out that "in accordance with the new historical conditions and experimental experience, a series of new and important economic measures are to be adopted to reform in real earnest the economic administration system and business operation methods. On the basis of self-reliance, we need to actively develop our mutually beneficial economic cooperation with other countries in the world. We need to make our best efforts to adopt the world's advanced technology and equipment." This treated opening up to the outside world as a grand strategy to promote China's social development, prosperity and progress. Ever since then, China has entered the new episode of reform and opening up to the outside world.

---

[1] *Selected Works of Deng Xiaoping (Volume III)*. Beijing: People's Publishing House, 1993: 64.
[2] Ibid., 117.

II. Foreign cultures during China's opening up to the outside world and their impact on China's traditional culture

With China's across-the-board reform and opening up, foreign products and businesses keep entering the Chinese market. The exchange between foreign cultures and China's traditional culture becomes increasingly frequent. Foreign ways of life, habits, business ideas and thoughts are imperceptibly influencing the Chinese people, especially the modern Western culture that comes with the globalization of economies, and they keep impacting China's traditional culture.

In the course of China's cultural evolution, differentiation between people and the nature is not complete. As a result, although there were advanced art, philosophical theories, some degree of science and technology and other self-conscious cultural factors in ancient China, they usually represented conscientious acknowledgment of tradition, experience, common sense, habits, natural emotion relationship, blood relationship, patriarchal clan system and other free cultural factors that have very strong repellency toward foreign cultures.

The core concept in China's traditional culture is harmony between man and nature. However, when man and nature are not yet differentiated such harmony results in the emphasis on and preference for people as a whole or people's group or category. As a result, in China's traditional culture, neither rational spirit and religious consciousness in the Western culture were differentiated, nor technical rationale and individual selfish departmentalism were converted, which is a huge difference from the Western culture. First of all, the natural idiosyncrasy in China's traditional culture is group departmentalism. China's traditional culture's spirit lacks independent individual freedom and individual consciousness. In the Western culture's individual departmentalism, its core is independent individual freedom and individual consciousness. Secondly, China's traditional culture has the feature of rational naturalism. Its value of interpersonal relationship weighs more than the relationship between man and nature. In the group departmentalist culture, differentiation between man and nature and between man and man has not yet reached rational consciousness. People's survival lacks individual consciousness and individual freedom. In view of this, emphasis on ethical relationship must concentrate on hierarchy relationship that is composed of people's endowed identity and status, family background, family relationship and so on and blood relationship, emotion relationship or patriarchal clan system. In other words, ethical culture of China's group departmentalism is a naturalist culture that depresses individual freedom and individual creativity. But the ethical culture in the modern Western culture represents an equal, free and rational association relationship and ethical relationship based on contracts and rule of law. It is a rationalist culture that provides the necessary condition for individual freedom and play of creativity. Finally, China's traditional culture is an experimentalist cultural mode that features conservatism and "guided by the past". Owing to lack of individual consciousness and individual freedom, and embedded in the natural relationship of harmony between man and nature, it lacks the spiritual orientation to conscientiously conquer the nature, which results in the key cultural factors as tradition, experience, common sense, habits and natural rhythm dominating people's life and social activities. The result is that society lacks the internal driving force and vitality for development. In comparison, the modern Western cultural mode relies on rationality, science, freedom, subject consciousness and innovative spirit.

The substance of industrial civilization and modernization is the process of individualization and rationalization. Individual consciousness and individual freedom become modern people's guiding cultural spirit and internal survival mode. As China needs to modernize itself through reform and opening up, it must be subject to the impact of the Western culture. Its impact is centrally reflected in the market economy culture. As an operating mechanism, even though there is no thinking ideology question in the market economy, its creation is closely related to the Western economy's ethical views, private ownership of production means and capitalist social system. When such an economic order is introduced to China that features public ownership of property, and emphasizes group coordination ethical views and a unique socialist political system, it is inevitable to have contradictions and conflicts. Its specific representations are as follows.

First, the impact of market economy's utilitarian idea on the "ethical center" idea in China's traditional culture. The "ethical center" idea means it is people's supreme pursuit to better their moral culture and individual personality in their life.

It is advocated that spiritual pursuit prevails over material pursuit. This results in asceticism that severely obstructs development in the Chinese society. However, the subject basis that market economy relies on so heavily is individuals that are in pursuit of maximum profits. Its essence is attention to and pursuit of material interests, which is what we call utilitarianism. Shifting to market economy inevitably strengthens people's attention to material interests. So the ideas such as being happy to lead a simple and virtuous life and valuing justice above material gains and so on are challenged in an unprecedented manner.

Second, impact of market economy's "rule of law" idea on the "rule by man" idea in China's traditional culture. The traditional "rule by man" idea still has far-reaching influence today. "Rule by man" embodies to some extent a kind of hierarchy idea, which is in line with the need to safeguard the feudal economy. "Rule of law" is the safeguard and basic character of the market economy. The establishment and betterment of China's market economy is indispensable of "rule of law". The shift toward the market economy requires "rule of law" from us. This will inevitably have a great impact on China's traditional "rule by man" idea.

Third, the impact of the "science" idea in the market economy on the "experientialism" idea in China's traditional culture. The "experientialism" idea in China's traditional culture stems from group departmentalism and spontaneous relationship between man and nature and is an indication of technological backwardness and underdevelopment in commodity economy. The "science" idea is the evitable choice by individuals who pursue maximum profits in the market economy. Only with "science" can individuals be able to maximize their profits. Then, the shift toward the market economy must require us to abandon "experientialism" in the traditional culture and pay homage to the "science" idea.

Fourth, the impact of the "innovation" idea on the "admiration for the ancient" and "smooth and steady life mentality" in China's traditional culture. There exists in China's traditional culture historical rudiment of "only the ancient can be the law and only the ancient can be respected", which stifles people's thinking and behaviors and obstructs China's economic development. "Innovation" is a requirement of the individuals pursuing maximum interests in the market economy and also an inevitable reaction under the market economy's pressure of survival of the fittest. In the course of shifting toward the market economy, the pressure of survival of the fittest must require the economic subject to break away from the idea of "only the ancient can be the law and only the ancient can be respected and following the beaten track".

Fifth, the impact of "respect for the individual interests" in the market economy on the "divided equality" thought in China's traditional culture. There exists in China's traditional culture the equalitarianist thought of "Do not worry about scarcity, but worry about unevenness." The existence of this "divided equality" inhibits the unleashing of the economic subject's active and innovative role and obstructs our country's economic development. Acknowledgement of and respect for individual interests are the basis of the market economy's operations. The shift toward the market economy will lead to conflicts between the thought of "respect for the individual interests" and the "divided equality" thought in China's traditional culture.

The entry to the World Trade Organization accelerates the steps of China's economic system reform. The cultural ideas such as individual departmentalism, rationality, science, rule of law and innovation and so on that are upheld by the market economy will no doubt keep impacting the contradictory ideas in China's traditional culture.

III. Inheritance and innovation of China's traditional culture

The world development and China's reform and opening up and the advancing in the modernization construction urgently request us to broaden our horizon. Under the great background of globalization of cultures, China's cultural development requires good treatment of inheritance and innovation of China's traditional culture.

In the course of globalization of cultures, forgetting the unique characters in the Chinese national culture and any attempt to substitute the national culture with the foreign culture in its entirety will make the Chinese national culture lose its original groundwork and truncate provision channels for important cultural development. The inevitable outcome would be extinction of the national culture. What is more, China's traditional culture goes back to ancient times and is the accretion of the material and spiritual property and socialized behaviors created by the Chinese nation and is the identified bond and spiritual dependency. Although there are ideas in China's traditional culture that are contradictory to modern industrialization and post-industrial civilization, there are many excellent ingredients in China's traditional culture. Among the world's four great civilizations, other civilizations were interrupted, declined or even perished. The only one survived is the Chinese civilization that stretches long and unbroken. It has become more charming today with the highly developed science and technology and has been valued by more and more foreigners. The great vitality itself shown by the eternal value that defies both time and space is exactly the confirmation of the excellent ingredients in China's traditional culture.

These major concepts that represent the correct direction of the Chinese cultural development and embody the Chinese nation's vigorous spirit are composed of the basic spirit of the Chinese culture, and they are also the national spirit of the Chinese nation. This national spirit is the spiritual driving force and spiritual pillar for the national survival and development that the Chinese nation relies upon and it is the source that the Chinese nation maintains its vitality, creativity and cohesiveness. It is also the core and soul of the Chinese nation's culture and the most essential and profound representation of China's traditional culture. So far as the manifestations are concerned, the national spirit is just the excellent tradition of the national culture. Among China's traditional culture, the patriotic spirit of "Everyone should bear responsibility for the fate of his country", and "When the state is at stake, he would give his last breath. Would a homecoming soul fear to face death?"; the spirit of having both ability and political integrity, but with an emphasis on political integrity such as "Capacity, virtue's source; virtue, capacity's captain"; the enterprising and tolerance spirit such as "As the ever revolving heaven, the gentleman should persistently renew his strength; like the sustaining power of the earth, the gentleman should practice the great virtue of kindness to bear all things"; the spirit to uphold justice such as "Die to achieve virtue, and lay down one's life for a just cause"; the spirit of harmony between man and nature such as "harmony between man and nature"; the spirit to work selflessly for the public interest such as "the public interest prevails over one's personal interest" and the virtue of emphasizing reputation such as "reputation is the fundamental basis of all behaviors" and Mount Jinggang Spirit, Long March Spirit, Yan'an Spirit, Xibaipo Spirit, Daqing Spirit, Hongqi Canal Spirit, Lei Feng Spirit, the 64-Character Entrepreneurship Spirit, Kong Fansen Spirit, Flood Fighting Spirit, and Spirit of Atomic Bomb, Hydrogen-bomb and Manmade Satellites and so on and so forth. These virtues and spirits, as the embodiment and crystallization of the Chinese nation's spirit, cement our nation's survival and development and inspire greatly the initiative of the Chinese people to forge ahead. Even under the market economy, they are excellent culture worth advocating and promoting.

Inheritance of the excellent ingredients in China's traditional culture is not simple inheritance, but inheritance of transforming and making innovative use of the excellent ingredients in the traditional culture through blending them with the excellent ingredients in the foreign cultures. Those people who are called cultural conservatists think that as long as the national character is extracted from the traditional culture it can be used to establish the national identity and hope to find the factors with the modern meaning from history's accretion to reestablish the value system and they like to make new by going back to tradition. However, no matter how people annotate the traditional culture, in fact, they are simply repeating what many people in modern times had tried to do, but they all failed. As a matter of fact, those people who would like to make the culture function without doubt would explain it in the modern values. Just as Joseph R. Levenson profoundly pointed out, "Those traditional Chinese values that can be reconfirmed by the modern people are those that are still suitable to the individual values of the modern people. Among them are values that are confirmed by the people who know nothing about the traditions."[①]

In the course of globalization of cultures, forgetting the common characters of ratione personae in the national culture and blindly emphasizing the aboriginality and particularity, the national culture will inevitably lack openness and flexibility owing to the narrow nationalism, and fail to conscientiously absorb the nutriment for itself from other national cultures, which will very easily result in closed and backward culture and economy. In fact, the home national culture can be highlighted

---

[①] Levenson. *Confucian China and Its Modern Fate*. Trans. Zheng Dahua, Ren Jing. Beijing: China Social Science Publishing House, 2000: 94.

and the home national culture can be maintained and promoted in the waves of globalization only if those ingredients in the home traditional culture that are not suitable to the home country's economic and cultural development under globalization are eliminated and full absorbing and blending of the essence in the foreign national cultures that globalization of cultures has brought as well as innovation to develop the home national culture are achieved.

A history of human civilization is one from which cultures keep drawing strength and keep forging ahead. Only with constant innovations can cultures be endowed promptly and effectively with new contents and new spirit of the times and be brought full new vitality so as to obtain new values and meanings. As regards cultures that contain and function with intelligence, ethics, and thinking and spirit, any kind of conservatism and stagnancy mean the suppression on society's progress and removal of the national spirit. Innovation of Chinese culture is to make innovations with the requirements of the times and experiments as the point of penetration and on the basis of discarding the dregs in our country's traditional culture and in the foreign cultures and inheriting the essence in our country's culture and in the foreign cultures so as to add brand-new scientific contents and modes of representations to forcefully promote China's social development. Only in this way, can we find the solution to break the dilemma of "absorbing the foreign cultures and preserving the local cultures", namely, localization of foreign cultures and modernization of home cultures. Then the national cultures can be updated in the course of inheritance and then be passed on in the course of updating.

As a result, the Chinese culture can last a long time and is still full of vitality only if we base ourselves on the great cause of reform and opening up and modernization, inherit and promote our national culture's excellent traditions, constantly draw nutriment and strength from the traditional culture's extensive knowledge and profound scholarship, from high-spirited revolutionary culture, from the healthy and helpful foreign cultures and from the latest practice of advancing with the times, actively make innovations with the system, contents and forms, and keep exploring new paths that can maximize our country's advanced cultural development.

Section Three Various Subjects of Globalization of Cultures

Globalization of economies is an undisputed fact. The subsequent globalization of cultures, though still faced with many disputes, whether you acknowledge it or not, is a prerequisite for one country's economic development to correctly view globalization of cultures. Among them, to a country, whether globalization of cultures is an opportunity or a challenge, national culture's development, and China's advanced culture's construction, all of these are subjects that are in urgent need of extensive research.

I. Globalization of cultures, a challenge or an opportunity

Globalization of cultures, as a natural phenomenon of the world economic and cultural development, just as globalization of economies, is also with advantages and disadvantages. To a country's economic and cultural development, opportunities abound but challenges exist.

From the view of opportunities, first, the various national cultures keep breaking their respective territorial boundaries and limitations on the modes and march in the world, under the mutual conflicts and blending at the same time, the global cultural ingredients thus formed are some common human matters that are universally identified by the world, this is helpful to form a uniform identity and solutions. For example, globalization of market economy is helpful to the operation of economic activities in the global arena. The identity to the significance of environment helps the international community work out a more effective coordination mechanism. Next, globalization of economies and cultures force most nations to adopt a more open strategy. This provides a very beneficial condition for the various national cultures to penetrate the markets of other nations so as to help commodities that are enriched by other cultures to enter the international market. Finally, the essence of foreign cultures supplements beneficially the innovation and development of the national cultures.

Coexisting with opportunities, globalization of cultures is full of challenges. Globalization of cultures makes the national cultures suffer more from the impacts of foreign cultures. Harvard University political science professor Samuel P. Huntington published *The Clash of Civilizations* in 1993. The book said that the basic framework of today's world is primarily the Christian culture represented by Europe and the United States in the West, the Confucianist culture in the East, and the Islamic culture in Central Asia and the Arab area. He asserted that "the future global conflicts will be clashes of civilizations ... The next war, if any, will be between civilizations." [①] Even though many scholars think that Professor Huntington's theory of clashes of civilizations may contain exaggerated contents, clash between civilizations is obvious. With globalization of economies, the Western cultures brought to the developing countries a sense of curiosity about the heterogeneous cultures. Then practice of copying and pursuit was formed in a certain scope and a certain layer which promotes the reform in the cultural structure and impacts the passing on and sublation of the traditional cultures. This creates a very grave challenge to the status formation of the excellent ingredients in the national cultures and results in what was passed on are the outdated ingredients in the national cultures and what was blended with are the dregs in the foreign cultures. What is worse is that when the national cultures were impacted by the foreign cultures, owing to the fact that under such impacts, there is a difference in the degree or progress of the cultures passed on and the blended foreign cultures, it is extremely easy to result in the lack of identity in cultures among the people and it is difficult to form a systematic cultural architecture. Without a systematic cultural architecture, uniform value evaluation standards and selection standards were lost. This will weaken a nation's cohesiveness and cause chaos in the cultural and economic order and then damage a country's healthy economic development.

Globalization of cultures, as a dynamic process of the world cultural evolution, is featured with both opportunities and challenges. It is a subject that is worth constant research on how to go after profits and avoid disadvantages.

II. Development of the national cultures under globalization of cultures

In the course of globalization of cultures, various national cultures are enriched

---

[①] Samuel P. Huntington. *The Clash of Civilizations and the Remaking of World Order.* Beijing: Xinhua Publishing House, 1998: 155.

and developed in collisions and exchanges with each other. However, history proves that flow of civilization and information is asymmetrical, it is always that cultures from the economically developed regions expand to economically backward regions. Thomas G. Harding and others call this phenomenon "cultural advantage principle", namely, those cultural systems that can more efficiently develop energy resources in a determined environment will expand into the environment that the backward system relies on for its survival. "Every new-coming advanced cultural type will gain broader and faster expansion than the cultural type in the earlier period. So till today, we see the so-called Western cultures not only cover most of the globe with their advantages, but also try to expand into the outer space. The potential expansion space by the more advanced cultural types greatly influences the entire evolution process."[1]

In the 21st century, the Western cultures represented by the United States are the strong ones, and they are the leading force in globalization of cultures and pose a strong offensive and impact on cultures of other countries in the course of globalization of cultures, which results in crises and losses of the national traditional cultures. Development in information technology and the constant blending and innovation among the various national cultures are bound to accelerate the updating speed of the cultures. Frequent knowledge updates keep taking up the space of traditional cultures and substantially minimize influence of traditional cultures and keep traditional cultures away from people's daily life with each passing day.

As regards the national cultures in the backward countries, conflict between modernization and nationalism shapes the mutual conflict between historical rational yardstick and national emotional yardstick, which places the traditional values in the national cultures in a predicament. If we adhere to the historical rational yardstick and acknowledge superiority and advancement of modern rationalist cultural mode, and voluntarily use it to change the traditional cultural mode, we can provide a kind of driving force to some extent for the society. However, the national emotion and self-respect will suffer severely. If we adhere to the national emotional yardstick, continue to maintain superiority of the national culture, continue to keep to the

---

[1] Thomas G. Harding et al. *Evolution and Culture*. Hangzhou: Zhejiang People's Publishing House, 1987: 58-59.

traditional culture's departmental position, and reject the Western rationalist spiritual culture, we will be behind the times in our competition with the developed countries and place ourselves in a more disadvantaged position. This type of cultural mentality will directly impact one nation's cultural choice in the background of globalization.

Prior to the modern times, the cultural mode of China's traditional naturalism and experientialism with the harmony between man and nature at their core and the Western cultural spirit featured with rationalism supported in synchrony the Eastern civilization and the Western civilization. However, at the modern times, with the completion of the Western modernization and establishment of the modern industrial civilization, the Western culture transformed to the cultural mode of modern rationalism with the basic connotation of individual departmentalism, individual freedom, and technical rationale and so on. But China's traditional cultural mode still maintained its internal super stability structure and kept to the cultural mode of group departmental naturalism and experientialism. Difference in China's traditional culture and the Western culture changed from its original synchrony relationship to the two civilization eras that closely followed one after another, namely, the representative cultural mode of the traditional agricultural civilization and the modern industrial civilization. This is also the situation that most developing countries' national cultures are facing.

As regards this point, we should not only have the scholarly understanding, but also have the courage to face the reality. When Iranian President Mohammad Khatami advocated "Dialogue of Civilizations", he pointed out that "Although Muslims used to own a civilized world and play a certain role in the human history, now this position and function disappeared. If we do not possess the fruits that the Western European civilization created, our non-Western life would be impossible."[1]

As a result, how to find equilibrium in the conflict between the historical rational yardstick and the national emotional yardstick should be a question that the backward national cultures should face.

---

[1] Yamaguchi Masayuki. "Dialogue of Civilizations and the 21st Century Global Society". *World Economy and Politics*, Issue No. 1, 2001.

III. Globalization of cultures and construction of China's advanced culture

It is not until the final 20 years in the 20th century that China started to participate in the modernization process of globalization of economies in an independent and open posture. For China, all this came somewhat late. However, for the Chinese culture, all this came somewhat suddenly. China's modernization and its cultural development are at a special historical orientation: when the Western industrial civilization had been fully developed but showed some kind of drawbacks and crises and began to transfer to post-industrial civilization, China started its own industrial civilization process. When a country and nation suddenly faced a huge difference of level in civilization but was in a hurry to catch up with the advanced civilization, and owing to a great variety of complex internal and external conditions, had no alternative but to have a great leap forward, its largest dilemma may not be in the field of technology and materials, but in the field of culture and spirit. In order to transfer to the market economy, it needs a matching culture that is different from the planned economy as its support. Without a matching culture that is compatible with the market economy and without a culture that is suitable to the profound Chinese national cultural background, the market economy is hard to operate in China.

Culture is divided into advanced culture and backward culture in nature. Advanced culture is the crystallization of human civilization and progress and the rational sublimation of social experiments. It conscientiously represents the mainstream of the times, direction of the society's development and the ideological guarantee, spiritual driving force and intellectual support of the human social development and historical development. It forcefully promotes establishment and development of superstructure such as society's political system, economic system, ideological and ethical standards and so on and ideology. It is a forerunner in the birth of the progressive political and social system.

Advanced culture is a historical phenomenon. Advanced culture differs in its contents in different societies, countries, and times. In the views of Marxism, the historical yardstick, scientific yardstick and value yardstick need to be adhered to in judging whether a culture is advanced or not. By adhering to the historical yardstick, it means in the corresponding historical condition, from nature of the contemporary economic and political system, to see whether this culture is in line with the historical development's trend. It is an advanced culture if it is in line with the historical development's trend. Otherwise, it is a backward culture. By adhering to the scientific yardstick, it means to see whether a culture objectively reveals human's truthful knowledge of the objective world. If it can scientifically reveal the nature and human society's development rules and development trend, it is an advanced culture. Otherwise, it is a backward culture. By adhering to the value yardstick, it means to see what kind of functions that this culture plays in the specific society's economy and politics and for whom this culture serves. An advanced culture reveals and safeguards the advanced economic and political relationship and to sum up it is beneficial to the productivity development. In today's China, the fundamental yardsticks to gauge the cultural construction direction are whether it reveals China's advanced productivity's development need, China's advanced culture's direction of advance and the basic interests of the great majority of the Chinese people, which is the requirement of the times. To see whether it can adhere to the advanced culture's direction of advance, the main touchstone is to see whether it provides a strong spiritual driving force and intellectual support to the economic development and the full-scale development of the society, whether there is a notable improvement in the entire nation's ideology makings and scientific and technological makings, whether it can train new socialist talents with aspirations, ethics, literacy and disciplines that the socialist modernization construction needs, and whether the people's cultural needs are better satisfied. These yardsticks are undoubted. In addition, the 16th CPC National Congress's report also pointed out China's culture's development strategy: "based on reform and opening up and modernization construction's experiments, with an eye on the front of the world cultural development, promote the excellent traditions of our national culture, draw from the strengths of the various peoples in the world and be active and innovative in its contents and forms."

In a society which is in transition and whose economy switches to a market economy, the diversity and complexity in its economic and cultural life determine diversity and complexity in people's values and value evaluation standards. There is a diverse development state in different social groups' value orientation, mores and culture's choice. Feudal decadent and declining values and the Western individualist values pose a huge impact on the national traditional values and modern socialist value system that have been long in existence. It is difficult to form a uniform value culture system, namely, cultural identity. It is an extremely important task for China nowadays to construct an advanced culture that is uniform and matches its economic and social development, especially the advanced value system so as to meet the challenge of globalization of cultures. As regards the modern transition in the national spirit value, it is not only a question of the change in the dimensions of time and space, the most fundamental question is the mode or path on how to achieve this goal. All this is undoubtedly significant in its theories and reality.

Chapter Two   Formation of Globalization of Cultures and Its Influence on Economies

Globalization of cultures develops side by side with globalization of economies. Globalization of economies promotes development of globalization of cultures through flow of commodities and production factors, global distribution of the market economy system as well as cultural exchanges. As representation of the globalization in interaction between economy and culture, globalization of cultures also plays an important role in one country's economy as well as in globalization of economies.

Section One   Globalization of Economies Goes Hand in Hand with Globalization of Cultures

Culture and social ideology rely on social existence and develop with the social existence's development. The cross-country flow and deployment of production factors such as capital, technology, labor, knowledge, and information and so on are bound to cause in various degrees the corresponding changes in the various national cultures and values and to result in new development state in the various cultures to adapt to globalization of economies. It is fair to say that globalization of cultures develops with development in globalization of economies.

The major representations that globalization of economies promotes globalization of cultures are in three aspects, material, system and culture.

Firstly, in the material aspect, the function that globalization of economies promotes globalization of cultures is reflected primarily in the influence of cross-country flow of commodities and production factors on globalization of cultures. First of all, globalization of commodity production makes the various national cultures hidden in the production factors global with the global deployment of production factors. Globalization of economies makes international flow of talents and labor more frequent. These people in the flow themselves are carriers of the various national cultures. Their interaction with the host country and its people makes exchanges of the various cultures possible. The international flow of people as a result of globalization of economies becomes an important path to influence globalization of cultures. Second, globalization of commodity consumption makes global cultures that use commodities as their carriers through cross-country flow of commodities. Multinational corporations' global sales expand the variety of the commodities available in various countries. At the same time of consumption of foreign commodities, countries begin to understand, become acquainted with, reject and accept foreign cultures contained in these foreign commodities to make global some cultures carried by these commodities. This global feature is mainly limited to the consumer culture aspect. Finally, information globalization based on the rapid development in information technology promotes more directly communication among the various cultures. The information revolution marked by information highway construction is quickly rewriting the human society's landscape. The Internet all over the globe shortens the distance between the peoples. With the Internet, information is exchanged and shared quickly, which enhances greatly culture's penetrability.

Next, in the system aspect, the function that globalization of economies exerts on globalization of cultures is reflected in globalization of market economy. In the modern society, market economy is an effective means to deploy economic resources and is an economic operating mechanism that can be shared by the human being. In essence, market behaviors are cultural in nature, and are hidden with rich humane connotations. This is because the realization of exchanges is bound to be based on certain cultural rules that are recognized by all the parties involved, namely, the so-called market rules. When the market is confined to a specific country, what is required is cultural consensus within that country's territory. When the market is expanded globally, without doubt the corresponding consensus in the global scope is required. As a result, although some market rules were first formed in one specific region or a specific nation state, as long as they are helpful to realize exchanges among the various nations and countries, they will overflow its national boundaries to become one global cultural consensus or a global "customary rule" or "general rule". It is fair to say that globalization of economies is globalization that is established on the basis of market economy. In order to adapt to the development trend of globalization of economies and seize the opportunities brought by globalization of economies and attract multinational corporations to set up factories in their countries, these countries one after another reform portions in their own economic systems that are not suitable to market economy's development. This promotes popularization of market economy spirit in the world. As a standard culture, market economy's effective operation will not be possible without support from the corresponding culture. Then, globalization of economies is bound to cause global popularization of market economy culture.

Finally, in the cultural aspect, globalization of economies functioning on globalization of cultures is reflected in formation and development of global cultural ingredients. Globalization of economies makes people in different countries and nations face similar or even the same life experiences, which results in adaptability pressure and performance pressure that request all the local and regional cultures to develop in one specific direction. Thomas G. Harding et al. pointed out that "The special view toward evolution contains a view that treats culture as an open system or adaptability system. Adaptability includes relationship with nature and with other cultural systems (unless a society is completely isolated). Adaptability to nature will create one culture's technology and results in this culture's social ingredients and idea ingredients. Adaptability to other cultures also creates society and ideas and the latter will influence technology and determine its further development. All the results in the adaptability process is creation of one organized culture's entirety, one comprehensive technology, society and idea, and it deals with the dual influence of selectable nature and external culture. In a word, this is cultural adaptability mechanism."[①] Globalization of economies makes the human being face the same economic, technological, social, political and spiritual problems such as ecology,

---

[①] Thomas G. Harding et al. *Evolution and Culture*. Hangzhou: Zhejiang People's Publishing House, 1987: 39.

resources, population, drugs, AIDS and so on. These global issues require all the peoples in the world to tackle together. The solution to these issues requires the corresponding cultures and values such as global awareness, jurisprudentialism and institutional norms. This requires people to consider these issues from the perspective of the mankind in its entirety and acknowledge some common characters in human cultures.

Section Two   Influence of Globalization of Cultures on the Economy of a Nation

"How important are the cultural factors to economic development?" is a long disputed question in social science. Social scientists tend to believe cultural standards of behaviors are universal in economic life and without culture one cannot understand economic life. David S. Landes (1998) and Ian Buruna (1999) think that culture has the marked influence on economic performance. David S. Landes (2000) even thinks that "if we ever learn anything from economic history, the culture is almost very important".

In fact, culture is produced on the economic basis and later it penetrates and serves the economic development and becomes the leader in economy. First, people's economic activities can be viewed as a selective activity which is led by a specific value. Value determines orientation of the economic subject and provides selection standards and driving power to the economic subject. The economic subject with the selective activity based on a specific value fully shows culture plays a leading role in the economic activities. Next, ethics as the cultural core, through behaviors that dominate the economic subject, leads the economic development. In the course of social economic exchanges, owing to individuals' differences in the status and identity in their production and exchanges, there are often huge differences in their economic benefits and behaviors and there are even contradictions and conflicts. For the sake of the entire society's harmonious development and in order to safeguard each other's fundamental interests, in the long social experiments some rules of behaviors to constrain their behaviors toward each other are formed and ethical rules are formed to regulate interpersonal relationship by public opinions and folk force. Through the support of certain values, ethical norms that discipline themselves and laws that discipline others, society standardizes and regulates interpersonal relationship and safeguards the regular functioning of the society. The more developed a society is, the more powerful the self-discipline of the invisible ethics is. Just as former President of the World Bank Alden Clausen thought in early November, 1999 at an international economic conference on China's development and international economy, behind economic development is people's standards of behaviors, namely, ethical judgments. It is impossible that this will be observed by the people. But in the end it determines the level that economic development can achieve. Again, with the industrialization of science and technology, economic development relies more and more on cultures. Social productivity's development makes human beings' economic activities gradually shift from reliance on physical strength to primary reliance on intellectual power.

Then, globalization of cultures' influence on one country's economy is through its influence on the country's culture and then on the country's economic development. Specifically, an analysis can be made on globalization of cultures' influence on one country's system selection, opening up to the outside and resources deployment.

I. Globalization of cultures' influence on system selection

Before the introduction of new institutional economics, mainstream Western economists thought that economic development is the outcome of changes in material factors especially technology factors and "institution" is only economic development's set prerequisite and external condition. But one of the founders of "new institutional economics", Douglass North, thought that the key element of economic growth and development is institution including state-issued official constraints and socially-recognized unofficial constraints and their corresponding implementation mechanism. Official constraints refer to primarily laws, regulations and so on and they are compulsory. Unofficial constraints refer to internal restraints composed of cultural and traditional constraints such as social customary rules, social customs, ethical values, ideology and so on and they are not compulsory in nature.

The theories of institutional evolution all center on a common subject, namely, generation and changes in rules and orders. The core idea in the institutional evolution theory proposed by Thorstein Bunde Veblen is "cumulative causation" and he thought that social structure and social system are evolutionary. "The so-called economic system is a customary method on how to proceed when people is in contact with the material environment that they are situated during their social living process."[①] He thought that members in the society voluntarily adapt to the changed environment and gradually form a thinking habit and as social habit or culture deposited to form the basic rules in the society. He also emphasized that although the institution can adapt to the changed environment condition, this process is steady. So it is expected that there will be time lag and the remnant rules that are not suitable to the modern system will be kept. Richard Nelson and Sidney G. Winter in their book *An Evolutionary Theory of Economic Changes* also think that routines are formed by gradual evolution from the interactions between the members in organizations and their environment. Changes in routines are constantly inherited and mutated by mechanisms such as adaptable studies and replications and so on. For example, in one industry routines that different enterprises try are definitely different. There are routines with better profitability. As a result, routines with better profitability will replace those with less profitability. Friedrich Hayek in his books such as *The Fatal Conceit* and *The Road to Serfdom* discussed that an institutional change is a voluntary and evolutionary process but not a process of rational design. He thought that social welfare function cannot be summed up and if one system that is designed in accordance with one certain welfare standard cannot satisfy all the people's preference, this system will not be effective. Through pursuit of maximum profits, interaction and game playing, the disperse individuals create mutually recognized rules, namely, "internal rules"—cultural traditions such as ethics, customs, rules and so on and on this basis the voluntary social orders for people's contacts. The voluntary social orders may not only predict accurately other people's actions, and members in the society can supplement their rational insufficiency by

---

[①] Thorstein Bunde Veblen. *The Theory of the Leisure Class*. Beijing: The Commercial Press, 1981: 193.

following the orders so as to reduce their errors in decision-making. As a result, "the most helpful factor to the social functioning is these traditional rules that people accepted and not those that the instinct thinks is a correct thing."[①]

We can reach a conclusion from the institutional evolution theory: institutional formation and changes cannot go without cultures' support (unofficial constraints). As cultural traditions are deeply embedded in the society's economic life, institutional changes must be combined with the cultural forms and their evolutionary process during a certain period of time.

As regards the institutional function of ideology culture, North thought it has three presentations: First, ideology is a savings mechanism. People recognize the environment they are in and minimize "trial and error" cost and external "transaction cost". Culture with ideology as its core, on one hand, may use one kind of external influence (discipline of others) to suppress economic actors' "opportunism" tendency to prevent opportunists to transfer their own cost or fees to others and cause damages to others; on the other hand, it may raise the internal consciousness (self-discipline) to reinforce personality's reliability to reduce information asymmetry factor to reinforce certainty of people's behaviors. As a result, "the presence of institutions is to reduce uncertainty of people's interaction" so as to reduce "transaction cost".[②] Second, ideology is usually interweaved with evaluations of ethics on fairness and justice that people held when they observed the world. This is to say, sometimes a selection needs to be made among mutually opposed theories and ideology. Third, when people's original ideas or experiences are not in line with ideology, they may change their ideology to develop a set of new rational selection that is in line with their ideas or experiences. As a result, culture forms the value basis of official constraints that are formed and confirmed and also provides legitimacy support for existence and development of official constraints. Moreover, in the long run, unofficial constraints have determination significance including determining evolution's direction, mode, speed and so on. From a certain

---

[①] Friedrich Hayek. *Selected Works of Friedrich Hayek*. Beijing: Capital University of Economics and Trade Publishing House, 2000.

[②] Douglass North. *Institutions, Institutional Change and Economic Performance*. Trans. Liu Shouying. Shanghai: SDX Joint Publishing Company, 1994: 34.

period, whether unofficial constraints are promoting or obstructing unleashing of official constraints depends on whether official constraints' change direction and mode dovetail nicely and the degree of such dovetailing. As a result, culture is a mobility factor that influences institutional formation and changes.

Differences in cultures can in a certain extent explain differences in institutions. There are marked differences in various countries in importance of capital markets, enterprises' outside financing capability and ownership of public trading companies. Explanation for such differences is degree of protection received by investors who are free from encroachment by managers, controlling shareholders and governments. Rene M. Stulz and Rohan Williamson (2001) have found through quantitative analysis of 49 countries in Asia, Europe, North America, South America and Australia: First, common law countries are better than Roman law countries in protection of investors. The reason is that function of governments in common law countries is less than that in Roman law countries and common law countries leave more room for judges to adapt to economic changes and support fairness. Judges in Roman law countries interpret laws just as theologians interpret the Bible. As a result, common law's merits are that application of its laws is more suitable to economic changes. Second, one country's main religion can better predict countries' differences in creditors' rights than opening in foreign trade, languages, per capita income and legal system's source. Just as Tawney (1954) said, it is a basic principle in the medieval church to prohibit collecting interest and collection of interest results in being expelled from the church.[1] Calvinist doctrine views payment of interest as a normal part of commerce and so the modern debt market could develop. As a result, creditors' rights receive most protection in countries that Protestantism is the main religion. In the Roman law countries, the Catholic countries protect creditors' rights less than the Protestant countries. Furthermore, in rights application, religion, languages and sources of law all play an important role and Protestant countries are better than Catholic countries. Finally, in interpreting shareholders' rights, a country's source of legal system is more important than religion and languages. Nickell and Layard (1997) made a comparison of 20 countries in OECD and

---

[1] R. H. Tawney. *Religion and the Rise of Capitalism*. New York: Harcourt, Brace & World, Inc., 1954.

confirmed that relevance exists between cultures and labor market system. Catholic countries in Europe have the most labor market regulations. Protestant countries in Europe regulate less and English-speaking countries regulate the least.

Once we understand the function of cultures on formation and changes of institutions, influence of globalization of cultures on one country's institutional selection can be analyzed from influence of globalization of cultures on one country's culture, which is reflected in two aspects.

On one hand, globalization of cultures provides one country's national culture with an opportunity to absorb excellent ingredients in foreign cultures so as to provide a cultural basis to one country to construct independently a "good" system that is in line with its own economic development. Hayek's idea of voluntary social order has its reasonable inner core, but voluntary cultural evolution will not necessarily result in a "good" system. China's feudal society lasted more than 2,000 years and did not evolve voluntarily into a "good" system. The root cause is that the behavior norms formed by departmentalism and ethics centralism made China's feudal society stay as a "rule by rites" social where the entire society lacked effective system protection and incentives and China's feudal social order produced what North called "lock-in effect". If China wants to establish a modern market economy system, it must establish culturally a market economy ethics culture. "Smith had long pointed out reasonably that any market economy can only operate normally on the basis of shared moral outlook (abiding by contracts, honoring payment promises and respecting market partners)."[1] Amartya Sen also thinks that "capitalism's highly efficient operations rely on powerful values and normative system".[2] An exchange economy's successful operation relies on mutual trust and use of open or hidden norms. In view of this, Sen provided advice to developing countries that "developing countries must not only pay great attention to prudent behavior's fine virtues, but also pay great attention to these supplemental values' function."[3] Globalization of cultures is just providing an opportunity of the shared

---

[1] Horst Steinmann, Albert Lohr. *Business Ethics*. Trans. Li Zhaoxiong. Shanghai: Shanghai Social Science Publishing House, 2001: 25.

[2] Amartya Sen. *Development as Freedom*. Beijing: China Renmin University Publishing House, 2002: 261.

[3] Ibid., 265.

moral outlook, values and normative cultures that developing countries rely upon to absorb and construct their market economy successfully.

On the other hand, during globalization of cultures, conflicts between foreign cultures and national cultures may cause chaos in one country's national culture and then make the institutional operation difficult. What is worse is that conflicts between foreign culture value and national culture value may sometimes be presented as the coexistence of two kinds of cultures at the same time and the coexistence of market economy mode and traditional economy mode and even deficiency in market credibility. When Gunnar Myrdal surveyed in South Asia, he listed South Asian countries' 12 "modernization ideals", including ration, development, increase in productivity, equality and so on and 13 specific attitudes. But these ideals have to compete with the traditional values supported by religion. Douglass C. North pointed out in his book, *Structure and Change in Economic History*, that law and politics may change overnight, but unofficial constraints such as customs, traditions and standards of behaviors are hard to change. In the absence of powerful national guidance, resistance from traditional culture value and impact from market economy ethics are bound to result in some unhealthy outcome. For example, in China, with globalization and deepening of China's reform and opening up, Chinese people's economic consciousness strengthens, but their moral consciousness weakens. Weakened moral consciousness will result in deficiency of credibility so as to increase market transaction cost and will be detrimental to the effective operation of market economy system.

As a result, influence of globalization of cultures on one country's system selection has both positive and negative effects. System change is integration of evolution and construction. In the course of system construction, governments should pay full attention to the construction of culture and minimize the unfavorable influence of globalization of cultures on system construction.

II. Influence of globalization of cultures on opening up to the outside world

Opening up to the outside world is a comparison to closed-door policy and it is a policy act of a sovereign nation. Opening up to the outside world in the modern sense has developed gradually with the establishment of capitalist production mode, development of Industrial Revolution and formation of the world market. Under the modern conditions, one sovereign nation's economic development is inseparably connected with the world economy. No country can position itself outside the world economic connection and shield and isolate itself but develop rapidly. The half-century development experience of developing countries also shows that complete import substitution development policy does not work. The only way to faster economic development is by full use of the global market, introduction of advanced technology and foreign capital, and development of export-oriented economy. Recognition of this idea has experienced an important ideological liberation process in developing countries especially in socialist planned economies, namely, opening up to the outside world requires support from ideological culture. The more recognition of urgency of transition and openness, the stronger and more consistent reform and opening up to the outside world will be. China's reform and opening up process is a very good example. Many years of experience has told us that the extent of ideological liberation matches the extent of opening. No ideological liberation, no opening in economy. As a result, opening should start with that of ideas, ideological liberation, which is a shakeup to people's conservative and closed ideas and status. That is to say, ideological liberation and breaking with the conventional ideas should be the must-have contents in "openness".

While economic system reform is implemented inside the country, further expansion and deepening of opening up to the outside world and attracting multinational corporations' direct investment has become an important measure in economic development by large developing countries. In the same vein, opening up to the outside world and attracting foreign capital in large developing countries are not possible without matching cultural support. Now, multinational corporations' overseas investment decisions hinge more on the soft investment environment in addition to its hard investment environment. In the soft investment environment, host country's culture is an extremely important variant. First, host country's culture can influence the products and services that such enterprises provide. Multinational corporations must adjust the products and services they provide in accordance with the host country's culture. For example, lotus in China symbolizes "pure, noble and elegant" while in Japan it represents "memorial". As a result, differences between host country's culture and home country's culture of multinational corporations may increase marketing cost of such corporations in the host country. Next, the extent of host country's culture to cater for foreign-invested enterprises will also have an important influence on production cost of foreign-invested enterprises in the host country. It is well known that in the early days of China's reform and opening up, when people looked for jobs, most of them preferred to work in government agencies and state-owned enterprises. This situation had made foreign-invested enterprises attract their needed talents only with salaries that were much higher than state-owned enterprises. However, this situation changed unknowingly when people better knew and accepted foreign-invested enterprises. Finally, differences between host country's culture and home country's culture of multinational corporations may influence to some extent communication and understanding among employees from these two cultural backgrounds. The barrier in communication and understanding may affect the implementation of enterprises' decision-making and dissemination of innovative thinking so as to result in lower production efficiency, increase in production cost and loss of market opportunities. It is fair to say that this influence may sometimes even prove to be fatal to the operation of multinational corporations in the host country.

Globalization of economies makes most countries to accept market economy culture. Formation of globalization of cultures makes closed-door countries to recognize the significance of market economy culture to its establishment and improvement of market economy system. This recognition itself is just a liberalization of ideology. Recognition and blending of market economy culture will further promote this country to open because when market economy develops to a certain degree there will be internal demand for opening, which is the evitable outcome of capital's global pursuit for profit. Then voluntary opening may be said to be a wise choice in line with the internal demand of economic development. Meanwhile, localization of global ingredients in globalization of cultures makes this country to enjoy the cultural basis of its economic exchanges with other countries. This has facilitated its economy to blend with the outside world and objectively promotes its process of opening up to the outside world. For developing countries, the more their cultures are blended with foreign cultures, the more beneficial it will be for the deepening of reform and opening up. As a result, globalization of cultures is beneficial to one country's process of opening up to the outside world.

III. Influence of globalization of cultures on deployment and service efficiency of resources

Most scholars think that cultures impact people first and then through these people penetrate economic organizations and social structures so as to influence one country's economic development. John Maynard Keynes said in *The General Theory* that "economists' thinking ... whether they are correct or not, the actual influence made are all beyond imagination ... Politicians think they are free from the scholarly world. But actually they are usually at the direction of some late economists' thinking. Those who are in power and full of ambition listened to various opinions proposed by their contemporaries, but they made their policies under the direction of some late and bad scholars." Then, politicians who make social and economic policies under the direction of the economic knowledge that they regard as infallible will undoubtedly influence deployment of resources. In addition, consumers' preference for certain commodities is obviously closely connected to their own cultural background. Consumers from different cultural backgrounds view different quantity of the same commodity differently. Then influence of globalization of cultures on one country's culture is bound to reflect its policy changes and changes in consumers' identification system on the original commodity.

Economic growth can be achieved by combination of "things" and "people". Among them, superaddition of production factors, economic structure changes and production technology upgrades all belong to the "thing" factor category while in the factor category of "people", except objective constitution factors such as number of laborers, work time, and social division of labor and specialization, this can only rely on the unleashing of subjective initiatives. On one hand, cultural difference can lead to laborer's labor input difference. Max Weber thought in his often-quoted *The Protestant Ethic and the Spirit of Capitalism* that Calvin's predestination doctrine makes its followers to devote into commerce and world accumulation to show their social status whereas the work ethics that Puritans advocated abolished the idea of "one's income should be the property that is just good enough for its living well" that Aristotle and Catholics advocated. In addition, Max Weber also pointed out in 1930 that the presumption made by economics scholars that "a raise in piece rate will increase output" would yield an opposite outcome in some agricultural society. This is because workers in the agricultural society think that leisure is more valuable than the accumulated value. As a result, a raise in piece rate will instead reduce daily workload and cause a reduction in output. W. Arthur Lewis clearly realized that "economic growth relies on people's attitudes on work, wealth, frugality, child bearing, creativity, strangers, risk taking and so on. All these attitudes are produced from the bottom of people's brain."[1] On the other hand, the question of people has already become the core question that determines economic development and social reforms. People are the most active and most vigorous factor and people's making directly determines productivity condition and economic development level. Cultures get involved in social productivity development through its function on people, and cultures (unofficial constraints) may direct people's spiritual orientation and values judgement standards to the track of economic development to increase individuals' need for achievement[2], mobilize individuals' enthusiasm and confidence in engaging in creative activities, promote constant improvement of their education level, and make technology reform and progress in production experiments so as to increase the service efficiency in resources.

As liberation of people's creativity, cultures' active role needs to be recognized. With such intellectual factors as knowledge and skills, cultures constantly raise people's level of science and technology, expand subject of labor's recognition scope, and create and improve production tools so as to utilize more efficiently the limited natural resources, provide guidance on thinking, theory and public opinion to

---

[1] W. Arthur Lewis. *The Theory of Economic Growth*. Beijing: The Commercial Press, 1983: 11.

[2] "Need for achievement" is a word adopted by David McClelland, a Harvard psychology professor, when he explained dynamic force factors in economic development. The so-called need for achievement means the values, spiritual orientation and internal motivation to create their own fate. David McClelland conducted numerous surveys on relationship between ancient Greek development period and modern society's social achievement need level and economic development to reach the conclusion that "one country or nation's economic development is positively related to this country or nation's need for achievement's strength. Or put it in another way, need for achievement is an important reason for economic development." Refer to Zhou Tianyong. *Development Economics*. Beijing: Publishing House of the Party School of the Central Committee of the CPC, 1997: 348.

material production, circulation and consumption, specify economic development's direction and scale, correctly treat the relationship between man and nature and environment and achieve coordinated development of economic benefit and social benefit. But, certain historical category produces certain social culture. Formation of various cultural ideas matches certain social economic basis and production relation so as to result in the periodic character of cultural ideas in that in the glorious course of promotion of social development cultures also have deposits of some negative factors that are not beneficial to social progress. Cultures themselves have differences in being traditional or modern, and advanced or backward and so on. People that are influenced by different cultures may create different factors of productivity. When the high, low and fast and slow in creativity is presented to be a rigid mode to affect productivity development, it will change to a negative factor that restricts productivity development and then restrict economic development. For example, there is one central thesis in the large number of documents on "Appalachian" in the United States, lack of tall mountain culture brings or at least reinforces the economic backwardness and poverty in this area. Appalachian with a village feature is restricted by traditional values such as traditionalism, familism and fundamentalism. These values used to fit this area well but they no longer fit modern society with urbanization and industrialization.

As a result, as one country's culture has both positive and negative effects on service efficiency of resources, globalization of cultures also has the positive and negative functions on one country's service efficiency of resources. On one hand, globalization of cultures provides an opportunity to one country's culture to absorb the excellent cultural ingredients in foreign cultures that are beneficial to its service efficiency in its resources. On the other hand, harmful ingredients in foreign cultures in globalization of cultures that are not beneficial to its service efficiency in its resources can also affect its culture.

Section Three Influence of Globalization of Cultures on Globalization of Economies

Globalization of economies promotes globalization of cultures. As a representation of interactions between cultures and economies in globalization, globalization of cultures plays an important role in globalization of economies and the role is centrally represented in international trade, international investment and international economic cooperation.

I. Influence of globalization of cultures on international trade

The unfavorable influence of various national cultures on international trade is primarily represented in two aspects: First, differences in cultures result in differences in economic systems to some extent. Market exchange rules and degree of credibility and so on differ under different economic systems. These differences may be fatal to cross-economic-system transactions. Second, consumer behavior theories tell us that consumers' choice of commodity and service is to achieve maximum utility under fixed income on the basis of the principle of "marginal utility obtained from unit output spent on each product is equal". Consumers' preferences for various commodities and services are obviously closely connected to their cultural backgrounds. As a result, utilities obtained by consumers with different cultural backgrounds toward the same quantity of the same commodity or service are different. That is to say that shadow prices of the same commodity or service in the eyes of consumers with different cultural backgrounds are different. This is equal to the fact that invisible trade barriers exist in circulation among different cultural groups for the same commodity or service. The more different cultures are, the higher the invisible barriers will be.

From the influence of globalization of cultures on globalization, we know that globalization of cultures to some extent forms global cultural ingredients. On one hand, formation of global cultural ingredients supports globalization of market economy, promotes establishment of international trade rules and customs in the world, reduces international trade transaction cost, and expedites international trade development. On the other hand, they make various nations have the same or similar knowledge and value identification of some things and commodities, reduce the cultural barriers in the circulation of commodities and services among different cultural groups, and promote global circulation of commodities and services.

In addition, in globalization of cultures, exchanges among the various nations' cultures make these countries understand better other countries' cultures. The understanding of the differences between other countries' cultures and home country's culture is a prerequisite to commodity's international differentiation marketing. Then, although globalization of cultures forms global cultural ingredients and presents localization of national cultures at the same time, a phenomenon of highlighting various nations' cultural differences, cultural difference obviously is not beneficial to sale in other countries of commodities and services that contain home country's culture. But this localization of national cultures unfolds under the condition of mutual exchanges of various national cultures. Cultural difference, once recognized by home country, can make international marketing of this country's commodities and services be in line with cultural differences and to some extent in conformity with the differences with other countries' cultures so as to expand sale of home country's commodities and services in the world.

As a result, globalization of cultures helps to reduce economic system differences and invisible trade barriers resulting from cultural differences so as to promote international trade development.

II. Influence of globalization of cultures on international investment

Cultures have national characters. Misunderstanding of national cultures will result in ineffective cross-culture exchanges. This ineffective exchange will result in all kinds of contradictions and may bring disastrous outcome for production operations and management in multinational corporations. Alan M. Rugman asserted that "although some economic forces to promote globalization exist, even more cultural and political barriers exist."[1] Presence of cultural barriers makes the idea of "a shared management culture results in uniformity in commercial practices and then establishing a global village merely a dream and is very hard to make it happen".[2] A great number of examples on cultural contradictions and

---

[1] Alan M. Rugman. *The End of Globalization*. Trans. Chang Zhixiao et al. Shanghai: SDX Joint Publishing Company, 2001: 16.

[2] Susan C. Schneider, Jean-Louis Barsoux. *Managing Across Cultures*. Beijing: Economic Management Publishing House, 2002: 24. This is a conclusion made by former *Harvard Business Review* editor Rosabeth Moss Kanter on a large number of surveys on 11,678 managers in 25 countries.

misunderstandings show that even negligence of a slight cultural difference may result in failure in cooperation. At the early days of Sino-French Guangzhou Peugeot Automobile Company, from president, divisional managers to technology supervisors and other important positions, they were almost all French. The company adopted a rigid and compulsory production organization mode and implemented a complete set of French-style management mode. This resulted in strong complaint from the Chinese employees and led to a group strike. Even mediation by the Chinese government and French Consulate General failed to solve this issue. The essence of this incident was cultural conflicts, which led to the failure of the parties' initial cooperative project. Whirlpool Corporation from the United States had its presence in Dongguan as early as in the 1980s. But owing to its lack of understanding of the Chinese culture, the company only lasted for a short period and then had to withdraw from the Chinese market.

Adequate realization of the driving force and potential impact force of cultures on business operations is a prerequisite for multinational corporations to successfully make their strategic cooperation, implement their overseas operations and explore the local markets. Just as scholars who specialize in the study of international marketing warned, "all the major failures by multinational corporations stem without any exception from their negligence of cultural differences".[①] From this, although presence of cultural differences is not beneficial to international investment, their harm to international investment is the worst only when cultural differences are neglected.

On one hand, globalization of cultures promotes formation of global cultural ingredients and to some extent reduces the differences between home country culture and host country culture. On the other hand, it expedites exchanges among different national cultures, facilitates and deepens understanding by multinational corporations of the differences between home country culture and host country culture and allows multinational corporations to adjust their production operation modes in accordance with host country culture. It is fair to say that globalization of cultures reduces cultural differences while it reduces the ability of cover-up of

---

[①] Fan Hui. "Cross-culture Management of Sino-Foreign Enterprises—on McDonnell Douglas' Cultural Blending Practice in Shanghai". *International Economic Cooperation*, Issue No. 10, 2002.

cultural differences so as to reduce the unfavorable influence of cultural differences on international investment. Localized operations, which is more and more favored as a key strategic choice by multinational corporations to explore further their overseas operations and achieve their integrated growth, is exactly a representation on the role that globalization of cultures plays in international investment.

III. Influence of globalization of cultures on international economic cooperation

Culture's position in international economic relations has been constantly rising and increasingly become the basis of international economic cooperation. Currently, world economy is accelerating to develop toward the total globalization. Regional integration shows a very strong trend. Various economic integration organizations are coming up like bamboo shoots. It is not difficult to find that cultures play a key role in regional economic integration. The most obvious is that internationally, successful economic cooperation happened mostly in homogeneous civilizations. European Union's rapid development is based on European civilization and Western Christianity. Success of North American Free Trade Agreement depends on the blending process of cultures of the United States, Canada and Mexico. Differences in various national cultures in Northeastern Asian region are a key factor that obstructs economic integration in this region. Northeastern Asian region, as the most culturally colorful region in the world, contains various unique cultural forms. This region is home for the Chinese people, Russian people, Japanese people, Korean people and Mongolian people who all had great and glorious ancient cultures. Presence of cultural diversity results in diverse conflicts of economic interests in the region, which creates frictions in economic cooperation.

With the development of globalization of economies, economic interdependence among countries keeps increasing. At the same time, economic frictions among countries become more frequent, which makes economic cooperation increasingly important. International economic cooperation is represented in interpersonal communication and such communication requires the prerequisite of respect for all the parties' subject status and subject power. This is a kind of common standards of behaviors. During the long international communication, for the sake of communication, different countries have formed or are forming many "international customary rules". These customary rules are the result of recognition of mutual standards of behaviors among the countries and respect for the interests, sovereignty and honor of these countries in communication. Because of this, joint declarations by the United Nations are made and international law is drafted. These common standards of behaviors must be premised on common cultural assessment. Without the common ethics and values, it is impossible to establish the common standards of behaviors. As a result, the global cultural ingredients formed by globalization of cultures provide a necessary cultural prerequisite to international customary rules in international economic cooperation. Communication among the various nations in globalization of cultures also deepens the understanding by various countries of other countries' cultures. This is beneficial to reaching consensus by the countries on the basis of seeking common ground and reserving their differences so as to accelerate development in international economic cooperation. As a result, globalization of cultures helps the further development of international economic cooperation.

In summary of all of the above, reaction of cultures on economies makes globalization of cultures reversely lubricate development of globalization of economies. We may say that globalization of cultures is a necessary safeguard and precondition to globalization of economies.

Chapter Three The Renaissance and the Rise of Modern Europe

Usually, the Renaissance refers specifically to European civilization during the 14th and 16th centuries. It not only represents that European civilization had an upsurge in these centuries featured with dazzling brilliance and flowers blooming, but also shows a decisive turning point in the historical process. Just as Jules Michelet, a great 19th century French historian, said, the Renaissance is not only a cultural revival, but also a start in an era that the modern world is already in the horizon.

Section One The Renaissance and the Technological Advances in Europe

The Renaissance not only brought huge social changes at the time in various areas in Europe such as politics, religion, thoughts and culture and so on, but also laid a foundation for the Enlightenment, Industrial Revolution and capitalist development that happened later. The Renaissance became a model of forming advanced culture and an important source of globalization of cultures.

I. Formation of humanism world outlook

The Renaissance is a great thinking liberation movement in European history. In summary, the basic features of the Renaissance are "rediscovery of man and the world; new idea of enjoying life; asceticism and symbolism yielding to sensory pleasure and naturalism; realism substituting idealism; and experimental mode of pursuit of knowledge replacing traditionalism and obscurantism".[①] It made people shake off theological thinking's bondage and human nature was restored. People were once again the subject that created their own cultures and people's spiritual activities shifted to a brand-new direction, namely, with people as the subject and with people as the target of thinking. This recognition of one's self is a starting point of creation of their own culture by the people.

Different from the medieval Christian Church's theological world outlook, the Renaissance proposed the new type of world outlook and historical view of humanism. Specifically, there are the following three primary idea changes:

(1) Confirm man is great and its pursuit of realist life. Medieval Christian Church thought that god was supreme and above everything. God was omnipotent and almighty. Man was tiny and god's sheep and was subject to god's disposal obediently and held himself as god's servant. Man was destined to suffer in reality and god arranged all this. In order to escape from the hardship, church advocated man practice asceticism, discard all the material life pleasure in realistic society, sever all desires, and diligently cultivate oneself according to a religious doctrine. This way people were under the bondage of Christian theological control. Literature and arts were withered, scientific and technological innovation almost stagnated, and economic development slowed down. Only when man's desires and pursuits were recognized could capitalist development obtain its sources and driving force. As a result, humanism praised man's value, dignity, nobleness, power and greatness. People-centered became the starting point or prelude to the Renaissance. Raphael was one of the traditional trinity of great masters of that period. In his masterpieces, *Sistine Madonna*, *Madonna of the Meadow* and *The Virgin and Child with Saint John the Baptist* (*La Belle Jardiniere*), the Virgin was always depicted as a good wife and loving mother and little Jesus was a lovely ordinary baby. There was not even a trace of the color of mysticism and asceticism that were found in the medieval traditional icons. Humanism clearly recognized man as the creator and enjoyer of the realistic life, happiness in the present time is above anything else, life's purpose is to pursue personal freedom and happiness and people are

---

[①] John F. H. New. *Renaissance and Reformation*. John Wiley & Sons Inc., 1969: 53.

encouraged to pursue honor and fortune. Recognition of man and human nature are the breakthrough and inner core in the idea changes during the Renaissance.

(2) It is a key condition for people's civilization and innovation to emphasize free will and uphold political freedom. The medieval church proclaimed that it was god's arrangement to have the universe order and the different classifications of people in the society. People can only accept this arrangement and cannot change it. People were servants under the dual despotic power of temporality and magisterium and lacked and even had no free will and political freedom. In *Heptaplus*, Giovanni Pico della Mirandola went ahead to place people beyond the system of the three worlds of angels, heavenly kingdom and natural power and so on and put people in the fourth world. Once theology was removed from Pico's discussions, the free will theory he proposed not only severely attacked the strict medieval hierarchy, but also laid a thinking foundation for the later political reform with republic and democracy as the core.

(3) Advocate ration and science and oppose obscurantism and mysticism. In the "Dark Ages", in order to establish the sole respect of theology by Christian Church, it enforced the principles of "knowledge yields to faith", "philosophy yields to theology", and "revelation is above ration", and implemented policy of obscurantism. Some popes blatantly proclaimed that "being ignorant and incompetent is mother of pious beliefs". Humanism, in diametrical opposition, proposed the slogan of "knowledge is power". They advocated reason and intelligence, and upheld search for nature, studied science, pursued truth, used knowledge to benefit human being, used education to develop human personality, and fully developed human ability and wisdom. In a word, it is necessary to adapt to social life's needs.

As a thought, humanism strongly attacked the theological ideas that had occupied the controlling position for almost one thousand years, and played down the rich religious color that shrouded people's spiritual world. Initial recognition of man's desires, power, will and intelligence made possible restoration of the cultural structure in Western Europe. Man once again became the subject of cultural creation and start and end-result of all the social activities circled man. What is more important is that humanism provided a theoretical basis for the later society's evolution process that people shook off all kinds of spiritual bondage and thinking obstacles.

II. Establishment of natural science view

Attention to human nature and man's natural essence formed the key driving force for renewed research on nature and its laws. Natural science was freed from the status of a servant-girl of theology for the past one thousand years or so and became an independently developed subject and provided a basis for the new world outlook and new philosophy. Engels highly praised the significance of liberation of natural science and he said that "this is a great revolution that had never happened on the earth. Natural science was also born and formed in this revolution and it was a complete revolution."[①] Francis Bacon, founder of British modern empirical science, also thought that this is "a great revival of science".

During the Renaissance it was astronomy that first broke theological world outlook and in this area the first challenger to the church authority was a great scientist Nicolaus Copernicus.

Based on his over 30 years of actual observation and calculations on the earth, the moon and planetary movements, Copernicus founded "heliocentric theory" and toppled ancient Greek-Egyptian astronomer Claudius Ptolemy's traditional "geocentric theory" and delivered a heavy blow to the church-sanctioned fallacy that the earth was the center of the universe and theological world outlook. Publication of Copernicus' *On the Revolutions of the Celestial Spheres* in 1543 signaled birth of modern science and world outlook. Einstein wrote that "Copernicus' great achievements not only paved the way for modern astronomy, but also helped people to have a decisive reform in their outlook on the universe".[②]

Danish astronomer Tycho Brahe and German astronomer Johannes Kepler further confirmed and developed Copernicus' heliocentric theory based on their astronomical observations. Tycho Brahe built Uraniborg astronomical observatory on the island of Hven and designed his own instruments. One of the quadrants with a relatively higher precision was later called "Tycho Quadrant". Kepler, on the basis of Tycho Brahe's materials and after his own observations and calculations, found

---

[①] *The Completed Work of Marx and Engels (Volume XX)*. Beijing: People's Publishing House, 1972: 533.

[②] *Selected Works of Einstein (Volume I)*. Trans. Xu Liangying et al. Beijing: The Commercial Press, 1979: 601.

the three laws of planetary motion, the so-called "Kepler's laws of planetary motion" and laid a foundation for celestial mechanics. Giordano Bruno, a famous Italian astronomer, also defended and developed Copernicus' theory. Bruno believed that the universe was infinite and the solar system was only a celestial system in the infinite universe, the sun was not stationary and its position with other planets was changing. He criticized Ptolemy's "geocentric theory" and proclaimed that Catholic and Protestant preachers were "the biggest stupid donkeys in the world". If Copernicus' heliocentric theory delivered a fatal blow to Christianity, Bruno's universe outlook brought Christianity to the brink of despair.

Galileo Galilei was the world's first astronomer to use a self-made telescope to observe celestial bodies. Based on light's refraction principle and a Dutch spectacle-maker's revelations, he made the first telescope but only with 3x magnification. Through constant improvements, he later made an astronomical telescope with 32x magnification. Galilei used his own telescope to find a nova and started a new chapter in astronomy. In addition, he also invented a thermometer. Galilei devoted all his life to blaze the trail for revival of natural science and became a founder of modern natural science.

During the Renaissance, the reason that astronomers were able to break Ptolemy's "geocentric theory" was partially due to the fact that Copernicus, Kepler, Galilei and others used their mathematical knowledge to calculate precisely the stars' positions. The person that merits attention in the mathematics field was French mathematician François Viète who was called by the Western people as "the father of algebra". He was the first to use words as symbols in algebra and vowels to indicate unknown numbers and consonants to indicate known numbers and general formulas to indicate equations and their roots' nature. He also established a unified approach to solve quadratic, cubic and quartic equations. His mathematical achievements influenced greatly the later generations. René Descartes had benefited greatly from François Viète's works and successfully applied the latter's algebra achievements to geometry and founded analytical geometry. Descartes' pioneering work caused a profound revolution in mathematics. Later Isaac Newton and others applied Descartes' methods and used algebra to indicate a geometric point's motion algebra equation to describe geometric graphs and founded calculus. Pierre de

Fermat, a contemporary with Descartes, made notable contributions to mathematical research and he was best known for Fermat's Last Theorem which he wrote conveniently as notes when he was reading ancient Greek mathematical works.①

If humanism only aroused man's subject consciousness and individualism, natural science's glorious victory provided a reliable basis for people to despise authorities and doubt the sacred ideas. Man began to really understand the world and see clearly their own position in the world. They could no longer maintain their humbleness and quietness as they used to and they were full of confidence and in high spirits and were determined to control nature with their own strength. Ever since then, a profound reform happened in man's world outlook and values and the Western civilization had started its fundamental reform since that time.

III. Ideological liberation and scientific and technological advances brought by the Renaissance

The ideological reforms during the Renaissance made thearchy decline and people want changes. In the course of ideological liberation to advocate human nature, free will and oppose the church dictatorship, there was an unprecedented development in man's personality and talents. Engels once said that "this is the greatest and progressive reform that had never happened in mankind and it is also a time that giants were both required and born and of such giants in thinking capability, enthusiasm and character and in versatility and being learned."②

Leonardo da Vinci was a representative figure of giants in the Renaissance. It is well known that he was a painter, sculptor, engineer, architect, physicist, botanist, and philosopher and made a notable contribution in every scientific subject. Especially in natural science, his vision and scientific knowledge surpassed his times. The genius da Vinci had predicted those that modern scientists had spent several centuries to conduct research on. He boldly proposed that man and animals were very much the same and his idea was more than 300 years earlier than Charles Darwin's evolutionary theories. He ascertained that one of the causes that old people

---

① Chen Xiaochuan, Guo Zhenduo, et al. *The Outline of the Renaissance*. Beijing: Renmin University Publishing House, 1986: 448.

② Friedrich Engels. *Dialectics of Nature*. Beijing: People's Publishing House, 1971: 7.

died was arteriosclerosis, which is proven by modern medicine. He imagined that man could utilize solar power, which was made possible today, over 400 years later. He predicted inertia principle which was proven later by Galilei's experiment. He even described in a very vivid and lifelike manner the power of atomic energy "that thing will explode and rise from the underground ... make people die suddenly in silence and castles will also be destroyed completely and it appears that destruction is in the air".

da Vinci's achievements in military science was even more surprising. He invented machine gun, tank, submarine and double-hull warship, and so on and so forth. He designed a large ocean-going submarine and some scholars concluded that his achievement had reached the WWII level. Through observing birds' flight, he designed himself various kinds of flying machines, helicopters and parachutes, and so on and test-flied those himself. In order to memorialize da Vinci's contribution in inventing flying machines, a large sculpture of him was built in the waiting area's plaza in the newly constructed Rome International Airport.

da Vinci embodied and represented in the highest manner possible the perfect combination of humanism in the Renaissance and scientific spirit. His innovative capability in a great number of fields shows the great potential obtained after ideological liberation. Meanwhile, his research and findings in natural science blazed the trail for inventions and creations by the later scientists such as Copernicus, Galilei, William Harvey, Newton and so on.

The world outlook changes during the Renaissance and attention to man and its social life made scientific inventions develop toward practicality. All the technological innovations served as much as possible to raise social productivity and improve people's life.

First we need to mention inventions of cannons and firearms. Even though gunpowder was invented by the Chinese people, it was the Westerners who first used it in war. At first the cannons made were very primitive so that the one who stood after a cannon feared about his own safety more than the one who stood in front of the cannon. After the mid-15th century, performance of cannons was much improved. Later firearms with even more killing power appeared and their technology was also gradually perfected. In 1453, new weaponry showed its power on the battlefields. Ottoman Turks used German and Hungarian's cannons to break through the defense lines of Constantinople and Byzantine Empire perished. The French used gunnery to take over Bordeaux and ended the Hundred Years' War. When Western Europe started its overseas expansion, cannons' use was expanded to be on board the warships. In the mid-15th century, most European warships were installed with bronze cannons. At the end of the 15th century, inexpensive iron cannons replaced extremely expensive copper cannons. Establishment of the sea forces primarily equipped with ship-based cannons as their main killing weaponry credited the Europeans with the absolute advantage in the military technology for their expansion to the East.

In the mid-15th century, before Johannes Gutenberg printed Europe's first work with mechanical movable type printing, books were luxuries only for the noblemen. After the year of 1500 or so, Europeans may read and buy at leisure all kinds of books as invention of printing not only reduced cost of books but also facilitated exchange and distribution of ideology and cultures. Prior to invention of printing, owing to the great differences in dialects in various places, it was relatively difficult for internal exchanges among European countries, and this affected to some extent centralization in politics. After invention of printing, European countries started to form their own language standards and distributed them out through books. "Standardized English" was the language used in London printing, but it was distributed to Yorkshire and Wales.[①]

In his *Novum Organum Scientiarum* ("new instrument of science") Francis Bacon summarized scientific results since the 15th and 16th centuries: "The power, virtues and results of inventions are obvious. And nothing can compare with these three inventions that were completely unknown to the ancient people (namely, China's printing, gunpowder and the compass). These three inventions have changed the appearance and conditions of the entire world; the first in literature, the second in warfare, and the third in navigation; whence have followed innumerable changes, in so much that no empire, no sect, no star seems to have exerted greater power and

---

[①] Phillip Lee Ralph et al. *World Civilizations: Their History and Their Culture*. Beijing: The Commercial Press, 2001: 723.

influence in human affairs than these mechanical discoveries."[1] Exploration from god to natural science indicated major changes in science and culture and gave birth to and promoted rise of ideological liberation movement in Europe.

Section Two The Renaissance and European Economy

I. Science and technology transformed to productivity—industrial development

Einstein said that "science directly and to a great extent indirectly produced tools that have changed completely man's life".[2] Then science influenced human society's development. Indeed, countries in the world started their industrialization and modernization process with scientific and technological progress and then used such progress as their foundation.

In the 15th and 16th centuries, new technologies started new industries' rapid development. Industries like papermaking, printing, glassmaking, horological industry, coal industry and so on quickly developed. Take glassmaking industry for example, before 1560 the output of glasses was less than 20,000 cartons. In the 17th century, the output reached 100,000 cartons. Owing to constant technological progress in horological industry, the styles were more and more delicate and exquisite and their prices tended to be inexpensive and enjoyed wider uses. Clocks and watches were no longer decorations for public facilities but became available to common households. In the 16th and 17th centuries, horological industry passed from Augsburg and Nuremberg to Paris, Geneva and London. In 1680, output of clocks in Geneva was 5,000 and horological industry was a new industry there. By the same vein, after Gutenberg printing was invented, book culture became a basic aspect in European life style. By the mid-15th century, printing had become one of the key industries in Europe. At the time, handicraft workshops had started to yield to factory-style manufacture. In order to raise profits, handicraftsmen united to start factories. Because printing was a new industry, guild's control was less in

---

[1] Allen G. Debus. *Man and Nature in the Renaissance*. Trans. Zhou Yanling. Shanghai: Fudan University Publishing House, 2000: 1.

[2] *Selected Works of Einstein (Volume III)*. Trans. Xu Liangying et al. Beijing: The Commercial Press, 1979: 135.

comparison with those traditional businesses. As a result, printing became a capitalist industry at an early date.

There was a breakthrough in mining technology which made deep mining possible and the number of new deposits increased. According to statistics, during the period between 1460 and 1530, mining output increased fivefold in central European mining areas such as Hungary, Tirol, Bohemia and Saxony.[①] Mining of silver and copper made large-scale minting possible and expedited circulation of currency in the market. Coal and iron mining also developed and hydraulic bellows simplified work in iron casting factories and a great amount of iron was made in ironmaking furnaces in Styria and Liège. After 1453, alum mining saw a rapid development in Western Europe. Alum was primarily used in manufacture of dyestuff and was raw material for Europe's textile and dyestuff industries. So there was a demand for alum in the European countries. After death of the Byzantine Empire, Turkish people controlled manufacture and trade in alum, which resulted in price hikes. When alum mines were discovered in Italy's Volterra, soon it became the focus of European wars and diplomatic fighting. In order to monopolize the alum mining manufacture, Florence people did not hesitate and resorted to force. In 1472, Florence people occupied Volterra and since then controlled alum manufacture there. During 1460 and 1461, better deposits of alum were discovered in Tolfa, the Papal States and the Pope ordered mining start at once. By 1463, the mining began to take shape and there were four mines and more than 8,000 miners there. This not only solved Europe's demand for alum but also made the Pope obtain the dual benefits of finance and monopoly in mining.

Owing to a great number of challenges they faced in organization and technology, traditional textile industry started to decline but manufacture of luxuries and decorations developed to some extent. Industries such as tapestry, woodwork products, enamelware, fur and leather and metal processing, garments, weaponry, construction and others came in vogue to represent the above trend. Delft was famous for its colored and glazed ceramics. Augsburg and Nuremberg were known for their gold and silver products. Antwerp was famous for its tapestry. Garments

---

[①] Thomas A. Brady, Jr. *Turning Swiss: Cities and Empire, 1450-1550.* Quoted from Zhu Xiaoyuan. *Rise of Modern Europe.* Shanghai: Xuelin Publishing House, 1997: 176.

gained practical and important significance. Cotton cloth and silk were processed in a more and more delicate manner. Dresses worn by the general public changed from durable woolen fabrics to gaudy, lightweight and thin materials. As a result, coating fabrics rose by replacing coarse wool ones.

The ever increasing market in Americas promoted industrial growth in Western Europe. On one hand, Western European ports such as Seville, Lisbon, Antwerp and others imported a large amount of gold and silver, cane sugar, dyestuffs and so on from West Indies, Spanish colonies, Brazil and other places. On the other hand, they shipped manufactured products from places like France, Flanders, the Netherlands, Silesia and other Western European places to American markets. Manufactured products shipped to Americas and Western Africa were rich in variety. In addition to linen and woolen products, there were also metal products, guns and gunpowder, silk products and glass beads as well as paper, religious books and others from France and Italy. These export products stimulated development in Europe's industries in textiles, metal products, and shipbuilding.

The mercantilist feature as shown in some European countries also paved the way for industrial development. In the 15th century, in order to protect its own textile industry, England even issued some decrees: In 1455, import of silk products was banned. In 1463, export of wool by foreigners was banned. In 1464, restriction was placed on continental corduroy industry, which predicted firm protectionism and mercantilism of Henry VII of England, and at that time British industry gradually surpassed the advantage of its agriculture. This move by the British was met immediately with the revenge from Nederland. Duke of Burgundy (1419-1467) ordered to stop import of corduroy from England as Nederland's most important industry suffered losses. In addition, he encouraged Dutch merchant fleets to compete with Teutons' Hanseatic League and assisted Antwerp's development. Since then, Antwerp replaced Bruges' superior position and in one century became the largest commercial center in the world. Louis XI of France was also famous for his capability and energy of implementing his policies. In order to establish its own silk industry, in 1466, France imported technical workers from Italy and gave them preferential care. After the boycott by foreign merchants and church, the king spared no high price to move silk factories from Lyon to Tours as the royal power could directly control Tours. Finally, silk industry in France developed. In the early 16th century, the silk industry in France developed from 16 workers to 800 masters and 4,000 workers. By the mid-16th century, employees in the French silk industry doubled. Moreover, the king introduced mining to Dauphiné.[①] In a word, the countries' policies greatly promoted the industrial development.

In the year of 1500 or so, areas from Bruges in the north to Florence in the south, including Flanders, northern Italy and southern Germany, were developed industrial areas in Europe. Daily products such as woolen goods, silk goods, flax goods, glassware, ceramics, leather, paper and so on as well as weapons and armor enjoyed good sales in other parts of Europe. Meanwhile, agricultural products, raw materials and semi-finished products were being transported there. But, after industrialization happened in France, the Netherlands and England, geographical distribution of industries changed greatly. With their low cost and high quality, new industrial areas in the north quickly took over the market. The old industrial areas lost their leading position as they were squeezed out by the competition. The Netherlands and England took over Italy as the center in woolen goods, shipbuilding and metallurgy industries. Milan and Venice's silk goods industry was taken over by Lyon and Tours. Flanders, Bavaria and Lombardy's cannon making centers were frozen out by England and Sweden. Spain lost not only its domestic market, it also had its colonies edged out. At the end of the 16th century, Spain degenerated to a transport station of French, Dutch and English commodities. Of course, those old industrial areas with advantages in natural resources and technical skills continued to be very much developed such as the luxuries making industry. Industrial fields with extensive influence and expanding market such as Italy's papermaking industry continued to hold a relatively important share owing to its centralized production of high-grade paper. Some old industrial areas, backed with increased products' colors and styles and upgrading in quality, continued to be somewhat competitive. For example, woolen goods industry in Ghent and Bruges and silk goods industry in northern Italy and flax goods industry in Flanders and so on continued to hold their market shares owing to their shift to production of textiles with superior

---

[①] Refer to Henri Pirenne. *Economic and Social History of Medieval Europe*. Trans. Le Wen. Shanghai: Shanghai People's Publishing House, 2001: 205-206.

workmanship and quality.

II. Development in commerce and trade

Rise in industry during the Renaissance laid a foundation for the development in commerce and trade. With the continued development in urban economy and fair trade, commodity exchanges among various districts in Europe became more frequent and several major trading districts were formed based on these exchanges: in the Mediterranean trading district, some cities in Italy such as Venice, Genoa, Pisa and others were the largest trading districts in southern Europe and also the most important trading districts in the entire Europe. Owing to their superior geographical position, they not only influenced European commercial development, but also facilitated trade between the East and the West and became a distribution center of world products. The trading district with Flanders and Bruges as its center including northern Germany, Nederland, England, Scandinavia and Russia was the largest commercial district in northern Europe—the North Sea and Baltic Sea trading district. Fishes, lumber, hides and fur, honey and grains from northern Europe and eastern Europe, and western European's corduroy, wines and handicraft items were all traded here. The Hanseatic League was a trade bloc established in the mid-14th century and was composed of cities in northern Germany such as Hamburg and Lübeck and others and united with more than 100 cities in northern Europe. This district was located in the central position of northern Europe and southern Mediterranean and western Europe and Slavic East and enjoyed a superior geographical advantage. The Rus trading district was the largest trading district in eastern Europe. It not only connected with trading with European districts, but also was the trading medium between Europe and the East. The Rus' merchants broke Byzantine's monopoly of East and West trade and directly transported silk, spices and other Eastern products to western Europe. Britain trading district was another important trading district in western Europe and was closely connected with the Mediterranean trading district and the Hanseatic League. Italian merchants played a major role in Britain trading district. They set up many subsidiaries in Britain at an early date and transported spices, silk, jewelry, chinaware and tea from the East for sale in the Britain market. Meanwhile, they purchased wool, corduroy and minerals locally and transported them back to the Mediterranean trading district. The formation of these trading districts showed that European trade had developed to a certain degree in the 14th and 15th centuries and initially shaped a pan-Europe trading network.[①]

Another important change was merchants' operations at a fixed place. At first, merchants brought their products and traveled with them and were often accompanied with armed guards. Later, they not only had fixed places of operations, but also united to form some kind of associations and allowed such organizations to control their risks associated with their trade. Under the promotion of Italian merchants, the original one-time cooperation gradually developed into a relatively long-term commercial cooperation organization and they developed their business by setting up permanent branch offices and agency stores in important cities. In the 14th century, major companies in Florence established representative agencies in Barletta, Bologna, Genoa, Naples, Perugia, Venice, Avignon, Bruges, London and Paris. Many representative agencies set up branches in other places. During the period between 1440 and 1450, House of Medici opened branch stores in Rome, Naples, Venice, Geneva, Pisa, London, Avignon, Milan and Lyon. Ravensberg's large companies had their offices all over cities in Deutschland, Switzerland, France, Italy and Spain.

In the 14th century, owing to the trade development and new demands, the commerce portion was freed from the yoke of notary public and changed to validity guaranteed with private seals affixing and only the parties' signatures. Trade development also resulted in the issuance of some laws such as commercial law, merchant law and maritime traffic regulations. Meanwhile, there were regulations on special trade and maritime jurisprudence: in England, Court of Piepowders, and later Court of Chancery; in Venice, Genoa, Florence and Barcelona, maritime court and Commercial Court; and in Bordeaux, the L'Ombrière supervisors. They often used extremely fast and efficient procedures to try cases: some cases were decided "within one day", some were decided "between two high tides" and some were decided "among three high tides".

[①] Song Zexing, Fan Kang. eds. *History of World Trade (Volume I)*. Beijing: Economic Science Publishing House, 1998: 14-16.

The main payment method in commercial transactions was still cash. At the time, European countries minted their own currencies. Various kinds of currencies were circulated in the market. Although most currencies were undisputed in quality, some were adulterated. As a result, money exchange business became popular. Through money exchangers' business, on one hand, currencies in circulation in the market were examined, and on the other hand, traveling merchants' safety was guaranteed. Traveling merchants could save their money with money exchangers. In exchange, money exchangers issued these merchants one receipt proving the amount of money they deposited. In this way, money exchangers' business gradually changed to banking industry.[①]

The innovative spirit during the Renaissance was also reflected in the perfection of accounting techniques and development in credit instruments. As in many other fields, the Italians were once again the leaders in this field. From one ledger maintained by the Genoese firm of Massari, the Genoese invented the double-entry bookkeeping. Calculation and counting were also applied in the commercial practice. Based on the use of Arabic numerals, in the 14th century, "modern" date recording method (e.g. January 1) happened, which simplified bookkeeping procedures. One day and the clock were divided into 12 or 24 equal hours so as to facilitate more accurate time keeping, which was a model to use scientific management in businesses.[②]

Bill of exchange was a significant progress in credit instrument development history. In banks of the 14th century, bill of exchange was used to transfer one person's money to another person in a different city. Every bill of exchange contained a short-term loan with interest. Owing to the hardship in traveling at the time, even though the bill of exchange was payment on demand, it would also take several weeks for it to clear the payment. Meanwhile, because bill of exchange involved a relatively large amount and the payor needed time for such an amount, the payment date was often prolonged. Bill of exchange solved the issue of

---

[①] Frédéric Delouche, Jacques Aldebert, et al. *The History of Europe*. Trans. Cai Hongbin, Gui Yufang. Haikou: Hainan Publishing House, 2000: 264.

[②] Carlo M. Cipolla. ed. *Economic History of Europe (Volume I)*. Trans. Xu Xuan. Beijing: The Commercial Press, 1998: 266.

merchants paying the amount to a creditor in a different city and also provided some credit for the merchants. This greatly facilitated the trade development among the places. "Endorsement" appeared relatively late, probably in the mid-15th century. The reason was that an often quoted example was in 1430. Endorsement made bill of exchange have all the features of paper money. With acceptance after "endorsement", a bill of exchange became a transferable instrument. Antwerp started to use endorsement widely in 1570. Endorsement also became popular in the late 16th century in most commercial centers in Italy.

The check system, namely, the depositor issues a check to the banker for payment by the banker to a third party, appeared in Italy for the first time in the mid-14th century. Later, this system spread elsewhere through Italy and became popular in countries in western Europe in the late 16th century.

A simple loan method was also used in England and Nederland where a promissory note was issued to a debtor who was allowed to pay back this amount within a certain period of time. As early as in the 15th century, English merchants often issued promissory notes to creditors for payment of loans. This payment method was popular in the 16th century in cities in Nederland. Later, exchange banks in Amsterdam and Venice and goldsmiths in London all issued promissory notes to depositors who could cash them at any time. In addition, promissory notes issued by banks in Amsterdam could be circulated and transferred like currencies.

It is called discounting of instruments when credit instruments were sold to third parties below their face value prior to their due dates. As early as in 1536, discounting of instruments emerged in Nederland. Wider application was after 1550 and later in Augsburg and Hamburg. As for other commercial centers in Europe, discounting of instruments began in the 17th century.[①]

III. System change—establishment of capitalism

Increase in productivity in agriculture and handicraft industry as well as development in commodity-money relationship caused the production relationship in the feudal society to disintegrate gradually. In the 14th and 15th centuries, buds of

---

[①] Song Zexing, Fan Kang. eds. *History of World Trade (Volume I)*. Beijing: Economic Science Publishing House, 1998: 98-99.

capitalism appeared one after another in cities in northern Italy such as Venice, Genoa, Pisa, Florence, Milan and others; Marseille and Paris in France; Cologne in Germany; Bruges, Ghent, Ypres, and Ylläs in Flanders, southern Nederland; England's London, and other places. However, just as Marx mentioned, "capitalist times started in the 16th century".[①] The period between the 16th and 18th centuries was the time that feudal system collapsed and capital primitive accumulation and capitalist handicraft workshops developed and also a transitional period from feudalism to capitalism. The Renaissance played a critical role in promoting this transition.

First, the Renaissance brought a sense of liberation for early modern European civilization and provided a driving force for capitalist development. It endowed people with rich creativity that could be used to free productivity, and revitalize politics, economy and culture. It quickened people's life steps, and cut off the ropes that bound people. All kinds of backward things such as lack of attention to technological inventions, all kinds of relationships that entangled people, people's irrational treatment of political, economic and marriage issues, loss of humanity as people were controlled by the priests, passively yielding to hierarchy and so on and so forth, were effectively contained. It caused people to gain a kind of "spiritual freedom" and one kind of "worldly freedom". People started to emphasize man's free will. Europeans became full of energy, character, impact force and imagination. Western Europe was greatly energized as a result of application of scientific and technological inventions, especially printing, sailing, shipbuilding, gunpowder and compasses. Among them, sailing and shipbuilding were the most important as they enabled Europe to control the three continents' resources and to complete its primitive accumulation of capital quickly. Moreover, the 16th century was a pre-industrial period. Except northern Italy and some districts in the Low Countries, Europe was basically an agricultural society. So this was particularly significant.

Next, the Renaissance promoted combination of capital with power and created a condition for primitive accumulation of capital. The Renaissance opposed feudal separationist rule and advocated a centralized power state under the rule of

---

[①] *Completed Works of Marx and Engels (Volume XXIII)*. Beijing: People's Publishing House, 1972: 784.

enlightened despots. This is in essence a reflection that the new capitalist class hoped to seek its own development under the strong royal power. This lessened the conflict between consumer political system and productive economic factors because capital and power found a mutually promoting point of cooperation. In order to develop economy, the new capitalist class requested to abolish such medieval restrictions as tariffs, road duties, prohibition of producing to earn interest by the people and so on. The medieval economy was a self-sufficient natural economy. The feudal lords imposed severe restrictions on production and trade with an aim to earn profits. Meanwhile, some rulers with ambition found that development in their partnership with the new capitalist class could limit the vassals' power, strengthen the central government's power and establish a new and infinite power base. In this way, in the course of formation of modern national countries, evolution of the partnership between the national rulers and capitalist class strengthened the parties' fortune and power to make mercantilism happen.

Mercantilism is to rely upon the government's intervention to promote accumulation of profits. Mercantilists thought this would make the country prosper and the urban commerce class who made key contribution to mercantilism would also benefit greatly from this. In order to keep trade surplus, obtain gold and silver, export industry and foreign trade had to be developed and a strong merchant fleet had to be established and colonies had to be secured. English economist Thomas Mun (1571-1641) was the first one to discuss mercantilism. In his book *England's Treasure by Forraign Trade* he pointed out that although a country could become rich by receiving gifts or through buying from other countries, this is unstable; and the means to increase private fortune and public fortune is foreign trade with exports at a higher rate than imports.[①] As a result, it was required to set up enterprises with privileges and monopoly trading companies. Domestic duties and transit duties need to be abolished and uniform border tariffs system and uniform measures and weights need to be adopted. Efforts need to be made to construct a great number of projects such as harbors, canals, roads, and so on to revitalize the country's economy.

In addition, another important content in mercantilism was to establish overseas

---

[①] Li Shian. *History of Development in European and American Capitalism*. Beijing: China Renmin University Publishing House, 2004: 35.

colonies to ensure Europe's smooth overseas expansion. Country rulers and merchants in Europe all hoped to use this means to expand their power and increase their fortune. "Discovery of gold and silver mines in Americas, the wiping out, enslaving and burying in mines of the native people, conquering and looting of the East Indies, and putting Africa into a place of commercially hunting the black people, all this indicates the dawn of capitalism. These idyllic processes are the main factors of primitive accumulation of capital".[1] Portugal and Spain were the first to establish colonies. Although they were unable to use the looted fortune to develop their own capitalism owing to the still strong feudal power, Portugal and Spain's fortune, through trade channels, flew into the Low Countries and became the latter two's primitive capital. After Spain, the Netherlands, England and France established their colonies one after another. Dutch East India Company was at its heyday in the 1630s and 1640s. Dutch West India Company was founded in 1621 and enjoyed the privilege of monopoly in trading with African west coast, American east coast and the islands in the Pacific Ocean. Looting from its colonies provided a large amount of primitive capital for the Netherlands and promoted its economic development. In the mid-17th century, the Netherlands became the most developed capitalist country. It enjoyed a flourishing commerce, and its fishing, shipping business and workshop handicraft industry led over all the other countries in Europe. Its capital city Amsterdam was the then world trade center and also an international credit center. Marx described the Netherlands as "the standard capitalist country in the 17th century".[2] Owing to the looting in the overseas colonies, countries in Asia, Africa and Americas gradually became colonies and semi-colonies and their economies suffered heavy losses. But countries in western Europe completed their own primitive accumulation from this process and laid a foundation for the birth of capitalist production mode.

Next, birth of new economic organizations and management systems of western European capitalism relied to some extent on the promotion of the Renaissance. In the Middle Ages, christianity viewed observing poverty and temperance as virtues. But thinkers during the Renaissance thought that fortune was the source of

---

[1] *Complete Works of Marx and Engels (Volume XXIII)*. Beijing: People's Publishing House, 1972: 783.
[2] Ibid., 820.

happiness that would make people happy and greed for fortune was the motivator of all enterprises. Transmutation and improvement in the idea of fortune made merchants' pursuit for interests more rational and objectively promoted commercial prosperity. Expansion of commerce and trade required a stable currency supply as guarantee. As a result, financial organizations developed with it. For example, House of Medici in Florence used the profits from the wool trade and industrial production to make loans and became western Europe's first group of creditors and then they founded banks. In the 14th century, Florence became the center of banks in Europe. Very quickly, banks were founded in western European countries. Management of banks required special knowledge, currency in circulation and knowledge of currency minting and so on. In the long time of currency management, the Europeans developed the relevant techniques and management knowledge and founded international currency credit and loan network. Appearance of credit and loan service system made exchange of invoices possible. By the 16th century, countries in Europe started to use paper money. Birth of credit and loan and paper money promoted western European economy and its overseas expansion capability. Moreover, in their daily economic activities, people had found that if their resources were pooled they could achieve their respective profit-making goals. So they formed investment companies where investors put their funds into them and received dividends at regular periods. After companies were invented, the most efficient united share-holding companies were born. United share-holding companies meant that members of the companies pooled their resources and selected managers to manage them and then received dividends in accordance with their shares. These new organizations were the most basic economic organizations of the capitalist society and also they were the most vibrant economic organizations of the capitalist economic activities.

The Renaissance made preparations in ideology and public opinions for the capitalist class to seize the power. With the development and distribution of the Renaissance, capitalist revolution was staged all over Europe. By the late 16th century, Nederland first established its capitalist class power. Subsequently, capitalist revolution was completed in England, France and the United States. We may say that the appearance of the Renaissance was largely due to the rise of capitalism. In turn, rise of the Renaissance promoted capitalist development in the fields such as ideology, culture, politics and economy and so on. As a result, German scholar Alfred von Martin in his book *Sociology of the Renaissance* directly called the Renaissance a capitalist revolution.

In summary, the innovative thinking that was formed before the Renaissance created a good prerequisite for the formation of economic development and advanced economic operations system and promoted science and technology in the economic field and led to the progress in material productivity. From the perspective of globalization of cultures, formation and establishment of advanced cultures laid a foundation for the ideology liberation for scientific and technological revolution, economic development and then system changes.

Section Three   The Renaissance and Globalization of Economies

I. Seamanship's influence on international trade

After the 15th century, western Europe's shipbuilding technology saw a major breakthrough. Before that, western European ships were primarily equipped with single masts only. They were suitable for sailing in inland seas or along the shores but not for long-distance sailing well into the ocean. In the 1420s, northern Europe had snows and in the 1450s Genoa had schooners. These ships were able to sail with the wind or against the wind and suitable for complicated weather conditions in the oceans. Scientific and technological advances during the Renaissance greatly improved seamanship. In addition to sea compass, combined use of astrolabe, dogvane, improved winch, anchor, cable chain and other instruments made ocean navigation possible. Drawing of charts became more accurate. Application of astrological instruments enabled ships' positions in the ocean measured. Moreover, appearance and use of mass killing weapons such as cannons and muskets not only ensured the safety of western European exploration teams, but also enhanced the looting capabilities. The material conditions for new sea routes were ready. In 1487, Europeans rounded Cape of Good Hope in Africa. In 1492, West Indies were discovered. In 1499, India was reached and in 1500 Brazil was discovered. In 1519,

Ferdinand Magellan made the first circumnavigation of the earth. Vital communication lines of human civilization were changed from continents and adjacent seas to oceans. Various regions on the old continents changed from isolated to interconnected. The Eastern Hemisphere and the Western Hemisphere were combined and globalization appeared for the first time.

One of the major changes that sea navigation technology caused international trade was development in the means of transport, and overland trade yielded to sea trade. Overland transport relied on four-wheeled carriages drawn by oxen or horses. The road conditions were awful and extremely unsafe. Sea transport was featured by relatively large load and port docking and unloading charges were much less than road tariffs for overland transport and water transport. Moreover, improvement in shipbuilding technology, chart drawing and improvement in sea navigation facilities during the Renaissance enhanced ocean shipping and ships became safe and reliable means of transport. As a result, overland trade gradually declined and the absent treatment of fairs of Champagne was mostly due to this change.

New sea-lanes' influence on international trade was also reflected in the changes in trade corridors. Since the Middle Ages, there were primarily three trade corridors that connected Eurasia Continent and Africa Continent: the first one is from the north coast of the Mediterranean Sea to Constantinople, cross Turkey, along the Black Sea and Caspian Sea, through Iran and Afghanistan and then pass across Asia Continent to arrive at China; the second one is from the Syrian region on the eastern coast of the Mediterranean Sea, through Mesopotamia to arrive at Persian Gulf, then cross Arabian Sea to arrive at India; and the third one is from the southern coast of the Mediterranean Sea to go through Egypt to the Red Sea and then cross the Indian Ocean to arrive at India. These commercial routes all started with the coastal areas of the Mediterranean Sea. As a result, cities on the coast of the Mediterranean Sea became centers of international trade. After the new sea routes opened up, countries in western Europe could round Africa's western coast from the south to arrive at the East, they could also cross Central and South America from the west to arrive at Asia. These new corridors were all from the western coast of European Continent or started from England, so the international trade centers transferred from the coastal areas of the Mediterranean Sea to the coastal areas of the Atlantic Ocean. In the mid-16th century, Antwerp replaced Bruges and Ghent to become an international metropolitan city. Each year thousands of ships entered and departed this port and commodities from all over the world were gathered and scattered here. Trade and financial activities among European countries were also centralized here. Every movement and every action here influenced the entire Europe. Delays in Spanish and Portuguese ships could possibly cause chaos in Antwerp's commerce and could even result in bankruptcy of banks in Augsburg or Ulm. After the 17th century, with the rise of the Dutch Republic, Amsterdam replaced Antwerp and became the largest commercial port in Europe. In the 18th century, when the Netherlands was in a recession, England rose to become the world overlord with its industrial strength.

After Age of Discovery, the economic connection between Europe and other parts of the world strengthened greatly and the number and variety of commodities in the world trade jumped quickly. In the European markets, many new commodities such as tobacco, coffee, cocoa, tea and others that were unprecedented showed up. Import of commodities such as rice and cane sugar that were rarely seen before rose by many times. Spices, a high-end luxury that used to be enjoyed by the noblemen, were imported in a great quantity and then its prices decreased with such imports and became a popular item for the public. When the Portuguese first arrived at the East, the annual import of pepper to Europe averaged 1.5 million pounds or so. In the 17th century, its imports jumped to seven million pounds. In 1772, the import by the Netherlands alone was as high as 9.05 million pounds.[①] The case with textiles was even more impressive than this. During the period between 1618 and 1621, the average annual import of cotton cloth by Dutch East India Company was only about 10,000 bolts. During the period between 1684 and 1689, its annual imports rose to more than 200,000 bolts, an increase by nearly 20 times. During the period between 1600 and 1700, England's import of Chail from India increased from 240,000 bolts to 860,000 bolts, and its quantity was far greater than that of the Netherlands.

In order to monopolize international trade, countries in western Europe founded their commercial companies one after another. Some famous ones were English and

---

[①] Wei Ke. "Changes of Import Modes of Pepper and Spices to Europe". *European Economy History Journal*, Issue No. 8, 1979.

Dutch East India Company and French West India Company. These new commercial companies were unlike the commercial guilds in the Middle Ages as they were closely connected with their respective governments. Their governments provided various kinds of privileges to these companies for the economic returns they would receive. These companies even could mint their own currencies, own weaponry, declare wars with other countries, and enter into peace treaties. They were just like special organizations that had a state's functions. These commercial companies with trading monopolies looted precious products from Asia, Africa and Americas through various kinds of compulsory and fraudulent means and then sold these products in Europe to reap staggering profits. Their profit rates could be as high as 200% to 300%. Meanwhile, there was the so-called "Triangular trade" that ships loaded with cheap European products sailed from European ports to African ports and used industrial products to trade for slaves and then sold these slaves to Americas and finally shipped the raw materials bought from Americas back to Europe. Slave trade and looting from colonies not only provided suzerain states with a large amount of accumulated primitive capital, but also promoted the economic development in these suzerain states.

International merchants that were specialized in international trade appeared with the rise of international trade. International merchants' business scope was very extensive and included nearly every kind of staple goods that people would need from treasures, female slaves to alum, hides and wool and they were simply all inclusive. They even traded with heathens in remote places. The few surviving merchants' handbooks showed us how broad and complicated the knowledge the special international merchants had to master. Francesco Balducci Pegolotti wrote Pegolotti's Merchant Handbook on practical knowledge of trade that was widely distributed. He was a commercial agent in the service of the mercantile house of the wealthy and powerful Bardi family of Florence for over 30 years. His employer's business areas included all of the Mediterranean Sea and Central Europe west of the Rhine. He provided in the book detailed silver money value charts as well as weights and measurements, tariffs, commodities lists and general trade information, and market information. A careful reading of this handbook would make you hard to believe the sheer kinds of money and weights and variety of commodities in various places. He listed 288 commodities from the Near East, from fennel and ambergris to tin and pine gum. Accurate to a single penny, he calculated the fees required to transport one bag of wool from London to Aigues-Mortes in southern France. The most interesting portion of this handbook was on the merchant route to China. This route was not only followed by Marco Polo and other traveling merchants who aimed at large profits and also distributed for reading by few missionaries who aimed at winning more Christian converts.[1]

II. Coming of the first wave of globalization of economies

Discoveries of the new continents drew the curtain of globalization of economies. With the Spanish "discovery" of Americas and Portuguese's arrival at India and the subsequent European colonial expansion, connections between western Europe and other parts of the world were strengthened and scope of trade expanded in an unprecedented manner. Regional markets that were originally separated from each other were gradually connected to form global markets. Cities such as Antwerp, Amsterdam, London and others that were along the Atlantic Ocean became successively world trade centers and distribution centers. Trade between Eurasia and Africa increased rapidly. Pepper that was transshipped previously by Italian merchants to Europe averaged only 2,100 tons annually. After the new sea routes were opened, spices that were shipped to Lisbon immediately jumped to 7,000 tons.[2] In addition to traditional commodities such as spices, chinaware, silk and others, coffee from Africa and tea from China became key products in international trade. In the Atlantic trade, combination between specialization of regional economies and development in sea transport caused large-scale trade primarily composed of new staple goods to rise. Since the 16th century, Latin America gradually formed its "single product system" in its economy. American plantations produced tobacco, cane sugar, coffee, cotton and other products that were supplied to European markets, and then all they needed were imported from Europe including cereals, fish, cloth and metal products and meanwhile, they imported labor force

---

[1] Gene Brucker. *Medieval and Renaissance Florence*. Trans. Zhu Longhua. Shanghai: SDX Joint Publishing Company, 1985: 88.

[2] Zhu Huan. ed. *World Ancient and Medieval History*. Beijing: Higher Learning Publication House, 1986: 259.

from Africa. A new kind of global economic relationship was being formed with each passing day. Then the first international division of labor, "Americas and eastern Europe produced raw materials, Africa supplied labor force, Asia provided a series of luxuries and western Europe directed all these global operations and concentrated on industrial output with each passing day".[①] Production and consumption showed a global trend, and the world was becoming one economic entity. Just as Marx pointed out, "the world trade and world market in the 16th century revealed capitalism's modern living history".[②] With the formation of global economic relationship, Europe made phenomenal progress and rose rapidly to become the leader in world economy.

In the process of establishing the early world market, European colonialists' trading in slaves and using slavery labor to develop American resources and expanding colonies played a very important role. In addition, slave trade and slavery were critical to capitalist development and Industrial Revolution's emergence. According to statistics, in the late 17th century, the total English foreign trade profits earned annually averaged two million pounds. Among this amount, plantation trade contributed 600,000 pounds, plantation produce output accounted for 120,000 pounds, trade with India yielded 500,000 pounds, re-export of products from India was 180,000 pounds, and trade with Europe, Near East and Africa garnered 600,000 pounds. It is obvious that "no slavery, no cotton; without cotton, modern industry is without the question. Slavery makes colonies valuable, colonies produced world trade, and world trade is a prerequisite to large industries".[③]

Industrial Revolution brought unprecedented great development to productivity and caused major changes to the economy. Mechanized great industry broke the handicraft restriction in the past and laid a solid material and technological foundation for exploring the world market. Products provided by large industry were far better than those made by workshop handicraft industry. They were famous for quality products at a low price. They not only conquered the domestic market, but also quickly took over the international market. Backed by their powerful industrial

---

[①] L. S. Stavrianos. *The World to 1500: A Global History.* New Jersey: Prentice Hall, 1971: 169.

[②] *Complete Works of Marx and Engels (Volume XXIII).* Beijing: People's Publishing House, 1972: 167.

[③] *Complete Works of Marx and Engels (Volume IV).* Beijing: People's Publishing House, 1958: 145.

technological strength, capitalist countries actively expanded overseas and Asia, Africa and Latin America were all forced to participate in the world market and became sales market for industrial products from developed countries and were kept in subjection to supply of raw materials. Meanwhile, development in communication and transport and telecommunications industry shortened the circulation time and space distance of commodities in the world market and accelerated the expansion of the world market. By the 1860s and 1870s, commercial capital yielded to industrial capital and the world market in the real sense was formed and cross-border exchange of production, sales and raw materials was achieved. Based on steam engines, the first wave of globalization of economies featured with commodity trade finally arrived. Jacques Adda, a French scholar, pointed out that "we may say that globalization started in the Mediterranean Sea about 1,000 years ago and is continuation of a decisive great development with the Great Discovery in the 15th and 16th centuries".[1]

Section Four The Renaissance and Globalization of Cultures

I. Global distribution of the Renaissance culture

The science spirit advocated by the Renaissance extended to European and American countries. In order to encourage inventions, England founded Royal Society of London in 1662 with an aim to promote natural science. Its charter specifies that "Royal Society of London's task and mission is to improve knowledge of natural things and all the useful techniques, manufacturing industry, mechanic operations, engines and experiments for inventions, and try to restore these useful techniques and inventions that are now lost".[2] Later, inventions and patents that were registered with the English government increased with the passing of time. Natural science achievements that were pioneered by the Renaissance continued to develop. By the 18th century, celestial mechanics, classical mechanics and higher

---

[1] Jacques Adda. *Globalization of the Economy*. Beijing: Central Compilation & Translation Press, 2000: 74.

[2] R. J. Forbes, E. J. Dijksterhuis. *A History of Science and Technology*. Beijing: Qiu Shi Publishing House, 1985: 167.

mathematics had established their complete theoretical systems. Important progress was made in various fields in physics. Chemistry was freed from metallurgy and became an independent subject. Engels said that "in order to develop its industrial production, the capitalist class needs to have a science that explores the physical nature of natural objects and movement mode of natural power."[①] Development in science and technology liberated productivity, which promoted the shift from workshop handicraft industry to mechanized large industry. In the 1760s, England had its Industrial Revolution. Later, major countries in Europe and Americas had industrial revolution one after another. Backed with their strong industrial strength, Western countries forced open the gates in many countries in Asia, Africa and Latin America and accelerated the process of globalization of economies.

With development of the capitalist economy, humanism that was once the core thinking of the Renaissance gradually developed to humanitarianism and its target that was aimed at challenging feudal theocracy was redirected squarely at privilege of feudal hierarchy. After the 18th century, humanitarianism became the guiding thinking in the Enlightenment. The Enlightenment thinkers led by Montesquieu, Voltaire and Rousseau challenged "divine right" with "natural rights" and declared the idea of freedom and equality and elevated humanitarianism to a theory. In the 18th century, humanitarianism was spread to North America and saw further development. Capitalist political thinker Jefferson encouraged the North American people to oppose British colonial rulers with the slogan of "natural rights", on the basis of which he also drafted the world-shaking "Declaration of Independence". In 1789, French capitalist revolution produced *Declaration of the Rights of Man and of the Citizen* (in short "Bill of Rights"). These two declarations were both based on humanitarianism and declared will of the "people" in the format of a program.

The dissemination of the Renaissance was not only limited to European and American countries. Formation of the integrated world market promoted countries that were relatively backward in modernization to accept Western advanced science and technological civilization and then to accept the Western advanced ideology through commercial exchanges, which eventually led to a series of social changes.

[①] *Complete Works of Marx and Engels (Volume III)*. Beijing: People's Publishing House, 1972: 390.

Such an example was Japan which started the Meiji Restoration. As early as Ming and Qing Dynasties, with development in trade relationship with Eurasia Continent, China's cultural exchanges with the West became more frequent and scientific and technological civilization of the Renaissance already spread to China through Western missionaries, which promoted China's modern science development. In the late 16th century and the early 17th century, famous Western missionaries such as Matteo Ricci, Jules Garrigues, Jean Terrenz, Sabatino de Ursis, Johann Adam Schall von Bell and so on came to China.

In 1660, Matteo Ricci presented some exquisitely-made things from the West to Ming Dynasty Emperor Wan Li. Among these gifts was *Kunyu Wanguo Quantu* (A Map of the Myriad Countries of the World) which was based on a blueprint on *Shijie Yutu* (A Map of the World) that he drew in 1584 when he was in Zhaoqing and was made reference to China's then existing old maps. This map was really eye-opening to the Chinese people and made them know for the first time that the world had five continents and the earth we lived in was a globe. This map was very significant to the development in China's geography and cartography. Before 1640, the history on Western astronomy written in Chinese by Johann Adam Schall von Bell mentioned the Renaissance astronomers such as Galilei, Tycho Brahe, Copernicus, Kepler and others. However, owing to the restraints by Catholics, no public distribution was made. Until the Holy See lifted its ban, *Huangchao Liqi Tushi* (The Regulations for Ceremonial Paraphernalia of the Qing Dynasty) published in 1759 introduced two instruments that demonstrated Copernicus' heliocentric system. One was an armillary sphere with orrery and the other an orrery. The latter was equipped with a clock mechanism and could automatically demonstrate the earth and the other five planets to circle the sun. This is the first time China officially introduced the Copernican theory. Johann Adam Schall von Bell also brought telescopes to China and authored the book *On Telescopes* describing telescopes' manufacture, functions and nature with illustrations. This book was the beginning of introduction of optical theories in Western physics into China. *Exquisitely-made Instruments* dictated by Jean Terrenz described mechanics in physics, and such contents as gravity theory, Galilei-invented lever, pulley, spiral, rule, screw nut, screw wrench and so on. Moreover, physiology and anatomy appeared in the Renaissance were also introduced to China by him. Furthermore, gunpowder was invented in China and after it was introduced to the West, it was used as war weapons during the Renaissance and then introduced back to China by missionaries. Those who contributed most in introducing advanced weapons were Johann Adam Schall von Bell and Ferdinand Verbiest. They helped Ming and Qing Dynasty governments with making steel cannons, compiling military science works and promoting development in China's weapons.

In the early 20th century, in order to save China, some Chinese people with advanced thinking actively sought from the West the truth and the Renaissance ideology was again brought to their attention. Chen Duxiu published "On Literature Revolution" in *La Jeunesse* and it could be rated as the declaration of the New Culture Movement. At the beginning of this article, Chen Duxiu said that "where does today's solemn and grand Europe originate from? Well, it is a reward of revolution. Revolutionaries, in the European language, means eliminate the old and invent the new". And then he enumerated various revolutions since the Renaissance: "since the Renaissance, there is revolution in the politics, in the religious field, and in ethics. Arts and literature have also revolution and because of revolution they are rising and evolving." Obviously, the sponsors of the May Fourth Movement would like to stage a cultural renaissance movement in China with the Renaissance as the model. That is why some say that China's May Fourth Movement was "the Eastern Renaissance" that was rooted in China's soil. The difference is that the Renaissance destroyed Christianity Church's one thousand years of spiritual dictatorship while China's May Fourth Movement broke the yoke of more than two thousand years of Confucianism.

With European economic expansion and formation of the global market, ideology and culture of the Renaissance started to spread in the world. Humanism, science theories and innovation consciousness advocated by the Renaissance culture became the common spiritual fortune of the world. Owing to the confirmation of the uniform market rules, some ideas held by various peoples in the countries of the world tended to be similar and trend of globalization of cultures tended to be more apparent.

II. The Renaissance and transmission of world cultures

Closed environment is bound to influence process of cultural development because every country would have nothing to learn from. All would start anew, and little by little. General communication in a global nature could break this stalemate. A certain culture may directly draw fresh cultural fruits through learning from the outside world and avoid the "repeat", "waste" and skip "restart" in cultural invention and creation so as to accelerate the speed of cultural development. Culture in the Renaissance was actually an integration of diverse cultures. Through commerce and trade, wars, diplomacy, scholars' exchanges and other cultural communication channels, from Islamic-Arab culture, Byzantine culture and cultural fruits of various peoples in Near East, Europeans selected and distilled the cultural factors that were beneficial to them and, through repeated reforms and synchronizations, integrated them into their existing cultural modes and shaped culture in the Renaissance so as to move Europe from the Dark Ages to a prosperous modern civilization.

From the late 11th century to the late 13th century, a grand translation movement in the West rose. This was another upsurge in learning classical cultures and foreign cultures since the Arab's "one hundred years of Translation Movement" in the Middle Ages. As a result of this movement, Islamic-Arab culture and Byzantine culture made their way in a large scale into the West and played an important role in the beginning of the Renaissance culture.

Al-Battani, an Arab astronomer and mathematician, compiled *Book of Astronomical Tables* based on his more than 40 years of observation and research. After this book was translated into Latin and Spanish, its influence in Europe lasted for several hundred years. In his famous book *On the Revolutions of the Celestial Spheres* by Nicolaus Copernicus, founder of astronomy in the Renaissance, he cited many times Al-Battani's scientific research results and observation data. Works by Al-Kindi and Ibn al-Haytham, Arab opticians, prompted Roger Bacon to conduct scientific experiments on reflection and refraction theories of light and then founded the modern study of experiments. After *The Compendious Book on Calculation by Completion and Balancing*, an algebra book written by Muhammad Ibn Musa al-Khwarizmi, the greatest mathematician in the Arab world, was introduced to the

West, it had been used as a major textbook by students in the various universities in Europe till the 16th century. The portion on introduction on Hindu-Arabic numerals in the book had an inestimable role in the development of Western mathematics. Philip Khuri Hitti pointed out that "if we still used the old-fashioned numerals and would like to keep mathematics progress along certain roads, that is impossible. Today's progress of science of calculation should be credited with the zero sign and Arabic numerals." George Sarton also thought that use of old-fashioned numerals "already became obstacles to the road of progress; on the contrary, Hindu-Arabic numerals opened up this path."[1] Many Arab medical science books were widely read during the Renaissance. Such examples were Al-Zahrawi's *Kitab al-Tasrif*, Ibn Sīnā's *The Canon of Medicine*, and Muhammad Ibn Zakariya al-Razi's medical works that were repeatedly printed and published after printing was invented. *The Canon of Medicine* was not only used as university textbooks, but also worshiped as the "Bible" of medicine.

Literature and arts during the Renaissance were also heavily influenced by Arabic culture.

Miguel Asín Palacios, a famous Spanish scholar of Islamic studies, found that Dante's *Divine Comedy* and Muslim's eschatology had shared many surprising similarities both in general structure and details. He thought that Dante's illusion on heaven and inferno should be attributed to Muslims. In the art of architecture, bell towers in the late Renaissance in Italy and inspiration of design of spires in England both came from Islam's mosques. Arabic design decorations were very much favored in the Renaissance. Italian realism artists used the term of "Arabic design decoration" to refer specifically to this kind of design decorations. Founder of Italian realism Giotto, Da Vinci, the greatest artist in the Renaissance and other artists all adopted Arabic design decorations.[2]

Charles Diehl, the most famous French authority on Byzantine history, said that the great professors at the Palaiologos dynasty (the last ruling dynasty of the Byzantine Empire, note by this author) were the pioneers in restoring research on

---

[1] Philip Khuri Hitti. *History of the Arabs (Volume II)*. Beijing: The Commercial Press, 1979: 687.

[2] Xu Shanwei. *Chinese Culture Prevailing in Western Countries and Renaissance of Western Culture*. Shanghai: Shanghai People's Publishing House, 2002: 193.

ancient Greece and they prepared for the Renaissance.① In 1396, a famous Byzantine scholar Manuel Chrysoloras was invited to teach Greek in University of Florence and the Greek language that was lost for nearly 700 years in western Europe was rejuvenated. After Manuel Chrysoloras, some other Byzantine scholars came to Italy successively to teach and promote classical knowledge. Such examples were: Gemistus Pletho was actively involved in the founding of the famous Platonic Academy and taught Platonic philosophy; and Basilios Bessarion presented his own collection of a large number of early priests' works, theological theses and ancient manuscripts to Library of Venice. Many Italian scholars visited various places in Byzantine to collect ancient manuscripts and antiques. From 1413 to 1423, Giovanni Aurispa himself alone brought back from Byzantine nearly 250 manuscripts of ancient works including works by ancient Greek playwrights such as Sophocles and Euripides and historian Thucydides. In 1453, after Byzantine Empire's (also called the Eastern Roman Empire) capital Constantinople fell to the Muslims, Byzantine scholars who kept a relatively large amount of Greek and Roman cultures exiled in succession to Italy and brought with them important classics and manuscripts and tradition in research on Greek scholarship, which "promotes Italy's yearning for and research on classic cultures … makes Italy the origin of the Renaissance in the West".② "The manuscripts saved from Byzantine at its demise and the ancient sculptures excavated from the Roman ruins presented in front of the surprising West a new world—ancient Greece; in front of its glories, the ghost of Middle Ages disappeared; and Italy produced an unprecedented prosperity in its arts which appeared to be a reflection of the classic age and its level would never be reached again." ③ In the art filed, late Byzantine painting style influenced Italian fine arts. Byzantine painter Doménikos Theotokópoulos (most widely known as El Greco) brought to Italy the complete set of Byzantine icons such as use of colors and new spatial sense and enhanced the expression of Italian paintings in the Renaissance. In

---

① Chen Zhiqiang, Xu Jialing. "A Preliminary Discussion on the Role and Function of Byzantine Culture in Cultural Development in the Medieval Europe and Eastern Mediterranean Sea". *History Teaching and Study*, No. 8, 1986.

② Zhang Shangren. *History of Philosophy in Western European Feudal Society*. Chengdu: Sichuan People's Publishing House, 1983: 209.

③ *Selected Works of Marx and Engels (Volume III)*. Beijing: People's Publishing House, 1972: 444-445.

addition, during the Renaissance construction of churches in western Europe mostly adopted the Byzantine dome style and their interior was decorated with Byzantine mosaic style.

China, at the eastern end of Eurasia Continent, also provided much inspiration to the artistic innovation during the Renaissance. Ambrogio Lorenzetti, a famous Italian landscape painter in the early Renaissance period, was obviously influenced in his color use by Tang Dynasty painter Wu Daozi; Giotto, a master in Italy's realism, successfully transformed Mongolian letters into a decorative style; it is also apparent that Song and Yuan Dynasty painters left their marks on Simone Martini, a famous Italian painter. Likewise, decorative art in China's silk products also heavily influenced Italian painting. Description of China in *The Travels of Marco Polo* caused changes in contents, skills and color uses in western European paintings in the Renaissance, which in turn influenced reforms in the western European painting during the period from the 14th century to the 16th century.

China led the world in applied science. It is obvious to all that dissemination of Four Great Inventions of ancient China had a huge influence on the Renaissance and even the world civilization. Marx profoundly pointed out that "gunpowder, compass and printing, these three inventions predicted the arrival of capitalist society. Gunpowder exploded knights class into pieces, compass facilitated opening up the world market to establish colonies, and printing became tools of Protestantism and in general it became a tool of revival of science and became the strongest lever for the prerequisite of spiritual development and creation".[1]

With international trade expansion during the Renaissance, sugar and spices that were originally produced in the East flooded the West in large quantities, which changed to some extent Western people's daily life. When sugar was first introduced to the West, it was mainly used as a medicine and beyond the reach of the ordinary people. With appearance of various kinds of sweets, candies and sugar-containing drinks, the Western people quickly loved the sweets and spices became a sign of middle and upper class food culture in the West.

Cultures are dynamic and change constantly. Development in any culture is not

---

[1] Marx. *Machines, Forces of Nature and Scientific Application*. Beijing: People's Publishing House, 1978: 67.

accomplished in isolation but instead it happened in the course of conflicting and blending with other cultures. Nations that are in self-isolation and dispelling and opposing other cultures will be deserted sooner or later in the desert of times. Only those nations which are open-minded and good at learning and drawing nutrition from other nations can enjoy full vitality. It is due to its learning and absorbing excellent cultural fruits from various nations in the world that Europe could march to Atlantic Ocean from the Mediterranean Sea to achieve its shift from middle ancient time to modern time. Dissemination of the Renaissance culture in the world in turn kept its permanent charm.

In general, the Renaissance originated from rise of humanism and caused a new breakthrough in the civilization history of human being. This ideological liberation promoted the constant surge of scientific and technological inventions and greatly enhanced human being's capabilities in changing the nature and creating property fortune. Human being's pursuit for material civilization brought the spread of ideological liberation movement and yearning for material civilization brought generalization of spiritual civilization. The spiritual civilization in turn promoted further the great progress in medieval material civilization so as to allow human being to march into a new era—capitalism.

Chapter Four   Globalization of Cultures and Industrialization in Modern Japan

The Renaissance was learning and absorbing of achievements of various nations' excellent cultures in the world and a synthesis of multiple cultures. Cultures are dynamic and developing constantly and it is a process of developing what is useful or healthy and discarding what is not. Namely, it absorbs advanced cultures while maintaining excellent contents in traditional cultures. By way of various cultural exchanges such as commerce and trade, wars, foreign affairs, religion, scholar exchanges and so on, the Renaissance found its way into other parts of the world. Japan was the most successful nation in absorbing external cultures as the Japanese had a great tradition of learning foreign advanced experiences to build its country since ancient times. During the 7th century, Prince Shōtokutaishi's reform and Taika Reform successfully transformed the Japanese society to a feudal one based on absorbing the advanced culture from China's Sui and Tang Dynasties. During the Renaissance in the 16th century, Japan introduced western Europe's advanced culture. Emperor Meiji's government and the Japanese people, faced with the Western culture's impact on traditional Japanese culture, actively absorbed, digested and integrated the new culture instead of resisting and denying it. It is this extraordinary capability of absorbing the most advanced foreign cultures and transforming them into its own unique nationalist culture in an extremely fast manner that makes Japan realize the "marriage" between the Western culture and Japan's traditional culture while integrating itself into the world civilization gradually and taking full advantage of its late comer country, thus creating a success of disseminating the Renaissance into other parts of the world.

Section One   Meiji Restoration in Japan and Outside Culture

Meiji Restoration is the starting point of Japan's pre-modernization. It is a revolution involving politics, economy, and culture and so on. Ever since then, Japan strode speedily from a feudal society to a capitalist one, causing a complete collapse of Japan's traditional social order. In the course of opening up to the outside world, Japanese culture continually braced for the influence and impact of foreign cultures. Through a painful choice, Japan voluntarily accepted Western culture, successfully achieving its co-existence and integration with Western culture.

I. Post-feudal society economy and culture in Japan

From Taika Reform in the 7th century to Meiji Restoration in 1868, Japan almost isolated itself from the outside world and saw a long and peaceful feudal society. When Leyasu Tokugawa defeated its competitors in early 1603, he established his Shogunate with centralized power in Edo, which signaled the last days of the Japanese feudal society. Its basic characteristics are as follows:

a. A relatively stable centralized feudal political system

The traditional Japanese society had been a strict hierarchal status one, formed on the basis of the separation of soldiers (samurai) from peasants. The separation of soldiers from peasants resulted in the formation of social classes of samurai, the ruling class and peasants and chōnin (industrialists), the ruled class, which was unique to the Japanese society, with samurai and townsman comprising the two basic classes in the traditional Japanese society. As all samurai were hereditary, an unbridgeable gap was created between samurai and townsman. Hayami Akira and Miyamoto Matao made a summary of the distinction between the Japanese feudal lords under the Tokugawa Shogunate and the western European feudal lords: In Japan, "feudal lords and their manors were weakly correlated in that in principle such manors were being awarded in accordance with the Shogunate's policies from time to time, unlike seigneur in medieval Europe where they directly owned the land."① This is to say that Japan's feudal lords, whether they were the daimyo or retainers, all of their manors were "not unchangeable particular manors", so such manors did not enjoy "firm seigniory". This shows the separation of political power from economic power. According to the study by Takeyoshi Kawashima, prior to Meiji Restoration, samurai's basic social relationship is that of the relationship between the principal and the subordinate, which is the basis of the functioning of the Shogunate's order. This relationship was originally the integration relationship of individual personality of the feudal lord and his subordinates.② But under Shogunate system, this relationship was converted to the relationship between families and families, which was a non-elastic characteristic in the Japanese feudal society. What supported this system is Bushido. As a result, under the Shogunate, Japan's feudal society could sustain for a long time. It is in the name of the restoration of imperial rule to the emperor that Meiji Restoration was achieved. Supported by the Bushido spirit of "selfless devotion", Japan was able to transform from a feudal system to capitalism in a speedy and upside down manner.③

b. The cultural detailed content to draw on strengths from the others

Generally, the flow of culture is like flowing water from high places to lower ones, namely, nations with low development stage in social nature absorbs very easily cultures from nations with high development stage. It was just because Japan was historically at a lower potential energy position for a long time that it was able to absorb in a large scale China's culture in the ancient times and Western culture in a large scale in modern times. The earliest foreign culture that Japan accepted was Sui and Tang Dynasty culture in China. From Japan's characters, costumes (Japanese traditional dress—kimono is also called Wu dress) to Confucian ethics in its ideology, this culture's print can be found everywhere in Japanese people's way of life. But with commodity exchange and development in nautical techniques, pre-Meiji Restoration Japan started to accept the Western civilization. Since the 16th

---

① Hayami Akira, Miyamoto Matao. *Economic History of Japan (Volume I)*. Shanghai: SDX Joint Publishing Company, 1997.

② Takeyoshi Kawashima. *Family Structure of Japanese Society*. Tokyo: Nippon Hyoron Sha Co., Ltd. Publishers, 1955.

③ Li Yining. *The Origin of Capitalism—A Study on Comparative Economic History*. Beijing: The Commercial Press, 2003.

century, Japan introduced successively from the Portuguese and the Spaniards guns and cannons, gun powder and Catholicism. However, Confucianism and the traditional Shintoism and Catholicism could not co-exist. Conflicts between the heterogeneous Western culture and the Japanese culture abounded.

c. Growth of the capitalist economic factors

"The feudal society was by no means a static one." "Its economic activities at the early days of its establishment were not active but given the right opportunities such activities would happen."[1] The long-lasting peace under the rule of the Tokugawa Shogunate promoted certain development in social economy characterized by population growth and development of handicraft industry and commerce, thus making the business people class stronger in their capabilities. Japan's population skyrocketed from 18 million in 1600 to 26 million in 1725. With the economic development, cities saw an unbalanced development, in 1700 population in Edo was near one million, population in Osaka and Kyoto each reached 300,000. The rapid population hike increased demand for commodities. The government encouraged business people and rich peasants to invest their surplus capital into a new production method, including family contract system, i.e., processing method distributed to families. They provided raw materials and equipment to peasants and craftsmen and brought the finished products to the market for sale. At the end of the Tokugawa Shogunate, industry in certain areas developed to a stage that factories were set up. Specialization in areas where usable raw materials and local techniques were featured started to emerge. Some areas were famous for their lacquerware, ceramics, textiles or rice wine. Regional handicraft industry's development and products' increase led to the extensive exchange of commodities, and such exchanges promoted money economy's development. Development in commercial agriculture and handicraft industry caused villages' natural economy to disintegrate with time. In the first half of the 18th century, the buds of capitalism led to the emergence of the new production methods, thus shaking fundamentally the basis of the Shogunate.

---

[1] Hayami Akira, Miyamoto Matao. *Economic History of Japan (Volume I)*. Shanghai: SDX Joint Publishing Company, 1997: 29.

II. External impact and Japan's reaction

In the latter half of the 16th century, spearheaded by missionaries, the Western culture rapidly penetrated Japan. After Industrial Revolution, the Western powers quickened their steps of colonial expansion. They opened up the doors of Asian countries one by one. By mid-19th century, the powers conquered Japan by force. The feudal production method suffered heavy losses inflicted by the advanced production method. Japan experienced the painful process of denial and non-adaptation and eventually denied itself by accepting the new production method. Faced externally by the forceful impact from the Western colonialists, and pressured internally by bankruptcy of handicraftsmen as a result of the inflow of Western commodities, outflow of gold and popular revolts caused by price hikes and, additionally by the growth in opposition ranks by the princes in southwestern areas that were not satisfied with the rule of Shogunate, the Japanese feudal society system based strictly by the hierarchal classes collapsed quickly. Capitalism found its way to develop in Japan.

a. Invasions by foreign powers, rescuing the national crisis and ending of closing the country to international exchanges

Prior to the Tokugawa Shogunate, Japan's foreign trade was relatively advanced. Its merchant ships sailed to China, Korea and various southeastern Asian countries. In the latter half of the 16th century, Western merchants and missionaries began their activities in Japan. Spearheaded by missionaries, European colonial elements rapidly penetrated Japan. Catholics in Japan increased sharply from 300,000 to 700,000. Through their trade with Western countries, some vassal states strengthened their economic and military power. After the establishment of the Tokugawa Shogunate, in order to prevent invasion of Japan by foreign forces, Japan started to carry out the policy of cutting itself off from the outside world. Since 1633, Japan issued several "closed-door country decrees" to prohibit trades with foreigners, exchanges between Japan and the outside world, expelling foreign merchants and missionaries from Japan, only allowing trade with China, Korea and the Netherlands and so on but limiting such trade to Nagasaki only, and imposing strict limitations on commerce with the outside world. Since the early 19th century, owing to the increased business activities in the waters in northern Pacific Ocean, foreign countries exerted mounting pressures on Japan. Ships engaging in whale hunting and fur trade had to stop at ports so as to obtain provisions and maintenance and repair to their vessels. But such requests were all denied by Japan. In the mid-19th century, the necessity to establish coal ports owing to the use of steamships made the situation even worse. Eventually the US government took the first step to pressure Japan to make public its stand. On July 8, 1853, American Commodore Matthew C. Perry dropped anchor in Edo Bay and delivered a letter from President Fillmore demanding privilege of commerce, opening coal ports and protecting shipwrecked seamen from US vessels. Within one week, when Perry's fleet left Japan, he warned that he would return the next spring for the answer. When he returned to Japan, he made it very clear that a treaty or a war was the only option. Japan was forced to yield and signed the Treaty of Kanagawa on March 31, 1854. This treaty allowed US vessels' access to the ports of Shimoda and Hakodate for maintenance and repair and to obtain provisions, and shipwrecked seamen from US vessels were to receive the assistance of Japanese authorities to return to the US; it also allowed selection and posting of consuls when either Japan or the US considers necessary, and Japan promised to give the US any favorable advantages which might be negotiated by Japan with any other foreign government in the future.

In accordance with this treaty, the US sent the very capable Townsend Harris as the first US consul general to Japan. With his extraordinary wisdom and patience, he won the Japanese people's trust and signed the Treaty of Amity and Commerce with Japan in 1856. Subsequently, Great Britain, Russia, France, the Netherlands and other countries signed similar treaties with the Shogunate. The series of unequal treaties signed made Japan lose many of its sovereign rights and led to Japan's national crisis of falling into a colony.

b. Deterioration of Japan's economy after opening its ports

In accordance with these treaties, Japan opened its ports on July 1, 1859, the sixth year of Ansei. After this, Japan saw its trade expand rapidly. In 1860, Japan's export was about USD 4.7 million and its import USD 1.6 million. In 1867, Japan's export was USD 12 million and its import USD 21.60 million. In eight years its import and export volume increased by more than fivefold. Raw silk, tea, silkworm eggs and cotton were exported in a large quantity and their prices rose. Take the local raw silk price in Kiryū for instance, after the ports were opened, such price increased by threefold in October, 1859 than the previous several years. Owing to a shortage of raw silk and price hikes, silk industry in several cities headed by Kyoto Nishijin found it very hard to keep their business. As a result, weavers in Nishijin staged two revolts at the end of 1859. The sharp rise in export products' prices also affected prices in general merchandise. Rice price started to rise since 1857. Japan's gold and silver ratio was 1 versus 5 while the international ratio was 1 versus 15. So Japan's gold price was lower than that of the international market. Western merchants and diplomats from various countries used Mexican silver dollars to buy gold in Japan in order to take advantage of this difference and they made a windfall profit. Outflow of gold and devaluation in currency price also promoted price hikes in rice, wheat, salt and so on. This made peasants, poor people in the cities and lower-class samurai hard to live.

Imports were mainly cotton and woolen products. Import of large quantities of inexpensive cotton cloth seriously impacted Japan's domestic production of cotton cloth. In 1861, production output of cotton dropped to 5% of the output before the ports were opened while import of cotton cloth commanded 31.7% of Japan's domestic consumption. Cotton textiles industry in Kanto's Moka Shi (southwest of Tochigi Prefecture) totaled 380,000 tan before port opening but decreased to 120,000 tan after port opening, causing a large number of textiles workers to lose their jobs and become destitute.

c. New changes in class relationship

After the ports' opening up, life of peasants and poor townsfolk deteriorated and their anti-feudal fights expanded in their scale. The number of peasant revolts increased sharply, 43 revolts in 1860 and 55.3 revolts on average annually between 1865 and 1867. The nature of such revolts changed from all peasant revolts to revolts in "changing the manners and morals of the time", which was based on peasants' fighting with feudal Shogunate suzerain system, landlord system and commercial usury capital and so on. The manner of such fighting is no longer "bypassing the immediate leadership and presenting their appeals and complaints to higher levels" but outright actions such as destroying landlords and rich business people's residences, demanding reduction of land rent and taxes and freely selling their farm products. Peasants burned "Kenchi records" and distributed equally land and properties, thus making such revolts more in the revolutionary land reform trend of further negating the suzerain system than the early 18th century. The revolts staged by poor townsfolk rose sharply too. There were 16.6 such revolts on average annually between 1865 and 1867, surpassing the annual average of 7.2 during the Tenpō period.

The majority of townsfolk's revolts were "rice revolts" (revolts in robbing the grains) against hoarding the grain in market, speculation and price hikes by suzerains and business people.

After the ports' opening up, the price hikes made lower-ranking samurai's life even harder. The shogun rulers, instead of aiding them, continued to use "half salary" or "reduced salary" to pocket a portion of the salary rice, making themselves being "hated as if they were enemies by those who suffered". These lower-ranking samurai originally belonged to the privileged class in the feudal society. However, at the end of the Shogunate, they had been on the wane. Some of them engaged in business or handicraft industry, became doctors, authors or old-type private school tutors. Many even detached themselves from the Shoguante and became ronins. In reality, they transformed themselves to become city petit bourgeois professionals. Moreover, they were intellectuals who had some knowledge of economic culture, Western science and technology and political thoughts and they were sensitive to new things. They no longer tried to find a way out in the Shogunate but instead they, in varying degrees, wanted to seek hope from reform in the political and social system. Since Tenpō Reforms, in Satsuma Domain, Chōshū Domain, Mito Domain and the Tosa Domain, and Saga Domain and so on, most lower-ranking samurai dissociated themselves from the various cliques of power struggles and some were assimilated into the Shogunate reform. After the ports' opening up, their conflicts and struggles with the higher-ranking samurai representing families of power and influence intensified.

The ports' opening up also stimulated developments in the products manufacturing. Among the newly established social class under the commodity economy development, new landlords and rich peasants, some engaged in cultivation of cash crops, some were in silk making industry, and some were contract buyers in the trading stores business and in the transport business and so on. Some peasant manufacturers also acted as businessmen, and these people were called rich peasants and rich businessmen. Suzerains imposed products monopoly policy within their suzerainty and collaborated with privileged businessmen to monopolize transport and trade by exploiting producers. These policies threatened rich peasants and rich businessmen's immediate interests and the latter formed an anti-feudal awareness. However, most rich peasants and rich businessmen were concurrently village officials and attached themselves to the feudal system for exploitation purpose. A few of them even bought the samurai status or became officials. So they somewhat feared revolution and wanted to develop capitalism as long as the feudal system was not fundamentally changed. With the development of crises, at the end of the Shogunate, the thinking of various shoguns and samurai intellectuals became more and more active. The anti-Tokugawa Shogunate cliques, especially the four domains of Satsuma Domain, Chōshū Domain, Saga Domain and the Tosa Domain, the so-called Satsuma-Chōshū Alliance, staged attacks on foreign powers during the period of 1858 and 1865 under the slogan of "respecting the emperor and expelling the foreigners".

III. Absorbing and using for reference

Under the violent attacks by Western capitalism, Japan's stable feudal social structure underwent strong shocks and experienced constant unrest and reforms. As Marx mentioned in the Preface to *Capital* (first edition), "What countries with relatively developed industries show to those countries with less developed industries is the latter's future image."[①] The advanced culture and technology in Europe showed its charisma to the Japanese people with the result that the backward feudal system was eventually negated. As Japan's domestic conflicts and its national crises intensified, in the final years of the Shogunate, the movement of "respecting the emperor and expelling the foreigners" and "toppling the Shogunate and reforming" developed vigorously. The anti-Shogunate battles happened one after

---

[①] Marx. *Capital (Volume I)*. Beijing: People's Publishing House, 1975.

another. Through the Boshin War, the Tokugawa Shogunate that lasted for two and a half centuries came to an end. On January 3, 1868, the Decree for the Restoration of Imperial Rule in the name of the emperor declared the abolition of the Shogunate and the establishment of the new Meiji rule.

The new Meiji government, under the slogan of "Enrich the Country, Strengthen the Military", hoped to establish a country that was on a par with the West. At the early days of its government, it adopted as one of its guiding principles to "break away from the deep-rooted bad customs" and to "pursue knowledge from the world" and specifically stipulated to reform Japan's traditional bad customs and learn advanced foreign culture so as to discard the old and welcome the new and catch up with and then surpass the advanced civilization. With Japan's door opening wider and the visits by the Iwakura Mission to Europe and America, from the government officials to the ordinary people, they all realized more deeply the significance of "pursue knowledge from the world". Ōkubo Toshimichi, Inoue Kaoru, Itō Hirobumi and other government officials realized early that Japan was involved in the world capitalism, only the introduction of Western civilization could change Japan's backward position and make Japan to catch up with the advanced countries and become one of the world powers and compete with them. In order to achieve this goal, the Meiji government staged a cultural reform campaign all over Japan with learning and introducing Western advanced culture as the guiding principles to include politics, military, education, social life and so on. It is fair to say that matters as great as national major subjects and as trivial as people's daily life all were touched by the cultural reforms. Through a series of capitalist reforms, Japan achieved the "transplanting" between advanced Western market economy and Japan's traditional culture. This is called "Meiji Restoration". Japan transformed itself rapidly from a backward feudal society and a country at the verge of being a semi-colonial one to a capitalist society and the only country in Asia that achieved national independence.

First, after the establishment of the Meiji rule, while it continued to eliminate the surviving feudal forces, it adopted a series of measures aiming to solidify the new rule: setting up "three positions and seven departments", and promulgating the Charter Oath in the name of the emperor, the contents of which are: deliberative assemblies shall be widely established and all matters decided by open discussion; all classes, high and low, shall be united in vigorously carrying out the administration of affairs of state; the common people, no less than the civil and military officials, shall all be allowed to pursue their own calling so that there may be no discontent; evil customs of the past shall be broken off and everything based upon the just laws of nature; and knowledge shall be sought throughout the world so as to strengthen the foundation of imperial rule. The Charter Oath is both the administrative program of the Meiji government and the herald of the government's call for introduction of foreign cultures.

Second, in order to establish a country modeling after Europe and America, the newly-founded Meiji government adopted a series of policies to welcome the new and abolish the old, thus paving the way for Japan's adoption of capitalism.[①] Through the abolition of the han system, feudal separatist rules were eliminated so as to create conditions for a national unified market; through coordination and reform of feudal status system, everybody would enjoy the freedom of taking official positions, selecting jobs and moving to other places so as to allow capitalist enterprises to obtain the freed labor; through land reform, the suzerain system was abolished and land ownership by the rising landlords and owner-peasants was confirmed and it was free to buy and sell land; through the land tax reform, exorbitant gelds were eliminated, only single land tax which was uniform nationwide (tax rate of 3% on the land price) was paid in currency and by the land owner, a bumper harvest year would not result in added payment and a lean year would not necessitate reduction or exemption. The currency land rent accelerated the polarization of small producers. Bankrupt peasants became cheap labor of capitalist enterprises. The Meiji government, through consolidations of government salaries, changed the life-long annual salary of Kazoku and gentry to one lump-sum payment of government bonds and partial cash. Kazoku and upper-class elements of gentry, backed by this huge amount of government bonds and cash, became investors in banks, railways or other enterprises. In this way, the Meiji government used government power to transform the income primarily from land tax (Over 80% of

---

[①] Shao Yanmei. "Historical and Cultural Reasons of Japan's Modern-time High-speed Development in Economy". *Langfang Normal College Journal*, Issue No. 1, 2001.

Japan's national tax revenue came from land tax.) to capital by way of paying Kazoku and gentry their government salary and compensation and other measures, thus speeding up the primitive accumulation of capital. Moreover, through rewarding trade, constructing railway, abolishing checkpoints of the various Shogunates, eliminating business people's monopoly guilds, the government unified and protected the national remittance business, set up model business and provided interest-free loans to capitalists to support private business and so on, thus effectively promoting the development of industry and commerce and expansion of the national market. Meanwhile, the personnel use standard of families of high pedigree during the Shogunate was abolished. The hereditary system of officials was eliminated in the second year of Emperor Meiji and discrimination and persecution of common people was abolished in the fourth year of Emperor Meiji. Instead people who had enterprising spirit and devoted to developing modern industry were used to manage the national causes. For example, Itō Hirobumi, an ordinary person, was made a full councilor, Minister of Public Works; and Ōkubo Toshimichi, a low-ranking samurai, was made Minister of Finance and Minister of Internal Affairs, to name only a few. The Meiji government also attached significant attention to the training and transforming of lower-ranking samurai. Under the slogan of "swords to abacuses", samurai-turned officials were encouraged to learn as quickly as possible business operations and management of modern industries. The aid method of using small principal loan facilitated part of the lower-ranking samurai to become small producers and great efforts were made to attract samurai who lived scattered to newly-built factories, businesses and corporations. Those former lower-ranking samurai who knew nothing about science and technology and enterprise management quickly became entrepreneurs and industrialists who mastered both technology and management. In the government-owned industries, engineers, technicians, assistants, workers and so on were mostly former lower-ranking samurai. Most of those common people who voluntarily and successfully transplanted advanced European and American technology and equipment at the grassroots were former lower-ranking samurai too. They were indeed a key driving force in technology to build a modern industrial power.

Third, in order to develop capitalism the soonest possible, the Meiji government firmly abolished the blind self-importance and cutting off Japan from the outside world during the Shogunate and proposed "Enrich the Country, Strengthen the Military", "Flourish Industries and Start up Businesses" and "Civilization and Enlightenment" as the guiding principles of Japan's modernization. In November, 1871, Iwakura Tomomi, Minister of the Right, in the role of extraordinary and plenipotentiary ambassador, Kido Takayoshi, as Imperial Advisor, Ōkubo Toshimichi, as Finance Minister, Itō Hirobumi, as Minister of Public Works, and Naoyoshi Yamaguchi, Junior Counselor to the Foreign Ministry as vice-envoy, were sent as a delegation to visit the United States and Europe for a planned period of two years with a very broad goal. This visit suggested strongly the determination of reforms by the Meiji government. Between May and September, 1873, delegates returned to Japan one after another and proposed the slogan of the goals of "Enrich the Country, Strengthen the Military", "Flourish Industries and Start up Businesses" and "Civilization and Enlightenment" as the guiding principles of Japan's modernization. However, officials inside the Meiji government had different opinions among themselves. Saigō Takamori who had military merit during the Meiji Restoration opposed to the reforms and staged a revolt openly in February, 1877 to start Satsuma Rebellion. The Meiji government suppressed this rebellion resolutely and paved the way for modern reforms. In the early days of the Meiji Restoration, Japan's gap with the various European countries was very wide. This caused the government and the public an urgency to learn from Europe and they proposed the slogan of Occidentalism for wholesale Westernization in politics, economy, military and culture, which was spearheaded by the new Minister of Foreign Affairs Inoue Kaoru. He proposed to transform Japan to a Europeanized country and Japanese people Europeanized people and this proposal was named "De-Asianization and Europeanization". Under "De-Asianization and Europeanization", the Meiji government had taken a roundabout course in its "transplanting" efforts in "directly copying" Europe and the United States. Later, it changed this course and proposed combination of Japan's national characteristics and its society and economy's needs and selectively learned proven foreign experiences and advanced science and technology and called people of all walks of life to suggest ways and means. It also organized specialists to survey closely

Japanese society's actual economic situation and its domestic products. People of various backgrounds proposed a multitude of advice and directions to promote starting up businesses. Moreover, it drafted "Encouragement of industry" based on site visits and surveys, which was a 30-volume industry promotion plan that covered industry, commerce and finance. These efforts corrected its "transplanting" policy of "directly copying" Europe and the United States. Furthermore, at the early stage of the founding of Japanese troops, it copied from foreign countries everything from imported weapons to training systems. However, after some time, they found it not workable. So in 1880, Murata Tsuneyoshi made changes to Western rifles in accordance with Japanese physique and manufactured its own Murata rifles. They also designed their own technical standards and manufactured their own equipment. In the early 1900s, Japan had already formed its own system based on introducing and digesting imported technologies.

Fourthly, the government actively developed modern education to train scientific and technological talents for industrial modernization. In order to educate and train talents for the industrial modernization, the Meiji government proposed "No uneducated family was in this town as well as no uneducated person was in each family" and stipulated that Japanese people, both genders, should receive compulsory education. It set up a normal school in Tokyo in 1871 so as to train more teachers. In 1874, it set up a female normal school. Normal schools were founded successively in other cities. While it rejuvenated elementary school education, the Meiji government also attached great significance to college education. It formed the University of Tokyo in 1877 to have four faculties of Law, Science, Letters and Medicine. It also took two emergency measures, namely, to hire foreign experts and select students to study overseas. In 1872, it hired 214 foreign experts and in 1874 it employed 503 which more than doubled its original employment. These foreign experts came from the United States, Great Britain, Germany and France and were posted in education and industry agencies and so on, and also in administrative agencies. However, the Meiji government emphasized seeking assistance only instead of total reliance on these foreign experts. The Meiji government promulgated "Rules on Employing Foreigners" in 1870 and stipulated that "Those who persecuted Japanese employees and disobeyed Japanese orders shall be fired." Those foreign experts were mainly hired to share science and technology that were in urgent need but Japan was unable to solve at the time. Even those foreign experts that were posted in the administrative agencies were consulted, they had no power of decision-making. Ōkubo Toshimichi reiterated that management was required for employing foreign experts and in no way should Japan lose its power to those foreigners. He instructed his subordinates that delegating powers should be centralized and those hired foreigners should not be unreasonably relied upon. However, remuneration for foreign experts was generously provided. At the time, the only university in Japan was the University of Tokyo. One third of its annual budget was earmarked for remuneration for its foreign experts. Foreign experts' remuneration was generally higher than that of Japanese high-ranking officials. The Meiji government's goal of doing so was to train Japan's own advanced professional technology talents and then replace gradually those foreign experts. This was shown in the rise and decline of the number of such foreign experts in Japan. In 1874, 103 foreign experts worked in Japan's public schools. 30 years later, in 1907, only 55 remained. The government's adherence to the policy of seeking assistance only instead of total reliance on these foreign experts had benefited Japan greatly and minimized any potential damage. In order to substitute Japanese talents for foreign talents as soon as possible, one of the key measures that the Meiji government took was to send its students overseas. In 1870, it sent 115 students overseas, in 1871, 281 students, in 1872, 356 students, and in 1973, 382 students. At the beginning, owing to lack of experience, examination was slack. So the number of students sent increased each year but its benefits received decreased. In 1873, someone submitted a report to the emperor claiming that "currently most students that were sent to Europe started with learning ABC and the annual cost of 1,000 taels of sliver is by no means reasonable to study only 26 letters." Additionally, one newspaper disclosed the test result of four returned students: two students had hardly learned anything and were not in a position even to take a test, and the other two students scored no more than middle school level. At that time, the remaining feudal elements were still very powerful. Kazoku abused its influence to send its sons overseas to study. *Tokyo hanjoki*, a book published in 1874, sarcastically said that "sons from noble families went abroad to study with huge amount of money, but they wanted to complete their studies the soonest possible so that they can return to Japan to assume high-ranking officials' positions" and "as some have not learned any skills abroad, only few can do their job well after they have returned to Japan." This situation caused reproach in the society. The Meiji government also felt deeply that it was imperative to change this situation speedily or its goal of training talents without any delay would fail. The government decided that all the government-funded students should be selected strictly by taking tests and managed centrally by Ministry of Education. Ministry of Education started in 1875 to send rigorously-tested students to study abroad. There were 11 students in 1875, 10 in 1876, and no student in 1877 owing to the suppression of Saigō Takamori's Satsuma Rebellion. In 1878, 11 students were selected from the Ministry of Public Works School to study abroad. During the 20 years prior to Sino-Japanese War of 1894-1895, Japan sent in total 118 students overseas to study, six students on average every year. After Sino-Japanese War of 1894-1895, Japan sent more students overseas. But during the 16 years between 1896 and 1912, Japan sent only 565 students, 35 on average every year. The Meiji government had high expectations of these students and had strict rules for them too. Since 1880, these students returned gradually and in turn replaced foreign experts once hired.

Each reform in social system in history came hand in hand with reform in thoughts and cultures. Meiji Restoration made possible the change from traditional Japanese culture to modern Japanese culture. Cultural modernization in turn promoted Japanese society's economic development and put Japan on a fast track to modernization.

Section Two   Meiji Restoration and Industrialization in Japan

I. Western influence spreading eastward and liberalization of thoughts and liberal civil rights movement

The 15th and 16th centuries were the point of division in the world history and a key turning point in the history of human being's civilization. The Eastern and Western civilization began to reverse, the ancient civilization nation in the East—

China started its decline and Europe that represented Western modern civilization began its speedy rise since this period and its advancement toward modern capitalist society. Western nations that led their way into modern capitalist society quickly started to expand and colonize the East by aggression. Meanwhile, they spread Western culture to the East and brought immense impact on the ancient but conservative Eastern culture.[①]

a. Dissemination of Catholicism and Rangaku in Japan

Japan's earliest contact with the Western culture began in the mid-16th century. The establishment of the Meiji government was the early period of Western culture's distribution to Japan. During this period, dissemination of Western culture had two main paths, namely, Western culture transferred with the dissemination of Catholicism and Western culture transferred with the rise of Rangaku. Portuguese merchant ships arrived at Japan the earliest in 1543. Portuguese missionaries came to Japan the earliest in 1549. The Spaniards arrived in Japan more than 30 years later than the Portuguese. They transported guns and cannons and did missionary work in Honshu. By the end of the 16th century, it was said that the number of Catholics totaled 150,000 in Japan. These Catholics were merchants, handicraft workers, peasants and samurai. Because Toyotomi Hideyoshi feared that expansion of Catholic influence might erode his own rule, he ordered ban on Catholicism in 1587. However, this ban was not implemented to the letter. In the early 17th century, namely, Tokugawa Shogunate, Japanese Catholics numbered as many as 700,000 to 750,000 and even some trusted followers of Tokugawa Ieyasu were Catholics. By the end of 1613, the Shogunate ordered a nationwide ban on Catholicism and condemned Catholicism as cult. From 1614 to 1635, it was said that 280,000 Catholics were killed because they refused to change their religion. The concern of the Shogunate toward Catholicism was that Catholicism may be deep-rooted in people's minds and become a spiritual force for revolts.

Dissemination of Rangaku in Japan was after the 18th century. At that time, influence of Catholicism spread by the Portuguese and Spanish missionaries decreased tremendously in Japan owing to fierce suppressions. Rangaku initially

---

[①] Tang Chongnan. *Japan's Culture and Modernization*. Shenyang: Liaohai Publishing House, 1999.

distributed natural science, medicine and geography. It was not until the early 19th century that distribution of political science knowledge expanded to some extent. As a result, the Shogunate was more permissible with initial dissemination of Rangaku than that of Catholicism because its rulers believed that natural science, medicine and geography spread by Rangaku would not pose a threat to its rule.

b. Upsurge in introducing Western capitalist thoughts

Faced with the penetration of Western culture, Japan began to accept and absorb Western civilization. The Meiji government developed capitalism and at the same time it staged an upsurge of introducing Western capitalist thoughts and translated and published many famous Western books. These books were broadly based. During the course of introducing Western thoughts, many social activists and enlightenment thinkers that promoted Western civilization appeared. Among them, Fukuzawa Yukichi was the most famous one. Fukuzawa was born into an impoverished low-ranking samurai family of Nakatsu. He began to study Western learning at youth. He traveled with the Shogunate missions to visit Europe and the United States many times and was keenly aware that Japan had to open itself to the outside world and be enterprising. After the Meiji Restoration, he founded Keio Gijuku (forerunner of today's Keio University) and started to write books and tried his best to advocate civilization and enlightenment. In his *An Encouragement of Learning*, he proposed the principle of equality of opportunity, which became his best-known words. In addition, in 1870 Katō Hiroyuki's *The Substance of True Government* advocated natural rights and he further emphasized this idea in his 1874 book *New Theory of the National Polity*. Even though Fukuzawa later changed this idea, natural rights remained very influential in Japan.

c. Upsurge of Freedom and People's Rights Movement

Western influence spread eastward. This blew fresh air into Japan's traditional society and brought strong shocks to the traditional small country's civilization. The early dissemination of Western culture not only made the Japanese people in initial contact and understanding of Western culture, what is more important is that it greatly expanded Japanese people's field of vision and imperceptibly influenced their world outlook with these changes and transfused fresh blood into the Japanese national culture. In the early days, Japanese people's attitude toward Western culture was rather contradictory. However, new things have their vitality after all and the advanced culture would prevail over the outdated one. As a result of Western influence spreading eastward, under the influence of free democratic thoughts, with Councilor of State Itagaki Taisuke who was defeated in the Seikanron (debate to conquer Korea) and retired from public office and others as representatives, and the background of extensive peasant uprisings, backed with Western capitalist thoughts, especially the natural rights, a capitalist democratic movement was staged in Japan.

In January, 1874, Itagaki and Kataoka Kenkichi and others published "the original covenant" (namely, guiding principles) of Aikoku Kōtō (Public Party of Patriots), believing in "endowed rights" (namely, equal rights as called in China) that were eternally bestowed on the people by the heaven and declaring that we are all equally endowed with certain definite rights. People are not slaves of the government and the government is established for the people. Only when people's endowed rights are upheld can "our country's national pride be made and our people be enriched". This should be the way of "loving the emperor and the country". Then (on January 17), Itagaki Taisuke, Soejima Taneomi, Gotō Shōjirō, Etō Shimpei, Yuri Kimimasa, Okamoto Kensaburo, and others petitioned in *The Petition to Establish an Elected Assembly*. The drafters were Furusawa Shigeru and Komuro Shinobu who were returned students from England. The petition criticized "Yushi Sensei" that was controlled by Iwakura and Ōkubo, which may lead the country to its demise, and proposed that the only way to "save" the country was to establish a "Minsen Giin" (a popularly-elected assembly) to give voting right and right to discuss rent and taxes to the people. When Itagaki and others petitioned to establish a popularly elected assembly and to give voting right to the people, what they meant by the people were not ordinary people but "Shizoku and wealthy farmers and merchants". The goal to establish a popularly elected assembly was to safeguard the emperor's country with "the top and the bottom will work together; lords and vassals will respect each other". Objectively, this may indicate that it meant to reform the emperor system and in essence it was the request from the opposition in the government.

In Japan where a ban on assembly was in effect then, it was the first time that a bourgeois party, "Aikoku Kōtō", was founded and it published its guiding principles requesting equality and criticized publicly the Meiji oligarchy, started to petition people's right to participate in government administration and specifically proposed to establish a legislative body by the people's elected delegates. This reflected the calls from various classes that were unsatisfied with the government and signaled progress. When *Minsen Giin Setsuritsu Kenpaku Sho* was rejected by the government and its contents were published in *Nisshin Shinji Shi* newspaper by Scotsman John Reddie Black, an argument that was against or in favor of the establishment of such an assembly started immediately. Ever since then "the Freedom and People's Rights Movement" in Japan's modern history, a bourgeois democratic movement, started with this petition as its fuse.

On April 10, 1874, in order to establish the movement for a popularly elected assembly, Itagaki Taisuke, Kataoka Kenkichi, Hayashi Yūzō and other early leaders in the people's rights movement founded the Risshinsha (Self-reliance Association) in their hometown Kōchi Prefecture. They advocated the natural rights and proposed "people are all equal and no difference in their social status". In order to uphold people's rights, people's assembly (parliament) must be established. But at the same time they emphasized that the goal to establish such an assembly was to "promote the Emperor's dignity and the Empire's welfare". They also claimed that Shizoku as intellectuals were leaders of farmers, workers and merchants. Under the influence of the Risshinsha, Komuro Shinobu founded the Risshisha (Self-help Society) in Tokushima Domain. Similar democratic organizations were founded in other cities successively.

On February 22, 1875, with the Risshinsha as the center, a combined group of 40 people from various political organizations in Japan (all were Shizoku) convened in Osaka to found Aikokusha (Society of Patriots). They proposed that "everyone promotes his right of self-determination, completes obligation of his own; at least they will safeguard themselves and their families, at best they will safeguard their country so as to promote the Emperor's dignity and welfare and make our country stand in pride side by side with the countries in Europe and the United States". They integrated the theory of people's rights on the basis of the fundamental human rights with the theory of state rights with an emphasis on the Emperor and the country and combined them as the outside and inside and then made propaganda all over Japan.

The government feared rise of the Freedom and People's Rights Movement and the establishment of Aikokusha and its activities. In order to crumble the Freedom and People's Rights Movement, Ōkubo Toshimichi induced Itagaki Taisuke who retired from public office owing to the Seikanron to rejoin the government. On March 12, Itagaki joined the government as a Councilor. On April 14, the emperor issued the Imperial Rescript Establishing a Constitutional Form of Government, and on the same day, the Chamber of the Left and the Chamber of the Right were replaced with the establishment of the Chamber of Elders (Genroin) and Daishin'in (Supreme Court).

After Itagaki rejoined the government, Aikokusha was disbanded in April, 1875. As Ōkubo Toshimichi and others insisted on centralization of powers and autocracy and there was no trace of democracy at all, all classes felt discontented and angry. The Freedom and People's Rights Movement was active again. During this period, liberal rights groups founded radical newspapers and journals such as *Review News*, *Collected Works News*, *Lake and Sea New Papers*, *Recent Things Review*, *Wilderness Journal* and so on. They promoted extensively in these publications people's right to resistance and revolution based on the natural rights and freedom and equality. In June, 1876, Ueki Emori published the article "Freedom is worth purchasing with one's own blood" in *Lake and Sea New Papers* and believed that if the government oppressed the people excessively, people cannot rely exclusively on speech, instead they must use "means to crumble the rocks and smash the earth chunks to overthrow the dictator government".

With the rise of the bourgeois democratic thoughts, the government's persecution intensified. On June 28, 1875, the government issued *Press Ordinance of 1875* that severely restricted speech and punished the offenders with fines or imprisonment. At the same time, it issued *Libel Law* that banned all criticism on officials' work or life, public or private and the offenders would be punished. Between 1875 and 1876, there were more than 60 cases of editors and journalists being sentenced. *Review News*, *Wilderness Journal*, *Lake and Sea New Papers* and other newspapers and journals were ordered to shut down. In October, 1875, owing to government's failure to comply with the agreement of constitutional monarchy, Itagaki Taisuke withdrew from the government and again got involved in activities to set up popularly elected assembly.

However, as the Freedom and People's Rights Movement led by the liberal organizations was integrated with the immediate interests of the people, during the course of their struggles against the state power, the movement gradually grew to a large-scale peasant uprising, which made it revolutionary in nature and reached its peak in 1884. Owing to the betrayal by landlords, bourgeoisie and suppression by the government, the movement declined eventually. By 1887, the Meiji government issued the Peace Preservation Law of 1887 to suppress the movement organizers and this movement came to an end.

In summary, during the 14 years from the organization of Aikoku Kōtō and *The Petition to Establish an Elected Assembly* in 1874 to the Meiji government's issuance of the Peace Preservation Law of 1887 to suppress the movement organizers in 1887, the Freedom and People's Rights Movement experienced an entire process of rise, surge, decline and end. The movement participants included Shizoku-turned intellectuals, small landlords, wealthy peasants, bourgeoisie and poor peasants. The movement requested, politically, a national assembly, disbanding Meiji oligarchy; economically, reduction in land tax, opposition to the government's excessive demands; and in terms of foreign affairs, amendment to treaties, opposition to the government's obsequiously submissive position. What they opposed was the Meiji government's incomplete bourgeois reform. Owing to the united front's breakup, betrayal by the upper class of the movement and the government's suppression, this bourgeois democratic movement failed. However, the 14-year-long movement forced the Meiji government to make some changes: politically, it promised to make a constitution, provide strictly-restrained basic human rights to its people; economically, it declared revocation of rules that every five years the land cost would be revised; and in terms of foreign affairs, it denied Minister of Foreign Affairs Inoue Kaoru's humiliating treaty amendment draft. In general, the Freedom and People's Rights Movement was a mind-emancipating one and to some extent expanded Meiji Restoration's scope and depth and was definitely somewhat progressive in the then Japan.

II. Using for reference and absorbing Western technology and Japan's industrialization

As Japan absorbed Western culture, it started to learn and transplant successful systems in the West and then digested and absorbed them to create one system that had Japanese characteristics. The economic performance and development speed made possible by the Meiji Restoration system arrangement were unique in the world economic development history.

a. Using for reference and absorbing Western technology and "Flourishing Industries and Starting up Businesses"

At the end of the Shogunate and early Meiji period, Japanese society's economy was still very backward. The capitalist family labor that was extensive nationwide was still dominant and its industrial production lagged far behind the advanced capitalist countries in the West and its heavy industry was almost non-existent. Meanwhile, its unequal treaties signed with the Western powers were not yet nullified and Japan was still threatened by the risk of being colonized or semi-colonized. In order to gain national independence and catch up with the advanced capitalist countries, well before the establishment of the Meiji government, the persons with insight in Japan understood well the advancement of science and technology in the West and they revealed the view of "Japan's ethics and West's technology" and actively advocated introduction of Western technology. Through a series of reform measures, the Meiji government abolished the feudal economic system and while endeavoring to promote capitalist development in Japan, under the slogan of "Flourishing Industries and Starting up Businesses", staged an upsurge of absorbing science and technology from the West. The details of "Flourishing Industries and Starting up Businesses" were to use the state power, through various policy measures and the national treasury funds to expedite primitive accumulation of capital and spearheaded by government-owned enterprises, to use Western models to support with might and main capitalist development. Marx said primitive accumulation of capital "is to use strong state power and use centralized and organized social violence to grow like in a greenhouse the transformative process from feudal production method to capitalist production method and to shorten this transition. Violence is the midwife for the old society's pregnancy with the new society".① Japan was exactly using its state power to accumulate capital from various sources and realized capitalist modernization from upside down.

The Meiji government implemented "Flourishing Industries and Starting up Businesses" from 1870 to 1885. It followed the Western countries' models to endeavor to develop capitalism. In October, 1873, Home Ministry led by Ōkubo Toshimichi was founded to rectify overstressing heavy industry development originally adopted by Ministry of Industry and instead to develop primarily agriculture, products processing, ocean-shipping industry and so on so as to set up the guiding principle of developing capitalism in Japan after the Meiji Restoration.

(1) Greatly promoting government-owned enterprises

At the beginning of the Meiji Restoration, the government took over the Shogunate and domains' military factories to transform and establish foundation of Japan's modern military industry by introducing the technology and equipment from the West. The period of 1868 to 1885 was the establishment period of Japan's modern military industry and also the period of policy to "Enrich the Country, Strengthen the Military" led by Ministry of Industry. At that time, the former Shogunate-owned factories included the Sekiguchi factory (predecessor of the Tokyo Arsenal), Yokosuka Iron Foundry (predecessor of Yokosuka Naval Arsenal), and Yokohama Iron Foundry (leased to a private party for operation in 1879). The former domain-owned factories included Mito Domain's Ishikawajima Shipyard and Satsuma Domain's Kagoshima Shipyard (both were predecessors of naval factories), Satsuma Domain's Shikine Powder Mill (later renamed as Army Powder Mill) and Wakayama Domain's Arsenal (later the affiliated factory of the Osaka Arsenal) and so on. Through mergers, reforms and adjustments, till 1880 or so, two army factories in Tokyo Arsenal and Osaka Artillery Arsenal and their affiliates as well as two naval factories in Tsukiji Naval Arsenal and Yokosuka Naval Arsenal and their affiliates were established.

The Meiji government also endeavored to develop communications and transportation and telecommunications industry. Railway topped in the government-

---

① Marx. *Capital (Volume I)*. Beijing: People's Publishing House, 1963: 828.

owned industries and its investment was nearly half of the total investment of the government-owned enterprises. In September, 1872, the railway between Tokyo and Yokohama started to operate, which is Japan's first railway. In May, 1874 and February, 1877 the Kobe-Osaka line and the Osaka-Kyoto line started business respectively. Meanwhile, the telecommunications and postal industry developed too. In 1869, the cable line between Tokyo and Yokohama was set up, which is Japan's first telecommunications line. In the same year, the telegraph line between Tokyo and Yokohama went into business. Initially, telegraph service was exclusively used by the government, but in 1878 the public was able to use this service too. In 1871, courier mail service (post of letters and goods) was improved and the state postal service was established. In January, 1871, mail service started among Tokyo, Kyoto and Osaka.

In industry and mining, the government issued *Notice to Mines* (1872) and *The Japanese Mining Law* (1873), and nationalized the mines owned by the Shogunate and domains. Major mines included Ikuno and Sado gold mines, Ani, Innai, Ashio, and Ogou copper mines, Kamaishi iron mine, Miike and Takashima coal mines and so on. Foreign technical experts were hired and machinery was imported and steam power was used in these mines. The government centralized its efforts to improve iron making techniques, imported equipment from England, and hired German engineers. An iron manufactory was set up in Kamaishi iron mine and began smelting operations in 1880. In order to increase the production of raw silk and silk fabrics and other products for export, silk-making and spinning model mills were established under the jurisdiction of Ministry of Treasury. In 1872, French technicians were hired, French machines were bought and the first model silk mill was set up in Tomioka, Gunma Prefecture. Meanwhile, the government bought the old cotton-spinning mill in Yokosuka and Nishi cotton-spinning mill. In 1876, a silk-spinning mill was founded in Shinmachi. In 1878, equipment was imported from England to set up two mills in Aichi and Hiroshima. In the same year, a corduroy mill was founded in Senju, Tokyo to manufacture woolen threads and corduroy (changed to a military factory in 1888).

In the silk-making industry, silk-making by machine technology was introduced from Italy and France. The machine silk-making mills quickly spread with Nagano

Prefecture as the center. In 1873, there were 14 such mills, in 1877, 50 such mills, and later they increased with each passing year.

In agriculture, Naito Shinjuku Experimental Agricultural Center was founded in 1872. In 1877, Mita Breeding Farm, Mita Agricultural Tools Manufacturing Company, and Tokko Breeding Stock and Sheep Husbandry Farm were founded to make breed and strain improvement and test-use foreign agricultural tools.

(2) Fostering private capitalism

By the 1890s, Japan had built up a large number of government-owned enterprises with the military industry as their mainstay, which laid a foundation for the future industry revolution with light industry as its focus. However, at that time Japan merely concentrated on transplanting modern capitalist industry but failed to take into account Japan's economic condition that it was a semi-colony. As a result, government-owned enterprises not only failed to lead private-owned enterprises, but also suffered losses year after year owing to its lack of financial expertise. So since 1880, the Meiji government decreased its fiscal expenditure and changed its original policy of government-owned enterprises leading and guiding private-owned ones to the policy of "disposing of at a loss" government-owned enterprises and directly supporting private capitalism. That November, it issued rules to dispose of government-owned enterprises and sold a great majority of government-owned enterprises to a group of capitalists at a very low price.

Later the Meiji government further fostered private enterprises, especially the light industry with textiles as the center. For example, it spent more than 220,000 yen to buy 10 sets of 2,000-spindle cotton spinners and sold them at the preferential term of 10-year interest-free loan to the public; it set up a total of nine cotton mills like Mayekawa, Obayama and others; and gave away free of charge to Mitsubishi Steamship Company 13 ships that it commissioned to the company when it invaded Taiwan and provided it with sea route grants. Moreover, the government bought 18 ships from Mail Steamship Company that was out of business owing to slack operations and provided them free of charge to Mitsubishi Steamship Company. With the full support from the government, Mitsubishi Steamship Company defeated the US' Pacific Mail Steamship Company and Great Britain's Peninsula and Oriental Steam Navigation Company and monopolized sea routes along the Japanese coast and between Japan and Shanghai.

(3) Introducing and training technical talents

In the course of promoting the policy of "Flourishing Industries and Starting up Businesses", the Meiji government paid special attention to the introduction of foreign experts and advanced equipment. In the early Meiji period, the employed foreign experts and technical professionals were mainly for the government agencies. In 1872, Ministry of Finance hired 19 foreign experts, nine for Ministry of Military, 24 for Ministry of Education, 153 for Ministry of Industry, five for the Bureau of Colonization of Hokkaidō, and in total 214. The year of 1876 witnessed the largest number of foreign experts, namely, 32 for Home Ministry, 21 for Ministry of Finance, 27 for Ministry of War of Japan, 55 for Ministry of the Navy of Japan, 67 for Ministry of Education, 221 for Ministry of Industry, 18 for the Bureau of Colonization of Hokkaidō, in total 469. The number decreased gradually after 1880. The largest employer was Ministry of Industry. The government provided very handsome payments but also was very strict with them over their work. *The Rules on Employment of Foreigners* issued in February, 1870 stipulated that foreigners hired who "indulge in sensual pursuits" and performed unsatisfactorily must be fired; and those who concurrently held other positions in addition to their full-time jobs to "promote their own inerests", especially who engaged in smuggling must be punished and so on. Owing to the government's position of vigilance and caution, most foreign experts played an important role in introducing and mastering advanced production techniques in Europe and the United States.

The policy of "Flourishing Industries and Starting up Businesses" was basically implemented in 1885. At the time government-owned factories and mines numbered 41, and they belonged respectively to Ministry of Finance, Ministry of Industry, Ministry of Agriculture and Commerce, Ministry of War of Japan, Ministry of the Navy of Japan, and the Bureau of Colonization of Hokkaidō. These government-owned enterprises were all large-scale and well-equipped artillery arsenals, shipyards, machinery manufactories and mines, which represented the development trend in Japan's modernization. At the time, small and medium-sized private factories numbered 1,981, among them textiles mills were 60.9%, kilns 12%, foodstuff industry 9.3%, metallurgical manufactories 8%, chemicals manufactories

4.6%, machinery manufactories 1.9% and the rest 3.3%. These factories were primarily handicraft works and rural handicraft works at more than 60% and urban handicraft works at less than 40%. In view of the number of employees in these factories, factories with 30 employees or less accounted for 83.4%. So a great majority of them were small-sized factories. Only textiles mills, chemicals manufactories and shipyards were relatively large-scale manufactories with modern machinery. Nevertheless, Japan's industrial development speed was astonishing. The average annual growth rate in Japan during 1866 and 1873 was 32.2% whereas its British counterpart (1851 to 1873) was 3.3%, its US counterpart (1861 to 1873) 5% and its German counterpart (1861 to 1873) 3.8%. During the period between 1874 and 1890, Japan's average annual growth rate was 12.1% while the British rate 1.7%, the US rate 5.2%, the French rate 2.1% and the German rate 3.5%.

After the implementation of the policy of "Flourishing Industries and Starting up Businesses", during only 15 years (1870 to 1885), Japan substantially changed its backward industry and Western science and technology took root and blossomed in various sectors in Japan. This forcefully promoted development in Japan's modern science and technology and laid a foundation for Japan's speedy modernization.

b. Japan's industrialization

Japan's absorption of the advanced Western culture and its imitation of technology eventually put Japan as a backward agricultural country on the market economy track and its indicator was just industrial revolution. Industrial revolution means the process of replacing handicraft industry based on manual skills with mechanized industrialization. It is both a revolution in production technology and a major change in social production relationship. With the backward production method being finally eliminated by the advanced one, Japan preliminarily completed transplanting Western market economy system.

(1) Features of Japan's industrialization.[①] The industrialization happened in England in the 18th century. Japan achieved industrialization as an Eastern and a less advanced country one century later than England. As a new-coming country, Japan's industrial revolution has the following general features:

[①] Refer to Wu Tingqiu. *History of Japan*. Tianjin: Nankai University Press, 1994.

Firstly, Japan's industrial revolution happened under the condition of "Western impact". In the mid-19th century, Western capitalist influence invaded Japan and forced it to open its ports and through "free trade" included Japan's economy into the world capitalist system with its status as a semi-colony. As a result, the significance of Japan's industrial revolution lies not only in realization of capitalist industrialization but also in its formation of an independent modern unified nation and an independent capitalist country.

Secondly, Japan's industrial revolution did not develop from its original capitalist buds or handicraft industry, but instead it made this happen through transplanting Western modern capitalist enterprises and economic system. The industrial revolution in the West happened after its original capitalist buds or handicraft industry developed to a mature stage. In Japan, although the natural economy under the Shogunate and domain rule kept its course to disintegration, the rice-dominant agricultural products tended to be commercialized and rural family-based handicraft works in green silk weaving and cotton spinning emerged. But these capitalist buds did not grow sufficiently under the Shogunate and domain rule and not until after the Meiji Restoration did it develop robustly and it existed and developed simultaneously with the modern mechanized industry transplanted from the West.

Thirdly, the Industrial Revolution's prerequisite is primitive accumulation of capital. In the origin of Industrial Revolution in the West, primitive accumulation of capital preceded Industrial Revolution. However, as a new-coming country, Japan was a different case. During the Tokugawa Shogunate, it was impossible for its closed small-scale peasant economy to have primitive accumulation. After the Meiji Restoration, on one hand, Japan transplanted capitalist production method and economic system through the state's industrialization policy, and on the other hand, through the government's policy and overseas plundering, it engaged actively in primitive accumulation of capital. So Japan's early industrial revolution and primitive accumulation of capital happened at the same time.

Fourthly, Japan's industrial revolution started with its military industry, which is a feature of new-coming countries in the East to achieve their own industrial revolution. In order to combat "foreign pressure" and get away from Western colonialist influence, Japan implemented the policy of "Enrich the Country, Strengthen the Military" to gain national independence. During the state's promotion of primitive accumulation of capital, it devoted its major efforts to developing its government-owned military industry and other factories and mines. These military enterprises and factories and mines were the earliest ones to introduce advanced Western technology and became the national bases of mechanized manufacture. This created conditions for later private capitalism especially the light industry characterized by cotton mill industry. Japan's industrial revolution with the military industry as its starting point and accompanied by overseas plundering stamped Japan's development of capitalism with the brand of militarism.

Fifthly, Japan's industrial revolution was promoted by the people who "adopted Western technology while preserving Japanese culture". That is to say, owing to the aforementioned historical conditions, Japan's industrial revolution after the Meiji government was established was basically a revolution promoted by gentry-born people that were with a certain amount of capitalist knowledge and business acumen. These people were generally divided into two groups: some were political officials in power, as they had controlled the state power and through site visits to Europe and the United States they felt the external pressure and proposed the policy of "Flourishing Industries and Starting up Businesses" and other guiding principles to foster modern industry from topside down; the others were gentry-born industrialists that were not in court such as Godai Tomoats, Shibusawa Eiichi who contributed directly and greatly to the establishment and development of Japan's modern industry. Only Shibusawa himself founded more than 50 enterprises of various types.

(2) Contents of Japan's industrial revolution

(i) Consolidating and developing Japan's fiscal and financial industry

After the Meiji Restoration, in order to implement the policy of "Flourishing Industries and Starting up Businesses" and solve fiscal hardship, Japan once adopted the inflation policy. The government issued a large amount of paper money that could not be cashed, especially owing to the issuance of Kinroku government securities and the outbreak of Satsuma Rebellion, the government also allowed banks to issue paper money which resulted in severe glut in 1881 or so. The inflation caused a series of chain reactions: commodity price hikes, government securities value decline, interest rate inflation, imbalance in exchange rate between silver coins and paper money and so on. Meanwhile, this directly affected further development of Japan's modern industry.

In order to change this situation, while the government was disposing of government-owned enterprises, it started to consolidate financial affairs. While it decreased expenditure and increased tax revenue and used other measures to expand its fiscal income, it increased its export so as to obtain gold and silver from overseas and increase its cash stockpile. In order to establish the system of the central bank's issuance of paper money, in 1882 it founded the Bank of Japan. It changed the chaos in its fiscal and financial status, and this financial retrenchment policy created the prerequisite to the rise of Japan's industrial revolution.

(ii) Focusing on developing military industry

After the Meiji government took over the former Shoguante-owned military factories, military factories were treated by the government as the key industry for development. These military factories were actually "one of the starters" of Japan's large mechanized industry. By the 1880s, owing to Japanese government's arms expansion, military industry became its key modern industry. This is also one of the indicators that Japan's capitalism was military in nature from its very beginning. The military industry that was operated as the key industry by the government supported its modern industry development. Meanwhile, it provided material prerequisite to its overseas invasion.

(iii) Developing light industry focusing on cotton spinning

In 1883, political entrepreneurs Shibusawa Eiichi and others pooled Kazoku and cotton merchants' capital to set up Osaka Spinning Mill. By 1889, it quickly developed itself into a giant enterprise with a capital of 1.2 million yen and more than 60,000 spindles. With the lead of Osaka Spinning Mill, from 1886 to 1890, Tokyo Spinning Mill, Kanegafuchi Spinning Mill, Hirano Spinning Mill and others were founded one after another, most with a registered capital of over 250,000 yen and number of spindles between 10,000 and 30,000, and use of ring-shaped spinners so as to increase the output of cotton yarns. In 1890 or so, Japan's cotton mill industry already occupied a dominant position in Japan's modern production. While the modern cotton mill industry was established, silk making, silk spinning, cotton spinning, paper making, sugar making and other light-industry sectors all achieved modern production.

(iv) Developing communications and transportation industry

As communications and transportation industry had military significance, the Meiji government always paid great attention to its development. Since the 1880s, the government mobilized the private enterprises to participate in railway construction. In November, 1881, backed with the Kazoku's Kinroku government securities, the private-owned Nippon Railway was founded. The government gave very preferential policy to this company. By the end of 1891, private railway in operation reached 1,165 miles, which more than doubled Japan's government-owned railway in length. During this period, private-owned railway's capital increased from 85,000 yen in 1881 to 44.57 million yen in 1891. The ocean shipping industry that also had military significance rose too with the assistance from the government. The communications and transportation industry grew rapidly with the government's support. By 1893, capital for the communications and transportation industry was 90.34 million yen, over ten times more than 6.89 million yen in 1884.

(v) Developing foreign trade

In the early Meiji period, while Japan implemented with might and main its policy of "Enrich the Country, Strengthen the Military" and "Flourishing Industries and Starting up Businesses", it also paid attention to its disadvantage in its foreign trade. After Iwakura Mission's visits to Europe and the United States, the government further realized the necessity of "Building up the State with Industry" and "Building up the State with Trade". This was very significant for the formation of modern Japanese capitalism. But as Japan's capitalism just started at the time, it endeavored to get rid of the trade structure as a semi-colony. So in the early Meiji period, even though the government made its best efforts to expand its exports primarily of raw silk and tea, it still faced with many years of import surplus. Its imports were largely machinery, cotton and woolen knitwear and so on. Before Sino-Japanese War of 1894-1895, Japan was successful in its industrial revolution focusing on light industry and actively increased its exports to China and Korea and at the same time increased its imports of cotton, steel, machinery and arms. In 1880 or so, Japan saw its trade structure changed. Japan supplied agricultural products and raw materials to Europe and the United States and imported industrial products and machinery, and it dumped its industrial products mainly of cotton yarns, cotton cloth and matches to backward countries in Asia and seized agricultural and industrial products from them.

Raw silk was a trump card in Japan's foreign trade. From the early years of Meiji government till Sino-Japanese War of 1894-1895, such exports were always number one in its exports every year. In 1895, raw silk was 5.2% of its total export. Raw silk contributed tremendously to the formation of Japan's modern capitalism. The largest importer of Japan's raw silk was the United States. In 1894 raw silk export to the United States was 52% of Japan's total export to the United States and in 1897 it was 53.2%. Among the four largest silk producers in the world (France, Italy, China and Japan), Japan rose to number one at the beginning of 1906.

In order to break away from foreign merchants' monopoly of Japan's foreign trade, Japan founded Mitsui & Co., Ltd. and other trading companies with Japanese features, which played a vital role in Japan's capitalist production and foreign trade.

III. System change and capitalism with Eastern features

The Meiji Restoration in the 19th century in Japan was an upside-down and compulsory system change. This profound social change made an earth-shaking change to the Japanese economy and social landscape. From the actual situation in the development at the end of the Shogunate, Japan's society produced a strong system demand which positioned the Japanese society in an inequilibrium in its system. Then the Meiji Restoration provided the system demanded and struck an equilibrium in the new system and put Japan on the capitalist development path of "Enrich the Country, Strengthen the Military". However, although the government-led compulsory system change made possible for Japan's economic leap forward development and squeezed itself into the Western powers, at the same time, it left a great number of feudal elements in its political and economic systems, which are the innate defects in the later Japanese economic system development.[1]

a. The topside-down compulsory system change and introduction of capitalist

---

[1] Refer to Jin Renshu, Feng Zhi. "Compulsory System Change and Meiji Restoration's Binary Effect". *Japanology Forum*, Issue No. 4, 2004.

system

The new institutional economics thinks that an institution is a code of behaviors that is written in advance to adjust conflict of interests. An institution may be designed as a tool by the human being to deal with uncertainty and to increase an individual's effectiveness. Choice of institutional arrangements will include calculations of costs and benefits. An institution exists to achieve an equilibrium in the institution, namely, to safeguard that benefit of the institution is greater than its cost and to benefit the behavioral agent that is subject to the constraints of the institution. The cause that leads to the institutional change is an inequilibrium in the institution. When the potential social net benefit in the new property rights is greater than the net social benefit in the original property rights, the motive and behavior to reform this institution appear. One major indication in an inequilibrium is the institution's shortage in supply, namely, institutional demand is greater than institutional supply. Then it requires an increase in institutional supply to solve this inequilibrium. Institutional supply can be divided into two modes: compulsory supply and inductive supply. These two system supply modes in the institution change process are called compulsory institutional change and inductive institutional change. The so-called inductive institutional change refers to the change and substitution in the current institutional arrangements, or the creation of the institutional arrangements is voluntarily advocated, organized and implemented by one individual or a group of people in response to profit-making opportunities. Inductive changes must be caused as a result of the profit-making opportunity that is not available in the original institution. Lin Yifu thinks that inductive institutional change has three features: (1) Spontaneity. The inductive institutional change is a spontaneous reaction by a relevant group or an individual to an inequilibrium in the institution. The inducement of a spontaneous reaction is presence of a potential profit. The institutional change process is the process of internalization of a potential profit. (2) Profitability. That is to say that only when the expected benefit of the institutional change is greater than the expected cost of the institutional change can a relevant group promote the institutional change. (3) Progressiveness. The inductive institutional change is an institutional change process that is topside-down and from part to the entirety. The transition and substitution of the institution requires a long process. As the institutional arrangement is a public product and a free rider is an issue that cannot be avoided by the institutional innovation, and meanwhile the transaction cost of the consensus reached by individuals is too high, if we only rely on the inductive institutional change, the supply of the institutional change in a society will be less than the society's optimum. However, the intervention by the state and the government will supplement the consistent shortage in supply. This is the compulsory institutional change. The compulsory institutional change means that the government proposes a new system's goal and contents and implements them compulsorily with the legal means. It generally shows the process that people accept passively and select the official institutional arrangements under the government's external pressure. The compulsory institutional change and the inductive institutional change also have a cross point such as on the basis of the state power, however, their greatest difference or the so-called feature of the compulsory institutional change is the grassroots organization or group's passiveness. The institutional innovation plan is all designed and proposed by the government. The grassroots organization or group is only a recipient. The interest of the government and the grassroots organization or the group's interest have nonuniformity and in case of conflict of interests between the two parties, the government will satisfy its interests first. The promotion and execution of the new institution do not have to go through an experimental unit and test but can be promoted as a unified whole and achievement of the reform goal within a short period of time is emphasized. It is radical and externalist in nature and may not be in line with the constitutional order or satisfy people's desires. It may be illegal under certain circumstances. The benefits of the compulsory institutional change can be summarized as: the compulsory institutional change is one that the government designs and drafts the institutional innovation plan and saves the transaction cost of the institutional supply. The radical and externalist nature of the compulsory institutional change may quickly satisfy the demand of the internalist institution to achieve an equilibrium in the institution. If the goal of the government and the grassroots organization has a public interest, the change may save organizational and coordination cost.

b. The motive to implement the compulsory institutional change

The Meiji Restoration is a bourgeois revolution carried out after the Meiji government overthrew the Shogunate rule. At the end of the Shogunate, the conflict inside the society intensified and the ruling party's inner circles also disintegrated. As a result, both the internalist and externalist causes of the compulsory institutional change appeared.

(1) The internal motive. The middle and lower-ranking samurai became the compulsory institutional change's unity of preliminary behavior subject and secondary behavior group. At the end of the Shogunate, the middle and lower-ranking samurai acted as the daring vanguard to overthrow the Shogunate, namely, the compulsory institutional change's preliminary behavior subject. During the Shogunate, the primary means of production were owned by the samurai class. The samurai class was one that enjoyed the political privilege. But so far as the inner circles of this class are concerned, the various strata and cliques had different ruling power. Owing to the noted differences in their political status, bitter conflicts existed. Moreover, with the development of commercial currency relationship and capitalism, samurai's parasitic life was severely eroded and disintegrated. Just as Engels said, "the knights' castle was destroyed by the currency long before it was opened up by the new-type cannons". The poverty and decline in the samurai class intensified its internal contradiction and fight. And the Shogun and daimyo often resorted to stopping payment or reduction in payment of the official salary to the lower-ranking samurai to solve their own financial hardship. At the time, the feudal lords relied primarily on the military forces composed of the lower-ranking samurai to rule the broad masses of the people. This contradiction and conflict inevitably weakened the power of the ruling class and became an omen of the collapse of the Shogunate. To the then capitalists that were both very weak and in the making, these were very good objective conditions that would help them make their reform requests possible. While the middle and lower-ranking samurai stayed away from their owners (the feudal upper-class rulers), some of them started to make close contacts with and then transformed to the capitalist class. The intellectuals at the end of the Shogunate were mainly composed of the middle and lower-ranking samurai. Their cultural knowledge and experience were much richer than the general capitalist class, especially some of them who came in contact with the advanced thoughts of the Western capitalist class through Rangaku, which made them more active and mature

in politics than the general capitalist class. As a result, some of them became key leaders in the anti-Shogunate and restoration movement. The middle and lower-ranking samurai acted as leaders in the secondary behavior group in the Meiji Restoration. The benefit in the institutional change by the Meiji Restoration was shown to a large extent in an increase in their future benefit. Among the lower-ranking samurai who monopolized the booty of this political revolution, some advocated embarking on the capitalist path, meanwhile, they also realized that if they failed to maintain their coalition relationship with the capitalist class and to gain the financial support from the capitalist class, they would not be able to keep their rule. As a result, when they were making national policies, they could not but prioritize the interests of the capitalist class. The class struggle inside Japan and the threat of colonization faced by Japan also forced the new government to implement reforms that were capitalist in nature and paved the way for capitalist development. We can see both the preliminary and secondary action subjects in the institutional change were shouldered by the middle and lower-ranking samurai. This made realization of the goal before and after this change more consistent. So the transaction cost resulted from the organization and execution also decreased accordingly.

(2) The external motive. Faced with the risk of falling into a colony of the Western powers, at the end of the Shogunate, Japan's internal conflict proved that it was nearing its fated end. So when the Western industrialization civilization arrived in Japan, the Tokugawa Shogunate rule really had too many difficulties to cope with at the same time. In the mid-19th century, the Western capitalist powers crossed the oceans from afar and had their fleet to set up the cannons to aim at the East. Under the influence of China's Opium Wars, the Tokugawa Shogunate started to realize that this world was really at the discretion of the state orders made by the West. Therefore, it had to abandon its closed-door policy and open up its doors to the outside world at an early date so as to avoid the fall of Japan. As a result, Japan's open-door policy was passive. But it avoided the damage of a large-scale war and it also did not meet the fate of ceding its territory and paying an indemnity. This laid a solid foundation for the Meiji Restoration. The external pressure forced Japan to open to the outside world. But it was exactly this pressure that made Japan realize

that the only way out was to copy the Western system the soonest possible and establish a new model country so as to shake off its national crisis and achieve its national independence in the real sense. As a result, an upside-down compulsory institutional change was on its timetable in history. The new-coming advantage reduced the cost of the compulsory system change. It is well known that the Western society realized the Industrial Revolution in the 18th century and that the revolution in its economy led to the revolution in its politics and that induced the inductive institutional change which was from down to upside and from a feudalist society to a capitalist one. In comparison, the late-coming Meiji Restoration was obviously new-coming in nature in relation to the Western system change. The new institutional economics thinks that the institutional change must take into account the cost and benefit of such a change. So far as the leaders in the Meiji Restoration were concerned, it would greatly save the cost of the institutional change if it studied and utilized the existing social, economic and political systems and massaged properly the Japanese national features into them. In view of this point, the Japanese people itself had a fine tradition of learning advanced foreign culture and technology. As a result, the Meiji Restoration chose the compulsory institutional change which is quick-acting and with lower change cost. In accordance with the principle of "making foreign cultures serve our purpose", through the Iwakura Mission, Japan took the Prussian political system and Great Britain's economic system for reference and built up a modern centralized capitalist country centered by the emperor. The result is that it took Japan only 20 years or so to achieve its modernization, shake off its national crisis and gain its national independence. It is clear that when Japan was apparently backward compared with the Western countries, the Meiji Restoration's choice of an upside-down and compulsory institutional change was a correct institutional change.

c. The Meiji Restoration built up an Eastern capitalist mode with the Japanese features

The Meiji government's series of major reforms formed a structural framework for Japan's modern economic society, and then completed the Meiji Restoration's historical cause. Ever since then, Japan walked away from an agricultural society and threw itself into the waves of modernization with a new posture.

Firstly, the identity of the institutional change behavior subject reduced the transaction cost. The new institutional economics proposes that preliminary behavior subject is generally the designer and executor of the system innovation and the secondary behavior subject is generally the executor of the institutional innovation. In Japan both of them were shouldered by the middle and lower-ranking samurai. This feature made the goal and mode of the institutional change more consistent. As a result, the transaction cost was greatly reduced in the execution process and the efficiency of institutional innovation was raised.

Secondly, the unity of the institutional supply and demand laid a foundation of good relationship between the Japanese government and the enterprises. The new institutional economics proposes that the government is generally the subject of the institutional supply and the institutional demand subject is generally the entrepreneurs. But during the Meiji Restoration, a compulsory institutional change, the task of both introducing and transplanting the Western system fell upon the Meiji government. Therefore, the government was the subject for both the institutional supply and the institutional demand at the same time. The government's compulsory institutional supply corresponded with the institutional demand of the micro subject, namely, for the great development of the capitalist industry and commerce. The Meiji government made its great efforts in establishing model factories and created a large number of market competition subjects and then it sold these factories at bargain to private people and made them privately-owned ones. At the same time, it provided preferential policies to encourage setting up factories. This compulsory system supply allowed capitalist privately-owned factories to appear and grow up very quickly. In reality, this system had produced an internalist induction and provided a deep-layered system innovation to the government's compulsory system supply from the point of property organization incentive and other points so as to ensure that the institutional supply conforms to the contents of the institutional demand. As a result of the policy of "Flourishing Industries and Starting up Businesses", the limited reason and preference of the earliest capitalists in Japan were always in line with those of the government. So the transaction cost of the two parties was reduced and their expected benefit shared an apparent public interest.

Thirdly, high-speed development was achieved through the optimization of the institution. Japan's capitalist development did not enjoy the original environment of the Western capitalist development. But on one hand, Japan learned and transplanted the successful models of the Western countries, and on the other hand, Japan formed its institutional environment with the Japanese features through digesting and absorbing the Western models. It adopted an upside-down institutional change mode, namely, in order to catch up with and then surpass the goals of Europe and the United States, the Meiji Restoration set up institutional arrangement of "Enrich the Country, Strengthen the Military" as the center, and "Flourishing Industries and Starting up Businesses" and "Civilization and Enlightenment" as the basic points. Obviously, the economic performance and development speed achieved by the Meiji Restoration's new institutional arrangement were unique in the world's economic development history. It is clear that this compulsory system change not only expedited Japan's modernization but also greatly reduced the institutional change cost and set up a development mode that is different from that of the Western developed countries for the institutional change of the later-developing countries.

Fourthly, Japanese people's frugal consumption idea expedited the process of capital accumulation and acted as a boosting function to the reforms in the Meiji Restoration. Japan treated better the relationship between "modern" and "traditional", namely, its domestic demand was satisfied by its traditional handicraft products and maintained its low labor cost to make its exports more competitive, and it used the earnings from its exports to develop its modern industry to satisfy the funding needs of its modern industry. In this way, Japan's traditional economic pattern was kept intact.

Section Three   Globalization of Cultures and Rise of Japan

Japan has been most successful in absorbing foreign cultures. Ruth Benedict, a famous American anthropologist, once pointed out that "in the world history, it is very difficult to find another independent people elsewhere that was so successful and in a planned manner to absorb foreign civilization". In summary, the reasons are twofold: One reason is the peripherality of Japan's civilization. Historically, Japan has long been a peripheral civilized country. This is especially true in the very early period of Japan when it was lonely located in the sea and independently developed its own culture. In comparison with China as the center of civilization in Asia, it was doubtless that the Japanese culture was a culture with a low potential energy that had a great potential difference. Generally speaking, the flow of culture is like flowing water, from high to low, namely, people with a low development stage in its social nature tend to absorb easily the culture from people with a high development stage in its social nature. It was just because Japan had historically long been in a status of low potential energy that it was able to absorb in a large scale Chinese culture in the ancient time and then to absorb in a large scale the Western culture in the modern time. The other reason is Japan's geographical location. Japan has been an island nation, with dense population and a very narrow territory, and with few natural resources and has been subject to severe and frequent natural disasters such as earthquakes, volcanic eruptions, typhoons, and tsunamis. This has forced Japan to keep learning as a necessity and making its very best efforts in catching up with and then surpassing the advanced cultures in order to pursue a beneficial living environment. In the ancient time, it caught up with China and in the modern time it caught up with the West. With its outstanding capability in absorbing very quickly the most advanced foreign cultures and then transforming them to its own national culture, Japan blended itself into the world civilization and at the same time it used to the fullest extent possible its privilege of being a straggler.[1]

I. Impact of the foreign cultures and the Meiji Restoration[2]

The conflict and blending of the Japanese and foreign cultures had been through the entire process of Japan's modernization. This process can be generally divided into three stages: The first stage is the introduction period, namely, the introduced technology started reforms in the surface culture. When the Shogunate was challenged by the foreign aggression, in order to utilize science and technology to meet its need of "Enrich the Country, Strengthen the Military", when Japan still had its country closed, it constantly kept learning Rangaku and useful medicine, geography, science and languages, and absorbed foreign knowledge of Germany,

---

[1] Shen Ren'an. "Meiji Restoration, a New Study". *Foreign Subjects Study*, Issue No. 3, 1986.

[2] Ye Weiqu. *History of Japan's Culture*. Nanning: Guangxi Normal University Publishing House, 2003.

Great Britain, France and other countries. At that time, several attitudes held by the foreign study scholars toward the Western civilization were: (1) only study those subjects such as geography and military technology that are indispensable in foreign relations and national defense and reject all the foreign study that is related to "probing the principle"; (2) in the area of learning the nature, also accept "probing the principle" in the foreign study but in the areas of philosophy and understanding problems, adopt the Eastern traditional Confucianism ideas; (3) substitute "probing the principle" for the natural philosophy that was used in the past, and try as much as possible to absorb the fruits of the Western natural science in the area of understanding problems. Although there is no "way" in the West, it may be outstanding in its "art" (technology). Even the non-foreign study scholars acknowledged that "there should be one or two points in the Western thoughts that need learning". Generally speaking, there was consensus in learning the Western technology from the above views towards the Western culture. But on the question of how to treat the Western culture excluding its technology, especially the Western spiritual civilization, differences existed. Among these differences, the above-mentioned second view was dominant. It is fair to say that at that period, the Japanese people's absorption of the Western civilization was confined to the surface layer and they basically rejected the Western spiritual civilization. The second stage is digesting and transplanting in a large scale. With the large-scale introduction of technology and then system and way of living and so on, the Japanese society started reforms in the middle layer and then into the deep layer. After the Meiji Restoration, the government implemented an open-door policy. Challenged by the influx of the Western culture, there were marked conflicts and imbalance in the Japanese people's treatment of the Western culture. There were the "Europeanization identification theory" that attempted to reject Japanese traditions with the Western culture and the "traditional nativism theory" that attempted to reject the Western culture with the Japanese traditions. These two theories were alternating repeatedly. The opposition between these two extremes made the Eastern culture and the foreign cultures in conflict in a more extensive scope. The third stage is "coexistence → blending" that furthered the deep-layer culture reform.

After World War II, the United States occupied Japan and forced democratization on it, which made the conflict between the Japanese culture and the foreign cultures intensify on an unprecedented width and depth and made possible the external combination to internal blending. Japan's anti-tradition Europeanization wave started in the Meiji Restoration and was through the different stages in Japan's modernization, especially at the early period of the Meiji rule and at the early period after World War II. During these two periods, two anti-traditional culture waves of Europeanization and Americanization happened. The first wave, Europeanization, happened after the Meiji Restoration. After Japan opened its doors, when its people found that the West had the modern culture featured with the advanced science and technology, democratic system and so on, they felt an extreme sense of inferiority on their traditional culture. They based their value judgment on the Western culture and attempted to use Europeanization to solve the modernization and traditional culture issues. Inoue Kaoru's theory of "De-Asianization and Europeanization" was a representative of this thinking mode. People who were in favor of Europeanization found that the Western culture was significant to transform the traditional culture and to promote the traditional culture towards the modernization. Although these thoughts had their active elements, they failed to correctly position in its entirety that the traditional culture also had its need to adapt to the modernization. So they proposed a complete breakaway from the traditional culture and instead to learn everything from the West from science and technology, system, social customs and behaviors to values and life style and so on. The emperor himself dressed in Western suits and ate Western meals in order to be a role model for his people. Mori Arinori proposed to have English as Japan's national language. Someone even proposed that the Japanese people should marry foreigners so as to improve their genes and so on and so forth. The second wave, Americanization, occurred after World War II. After Japan's unconditional surrender, the United States occupied Japan. The Japanese people's sense of national pride suddenly gave way to a sense of national inferiority. They thought that the traditional Japanese culture was absolutely backward compared with the modern American culture. While they reflected upon and criticized the emperor's tradition in its political, historical and cultural views, they treated the traditional Japanese culture as nothing but feudal and proposed to entirely reject the traditional Japanese culture. They attempted to use the American culture to replace the Japanese culture and someone even proposed that instead of suffering from all types of incomplete reforms, Japan should simply become a state of the United States.

II. The Meiji Restoration and the traditional culture conflict

At the pre-modern time in Japan, the Shogunate had put in place the locked country policy for more than 200 years and promoted the traditionalism. As regards their views on the Western modern culture, their consensus on learning the Western technology was the same. However, they took a rejection position on the Western spiritual civilization. During this period, the incidents of fumi-e① and the Gonin Gumi② and other similar incidents happened successively to reject the Western religion and these incidents were the most obvious of them.

After the Meiji Restoration, in order to promote the capitalist modernization and keep its door open, Japan proposed the slogan of "Civilization and Enlightenment" and, in accordance with the modernization need, continued to absorb the Western natural science and technological civilization, and learned the Western civilization at the surface level. However, the introduction of the Western spiritual civilization was strictly restricted within the remnant feudal structure and cultural structure as well as the politically allowed scope. This brought some passive impact on Japan's modernization. Under the political landscape from the mid-Meiji period to Showa period and the influence of the big unification ideology of the politicalized emperor system, Japan tried to maintain its quintessence of a country and implemented the policy of combining the so-called traditional Shintoism as its national religion and the state's modernization and to prettify the emperor system. It specified that "the Japanese Empire is ruled by the emperors who have 'reigned since time immemorial'" to establish and solidify the absolutism of the emperor system. At the same time, in the thinkers' circle, Society for Political Education (Seikyōsha) with Miyake Setsurei and Shiga Shigetaka at its center started with the

---

① stepping-on the holy picture: a wooden board with a likeness of Jesus or Mary was placed in front of an official and then suspected people were required to step on it in order to find out whether they were Catholics

② people who sheltered a priest would be executed by stake and their family possessions would be confiscated and a group of five households would be held collectively responsible

criticism of Europeanization implemented at the early Meiji rule and pointed out that the non-nationalism in Europeanization was not in line with the spirit of *Imperial Rescript on Education*. Then they staged a movement to fight against the Western modern culture and advocated nationalism and fanatically preached narrow nationalism. And even worse, during the wartime, this was the fundamental norm of the Japanese culture. The Japanese government took advantage of and strengthened this traditional thinking mode of monism and pushed Japan's conservative and feudal features to its extreme. From the experience of modernization of Japan's culture, any attempt to maintain the traditionalism from the conflict between Japan's traditional culture and the Western modern culture will usually be futile. The occurrence of Japan's traditionalism is not only due to its culture, but also due to its political motive and it attempts to achieve its goal of nationalism or super nationalism by combining the cultural traditionalism and the political nationalism. During the early and middle periods of Japan's move to its modernization, the above-mentioned elements had brought extreme limitation to Japan's modernization.

III. Blending of Japan's culture and the Western civilization[1]

After World War II, the United States occupied Japan, forced democratization on it, reformed the emperor system, family system and abolished aristocracy, and carried out a series of political and economic reforms, which resulted in the complete disintegration of Japan's traditional social order. Criticism of the emperor's absolutism in the sense of feudal politics, economy and culture, especially in the political, historical and cultural ideology promoted liberation of people's thinking and reform in their ideas. This formed a huge humane thought. People, as the individual existence in the society, fully awakened and were subject to the baptism of science and democracy. Freedom and openness dramatically attacked the traditional value system, which made the conflict between the Japanese culture and the foreign cultures intensify on an unprecedented width and depth and made possible the external combination to internal blending. During this period, although for a short time, the tradition was once viewed as feudal things and every traditional

---

[1] Ye Weiqu. *History of Japan's Culture*. Nanning: Guangxi Normal University Publishing House, 2003.

value was suspected and Americanization was proposed, the general trend was: while absorbing the Western material civilization, induced by the Western spiritual civilization, Japan's traditional value was reconsidered and the innovation of the traditional culture was reactivated. While adhering to the subject of the traditional innovation, the Western modern culture was introduced in an omnibearing and multi-layered manner so as to avoid the extreme mode of "identification" and "rejection". A brand-new cultural mode of "conflict→ coexistence →blending" was established so as to further expand and systemize the diversified structure. In this way, this cultural system has more tolerance and absorption capability and has created a more beneficial condition for the coexistence and blending of the Japanese culture and the foreign cultures. Specifically, politically, Japan adopted the Western system and rule of law, and economically, it adopted combination of the Western market system and the traditional society structure unique in the East so as to ensure that combination of the Western culture and the traditional culture is able to blend on the basis of the mode of thinking unique to the Japanese people. This mode guarantees that changes in the deep-layer culture are still rooted in the traditional basis. Without doubt, this has played a vital and even decisive role in completing the historical task of the Japanese-style capitalist modernization.

It is doubtless that Japan's modernization began with the introduction of the Western technological civilization. Technological civilization is important to modernization. However, it is simply a means. Without the safeguard of the democratic system, it is very difficult to use this means. But if Japan's modernization only stopped at these two layers, if it did not base itself on the transformation of Japan's traditional innovation, and if it did not have the reasonable elements inside the Japanese traditional culture as its foundation and let it play its subject role, it is also hard for Japan to achieve its Japanese-style modernization. Even if modernization was achieved at the two layers of technological civilization and the democratic system, this is nothing but a Western-style modernization, namely, a total Westernization. Shūichi Katō summarized this historical experience and proposed the mode of Japanese-style modernization: Japan's modernization can only adopt a mode to combine democratic principles, technological civilization and Japan's cultural tradition. The key in Japan's modernization mode emphasizes that

Japan's cultural tradition should become the internal dynamic mechanism of Japan's modernization development and be the decisive factor of Japan's modernization. That is to say, Japanese-style modernization is based on the Western democratism, with high technological civilization as the means, with the Japanese people's traditional culture as its root, and is achieved inside the innovatively transformed traditional value structure. This ensures that Japan's modernization was not a total Westernization. Even though one cannot say that Japan's cultural tradition is the only dynamic power for the Japanese-style modernization, one cannot underestimate its role of the dynamic mechanism and guide that it played in Japan's modernization.

Chapter Five   Globalization of Cultures and Opening up to the Outside World in Modern China

China is an ancient civilized nation with a very long history, a vast area of territory and rich natural resources. During its long history, China had formed an Eastern civilization with farming as its basic means of production. China's glory in its history made it the center of trade where envoys from vassal states or foreign countries presenting tribute to Chinese emperors. As a result, China viewed itself as Celestial Empire over history and prided itself on its mainstream culture of refusing to have exchanges with foreign countries. Since modern times, the Opium Wars pried open China's gate and forced it to be integrated gradually with the world market and started to change its closed-door status. In order to discuss the series of changes that happened to China under the open policies in modern times, we must begin with analyzing the inherent essence in China's culture.

Section One   China's Traditional Society and Its Closed Culture

China has formed its own unique culture in its history of several thousand years. This culture can be traced to the same origin despite the fact that it keeps changing gradually because its essence remains unchanged at all. In a certain sense, the stability in its culture has determined the stability in China's economic system over history.

I. Great unification and stability in China's traditional society

China's traditional culture can be summarized as ideology of "great unification". This ideology was formed in practice since the very beginning of the

Chinese nation, and was created, matured, perfected and distilled with creation, formation and evolution of the Chinese nation and its civilization. The so-called "great unification" can be summarized as ideology of extensiveness, diversification and universal unification; ideology of overall harmony and harmony with all the nations; ideology of respecting progress and harmony without sameness; ideology of respecting rules, orders and rituals, and coordination and stability; ideology of revering various virtues, people-orientation and protecting its people and making its country stronger; and ideology of pursuing unification and opposing separation.

(1) Vast territory and variety of its ethnic groups in creation, formation and evolution of the Chinese nation have determined the extensive and diversified and universal unification content in ideology of "great unification".

The Chinese nation originated from valleys of the Yellow River and the Yangtze River and is composed of ethnic Han and a great number of ethnic minority people over long time of integration and assimilation. Because all the ethnic groups of people lived and multiplied in the same areas, extensive and long-lasting integration and exchanges happened among their different social customs and cultures. As a result, strong cohesion, identity and centripetal force were formed. The extensive and diversified and universal unification in ideology of "great unification" was gradually reinforced and forged over long time of integration of ethnic groups. This content is the primary one in ideology of "great unification".

(2) Objective of "seeking common ground while reserving differences" in creation, formation and evolution of the Chinese nation has determined the content in ideology of "great unification" of the overall harmony and harmony with all the nations.

The "common ground" means primarily the basically same survival history and communicable cultures owing to living in the basically same areas and facing the basically same geographical conditions. Seeking common ground is a prominent feature of the Chinese nation's civilization. Distillation of seeking common ground has become the content of the overall harmony and harmony with all the nations in ideology of "great unification". During the period from pre-Qin Dynasty to Han Dynasty, people in the ancient Chinese nation that was composed of people of Xia Dynasty, Yin Dynasty and Zhou Dynasty but integrated with people of some parts of the other ethnic groups were further integrated with people of many other ethnic groups. During the Wei Dynasty, Jin Dynasty and Northern and Southern Dynasties, Tang Dynasty and Five Dynasties, and Song Dynasty, Yuan Dynasty, Jin Dynasty and Liao Dynasty, ethnic Han had integrated or assimilated with one ethnic group after another. This was made possible owing to the basically same living areas and geographical conditions and with the integration and assimilation and the increasing inclusiveness. Ethnic integration is a mutually penetrating process when "ethnic Han feature" of ethnic minority groups and "foreign or non-Han feature" of ethnic Han people often happened at the same time. This is exactly an important historical reason of formation of the ideology of the overall harmony of the Chinese nation. The early scholars of the Confucian school were the first to summarize this feature and this feature was elucidated successively in theory by thinkers over history. The proposition of "Amiability is highly valued" that was crystallized in ancient Chinese ideology and culture is embodied imperceptibly in the history and ideology of the Chinese nation.

(3) Establishment and deepening of the ritual system and centralization in creation, formation and evolution of the Chinese nation have determined the content in ideology of "great unification" of patriarchal clan system and respecting rules and orders and the ritual system and pursuit of macro-coordination and stability.

The ritual system and patriarchal clan system have maintained a significant place and played an important role in civilization history of the Chinese nation. The ritual system in ancient times included a series of systems, regulations and the ideology to implement them which were not only regulations and ceremonies in social life but more importantly those involving the country's political, economic and cultural systems. As this system had a far-reaching influence, Neo-Confucianists in the Song Dynasty mostly advocated restoration of the patriarchal clan system. After the Southern Song Dynasty, the study of family tree again flourished and this became an important tie to bind clans in the feudal times. The political system in the centralized feudal state in the alliance mechanism of the Xia, Shang and Western Zhou Dynasties and the unified absolutism from Qin Dynasty to late Qing Dynasty was characterized by effective historical experience, developed political division and long-lasting concept of check and balance on power, tradition of administrative legislation that formed a complete set of administrative laws and regulations, and accumulation of a complete set of relatively scientific human resources management experience. The traditional political system and the ritual system and patriarchal clan system formed the outside and inside that historically represented the relative coordination and stability between the basic social structure and institutional arrangement and then formed the binding force of the order that was universally rational and effective during a certain period and solved the social stability problem in a relatively good manner.

(4) Upholding of the nation and country's interests as paramount in creation, formation and evolution of the Chinese nation has determined the content in ideology of "great unification" of "reverence for various virtues", "people-orientation" and protecting the people and strengthening the country.

Strong impact from ideological emancipation movement during Spring and Autumn Period and Warring States Period made ancient Chinese history viewpoint stay away from the divine theory of Mandate of Heaven and started the path of an independent development. Later, during thousands of years of the feudal society, although the rulers still relied on the divine theory of Mandate of Heaven as their important tool to maintain and strengthen their ruling position, they had already realized strength and power of the people. After the introduction of the thought of "reverence for various virtues and protecting the people" or "reverence for the heaven and protecting the people" from the early Zhou Dynasty, later this thought was developed to the thought of "people-orientation" and "people-emphasis" which was carried out throughout the Chinese feudal society. This thought had played an important role in the social pattern of making the country stronger and its people richer and strengthening great unification, and safeguarding the feudal rule.

II. Stability of China's traditional economic system

The socio-political system of great unification determined the economic system characterized by high centralization and integration. The main characteristics of ancient Chinese industry and commerce system lied in the flourishing of officially-run industry and commerce and strict restrictions on privately-run industry and commerce, especially in the circulation sector. Viewed from ideological and action guidance preference, governments of the various dynasties always had direct control of certain industry and commerce sectors, especially those major ones that were critical to the national economy and the people's livelihood such as salt, iron and so on, and protected such operation privileges in the form of system regulations so as to obtain and maintain their monopoly status, which made the country's official arrangements in these sectors such as market system, commercial taxation system, and monopoly system, etc., more meticulous and consummate than those in the medieval century in the West. Its obstruction effect to the economic development was apparent too. Under the constraint of the country's power, private owners and operators in industry and commerce only had a humble social status and seldom had horizontal integration and free combination. As a result, there was a dire insufficiency of official or unofficial system arrangements that were not specified by the country's laws and regulations and in the nature of social contract. Chinese industry and commerce owners had long become accustomed to obeying and relying upon the centralized government and except family and clan coordination that was tied by blood relationship they found it very hard to accept system constraint from any autonomous consortium.

a. Flourishing of officially-run handicraft industry system

One main characteristic of ancient Chinese society was that it established at an earlier date centralized bureaucracy country system that the central government and local governments had a far more responsible economic function than the various royal families and seigniors in the medieval century in the West and that their direct operation of the handicraft industry was an important aspect of their various economic functions. In ancient Chinese society, the handicraft industry had gradually formed a relatively complete production and management system and corresponding system regulations.

The country's direct operation of the handicraft industry not only aimed to satisfy the direct consumption needs of the royal family and the government, but primarily resulted from the country's financial needs because such practice could combine profits and taxes, increase revenues and ensure the central government and local governments be based on a sound economic foundation.

Officially-run handicraft industry had played a progressive role in development of Chinese handicraft industry because it enjoyed technological advancement, sufficient financing, meticulous labor division and economies of scale. However, with the development of productive forces and commodity economy, its restraint of production development and its own malpractice became increasingly exposed, especially corruption in its management and side effect of the hereditary household craftsman system became more and more apparent. In the late period of the feudal society, officially-run handicraft industry gradually declined.

The power of the officially-run handicraft industry and its monopoly status added another layer of severe obstacle to the development of the privately-run handicraft industry in China than its counterpart in the West. In terms of market, labor force, capital, technology and equipment, the privately-run handicraft industry was all at a disadvantage in its competition.

b. Monopoly system and other officially-run commerce systems

In ancient Chinese society, governments had a tighter control in the circulation sector than in the production sector in the national economy. The flourished monopoly system is one of the representations. Although in the monopoly system governments sometimes also had direct control of the production process in specific commodities such as iron, for most commodities and in the long-term perspective, governments only had control over the circulation sector while production was carried out by private persons such as in salt. In the medieval times in the West monopoly by countries or business people that were authorized by countries to have monopoly over operation of certain commodities existed too. But such monopoly's scope and degree as well as its history are not comparable to those in China.

In addition to monopoly over certain commodities, feudal governments in certain dynasties also had direct operation of other commodities especially those that were most closely related to people's livelihood such as grains and so on. However, the difference in this practice from the monopoly system is that while countries operated directly in these commodities, they did not restrict operations by private persons. Flourishing in officially-operated commerce just as officially-run industry's monopoly status is a characteristic of ancient Chinese economic system, which is especially true in the early stage of the feudal society.

c. Official industry and commerce administrations with their major functions as leading officially-run industry and commerce and collecting commerce taxes

In ancient Chinese society, the main functions of governments were to safeguard national security and to ensure that taxation by governments could maintain normal operation of countries. As industry and commerce were not well developed, official industry and commerce administrations were simple-structured. These administrations were often affiliated with political organizations and led by officials at various levels. However, as these officials were not professionals in economic sectors, they usually lacked knowledge and experience in the sectors they were in charge of. For those officials that once worked in such administrations, their term there was merely a stepping stone in their official career.

Comparisons between industry and commerce administrations in ancient Chinese society and those in the medieval times in the West or industry and commerce administrations in modern times show the following characteristics: (1) A major function of China's industry and commerce administration was to lead officially-run industry and commerce. (2) The government was mainly interested in collecting taxes from privately-run industry and commerce and imposed some necessary restrictions on them, but provided little or no service to them. (3) There was no vertical leadership system from the central government to local governments. The responsible organizations were local governments in privately-run industry and commerce instead of the central government. The administration mode was actually a type of "local administrations are primary and rules and regulations are secondary". (4) Administrations were overlapping, not clearly delegated, corruptive, overstaffed and not efficient. (5) Decision-making processes in official industry and commerce administrations were generally in the mode of suggestions by officials in the central government and local governments but final decisions by emperors only. As a result, such decisions were subjective and arbitrary in nature and lacked consistency in relevant policies. (6) Once decisions were made, no fixed organizations were responsible for implementing and supervising them. In summary, in ancient Chinese society, the ruling groups' decisions on industry and commerce development usually had to yield to their political goals first and not in the best interests of the development of industry and commerce. As a matter of fact, in ancient China, policies toward privately-run industry and commerce focused on taxation and its starting point was the financial condition of the country.

III. China's historical glory and hardship in its system change

It is well known that China is one of the four countries in the world that have an ancient civilization. The four great inventions in ancient China are famous all over the world. Up till the medieval times, China had been the economic and cultural center in the East. During the Sui and Tang Dynasties, Japan, China's close neighbor, sent many times its imperial embassies to China. That is why till today Japanese culture has been deeply branded with Chinese culture. As a unified Celestial Empire that was ruled by rites, in order to expand its influence, in the Ming Dynasty, Zheng He, as a peace envoy, sailed to the Western Ocean seven times with treasures of China's economy and culture such as exquisite chinaware and arts and crafts to visit countries in the West. China had been a world power till Emperor Kangxi and Qianlong Heyday in the middle of the Qing Dynasty. Statistics show that from the 6th century A.D. to the pre-17th century A.D. China's scientific inventions were more than half of the world. China's handicraft industry, agricultural production technology, total agricultural output and so on all prided themselves among the most advanced level in the world. Since the 15th and 16th centuries, with the development of tribute-paying to Chinese emperors and mutual trade, it formed Asia's system of tribute-paying to Chinese emperors that centered on China's tea, raw silk and coarse cloth, Japan's seafood, Thailand's rice, India's cotton, Philippines' granular sugar and so on and China was the center of this system. Since the 16th century, during the intercontinental trade where raw silk and tea that flowed from Asia to Europe and silver that flowed back from Europe to Asia, tea and raw silk were China's traditional products.[①]

The China-invented selection system of government officials from the common people (the imperial examination system) and so on still play a role today. Only from the post-17th century, with the development of Western natural science and technology, China's scientific and technological inventions were next to nothing in the world. The Industrial Revolution rose from the West and Asia's traditional

---

[①] Refer to Takeshi Hamashita. *International Opportunities in Modern China*. Trans. Zhu Yingui et al. Beijing: China Social Sciences Press, 1999.

tribute-paying trade network was broken and China, the ancient civilization in the East, gradually lost its edge.

a. The long history and glorious civilization in China have made the Chinese people in a dilemma on whether to accept overseas civilization.

China's glorious civilization of several thousand years has resulted in the Chinese people's self-important consciousness and cultural centrism. They often have excessive confidence in their own culture and treat overseas civilization with an attitude of superficial inclusiveness and essential despise or vigilance. When confronted with the Western civilization during the Ming and Qing Dynasties, intellectuals in China, namely, scholars, held the same attitude. For example, in the final years of the Ming Dynasty, Mr. Liu Zongzhou, a well-known Neo-Confucianist and President of the Censorate, in the crisis of his country's doom, still refused to figure out a specific solution but thought that the country was "not concerned with the lack of talented people" but was only "concerned with the lack of conscience" and blindly and strongly persuaded the emperor to adopt "the doctrine of Yao and Shun" and practice "the school of Yao and Shun". He thought it was not right to appoint a foreigner Johann Adam Schall von Bell to make cannons so as to strengthen the military forces and instead thought that "the way of using military is primarily benevolence and righteousness proposed by Emperor Tang in the Shang Dynasty and Emperor Wuwang in the Zhou Dynasty and secondly restraint and control proposed by Duke Huangong of Qi Kingdom and Duke Wengong of Jin Kingdom and all other things not in line with the above should not even be discussed" and that "firearms will not do any good for the outcome of battles".[①] This type of pedantic and empty thoughts and remarks is exactly a natural representation of the cultural self-importance mentality. In comparison, the false and boastful personality of the feudal rulers, scholars and the common people: They believed that China was the center of the world and the "Celestial Empire" and all other places were simply "barbarians". *Imperial Collections of Classics* revised during Emperor Qianlong's reign described the world as "China is located right in the middle of the earth and surrounded by seas at its four sides. Those who inhabit

---

[①] Refer to Shu Dagang. ed. *China's Great Confucian Scholars in Various Dynasties*. Changchun: Jilin Education Publishing House, 1997.

near the four sides and seas are called descendants. So descendants mean the sides of China."[①] This thought is both deceptive to oneself and others and when it was reflected in foreign affairs it was just in pursuit of vanity for the sake of "Celestial Empire".

Since the Ming Dynasty, China had imposed a ban on maritime trade and foreign trade administration was Sup Sam Hung. Western merchants were all confined to Canton. During the late Ming Dynasty and early Qing Dynasty, Westerners traveled to Zhangzhou, Quanzhou, Fuzhou, Xiamen, Ningbo and Dinghai. Later, owing to first de facto inconvenience and second ban imposed by Qing Dynasty imperial decrees, "the one-trading-port system" was established. Even in Canton, foreigners were not free. As summer and fall were business seasons, they could live in Sup Sam Hung, Canton. When they finished their business there, they had to return to Macao in winter. According to Canton Maritime Customs' regulations, foreigners were unable to meet local governors and inspectors directly. When they had any official business, they could only ask "hongs" to do so on their behalf because this was related to national prestige. This is one instance of many similar things that show Qing Dynasty rulers' self-importance and their refusal and denial attitude toward outside cultures. Before the 19th century, China and the West did not have diplomatic relations. The West did not send envoys to China and China did not send ambassadors and envoys to foreign countries. The reasons were very complex. However, one reason was that China did not recognize equality of other countries. If foreigners did not come to China, Chinese governments would not force them to do so. If foreigners did come, they had to respect China as the "Celestial Empire" and viewed themselves at vassal countries of China. Then propriety and ceremony would become major obstacles to diplomatic relations because the "Celestial Empire" absolutely would not accommodate anything otherwise. At that time China did not feel it necessary to communicate with foreign countries. If foreigners came for profits, the "Celestial Empire" would bestow benefits on them and allow them to trade with China and at the same time China would merely take this opportunity to keep under control and appease these countries but nothing else.

[①] Refer to *Imperial Collections of Classics (Volume CCXCIII)* (Emperor Qilong's official revised edition). Hangzhou: Zhejiang Ancient Books Publishing House, 1988.

At that time Europeans viewed Emperor Qianlong as a model and enlightened monarch. The British thought all the hardship they met when trading in China was created by local Cantonese officials. If such hardship could be made known to the emperor, he would definitely make some reforms. In 1793 (the fifty-seventh year in the reign of Emperor Qianlong), he would be 80 years old. If England could take this opportunity to send an envoy to China to celebrate his birthday, they would obtain an opportunity to negotiate with China and promote Sino-British friendship. As the Cantonese officials knew Emperor Qianlong's vanity, they spared no effort in instigating England to send such an envoy for this event. Then England sent Lord Macartney as the envoy plenipotentiary to China. His preparations were painstaking indeed. The envoy rode on a first-class ship of war and took with him guards. His gifts for Emperor Qianlong were all first-class British-made such as astrological and geographical instruments, machinery, guns and cannons, vehicles, ship models and so on, totaling 600 cases. The intention of such gifts was to showcase to China that England was a country with strength and civilization. The instructions given by the British government to Lord Macartney were for him to yield as much as he could to the Chinese rituals but to show equality of England with China. The goals for negotiations were the following: 1. England would like to send an ambassador plenipotentiary to China and station in China. If China would like to send an ambassador to England, the British court would treat him with the utmost respect. 2. England hoped that China would add more trading ports. 3. England hoped that China could have a fixed and transparent customs tariff. 4. England hoped that China could provide a small island for the British to live on and to store their goods there as China did with Macao for the Portuguese. Emperor Qianlong was very happy to meet the British envoy but he treated him just like another tribute envoy from a vassal state and asked him to kowtow. Lord Macartney initially declined but later he yielded with conditions. His conditions were: When the Chinese envoy came to London, he had to kowtow to the British king or China sent its officials to kowtow to the portrait of the British king that he brought with him here. His such conditions were nothing but to show equality of England with China. Emperor Qianlong believed that such gifts were "merely for exaggeration purpose only because instruments made by the Imperial Household Department are both exquisite and taller and we are in no short supply of them. In my opinion, those things you called exotic and unusual are only ordinary ones."① As a result, Emperor Qianlong was very unhappy. After their meeting, he ordered Lord Macartney to leave Beijing to return to England. In his edicts to King George III, he stated that "Our Celestial Empire possesses vast territories ... strange and costly objects do not interest me ... Our dynasty's majestic virtue has penetrated unto every country under Heaven, and Kings of all nations have offered their costly tribute by land and sea ... we possess all things. I set no value on objects strange or ingenious, and have no use for your country's manufactures."② "Our Celestial Empire possesses all things in prolific abundance and lacks no product within its borders. We do not value your strange or ingenious objects as treasures."③ As regards Lord Macartney's requests for establishment of trade relations and diplomatic relations, naturally China refused both. In this way, China brushed past the opportunity with the modern Western civilization.

During the Westernization Movement, many officials in the court did not favor "learn advanced techniques from foreign countries" and thought it had much more harm than benefits to learn foreigners' diabolic tricks and wicked craft. Grand Secretary Wo Ren opposed introducing science and technology from the West. In his memorial to the emperor, he stated that "the way to build up a nation lies in respect for rituals but not for diplomacy, and what really matters is social mores, not techniques." He was of the opinion that science and technology "only degenerate and harm social mores, only confuse and poison people's minds, and only use and waste money and at peaceful time they breed treachery and at war time they aid and abet the enemy and they can hurt our national livelihood and do not help us". Li Hongzhang stated in his official letter to Tsungli Yamen that those people who opposed "learning advanced techniques from foreign countries" "sneer at advanced foreign techniques and instruments as diabolic tricks and wicked craft and believe

---

① Refer to *Qianlong Imperial Poems (Book V) (Volume XLVIII)*. Hangzhou: Hangzhou: Zhejiang People's Publishing House, 1989: 13-14.

② Refer to Liang Tingzhan. *History of the Cantonese Maritime Customs (Volumes II and III)*. Guangzhou: Guangdong People's Publishing House, 2002.

③ Refer to *Annals of the Period of Jiaqing (Volume CCCXX)*. Beijing: Zhonghua Book Company, 1986.

we do not need to learn them at peaceful time but at war time they are surprised at these advanced foreign techniques and instruments as strange and exotic and believe we are unable to learn them."① In view of the above, this is by no means strange.

b. Relationship between centralization characteristic in culture and individual ideology results in hardship in system transfer.

Commodity economy in ancient China was more developed than that in the medieval times in the West. Markets played a more important role in China's national economy. Rulers in each dynasty generally viewed social division of labor as an objective existence and a necessity. As a result, it was a basic link in a society's economic life to have a smooth production and consumption through commodity exchange. However, in order to safeguard traditional natural economy and to inhibit excessive development of industry and commerce and to maintain social economy's stability, rulers also thought that market exchange activities should be done in an orderly and normal manner under the governments' control.

During the early and middle periods in ancient Chinese society, markets in major cities were established by the governments. In most dynasties, market establishments were done in compliance with the court decrees both in the capital cities and at the various political subdivisions. These markets were administered by officials appointed by the governments. In the central government, separate organizations and people were responsible for this matter. As a result, to some extent, those markets could even be said to be directly administered by the country. One of the main functions of these markets was to satisfy the demand of governments, royal family, aristocrats, scholars, gentlemen and those people who served them and so on to use their currency to buy products from peasants and handicraftsmen.

From the pre-Qin Dynasty days, the country enjoyed very specific provisions for the market system. Till Han and Tang Dynasties, these administration systems became even more detailed and complete. The ancient market system stated in *The Rites* of the Zhou Dynasty and *The Book of Rites* gave the impression that these rules were branded with strong ethics and were used by the country as its tools to restrict business activities. But these rules were mechanisms to regulate market

---

① Refer to Xu Hua. *Sacrificial Offerings to Sea for the Sino-Japanese War of 1894-1895*. Beijing: Huaxia Publishing House, 1996.

activities from the view of politics and culture but were not rules that were made from the objective needs of economic activities. As China was unified politically at a very early time, its politics and culture had an extremely strong standardizing force over economic activities mechanism. These rules minimized uncertainty and transaction cost in market transactions, provided information and standardized some business acts, and on one hand they had some benefits over promoting development in production and transactions but on the other hand their various restrictive provisions had obvious constraint functions over distribution activities. These rules had the nature of idealism to a great extent and suffered from great hardship in their execution. Even if thoughts of adjustments were available, stability in policies would make it hard to implement.

Section Two   Outside Impact on Modern China

After the Opium Wars, the Western invaders forced open China's doors by guns and cannons to bring in not only their industrial products, they also brought advanced systems in politics and economy. All this had brought great impact to the traditional Chinese society and left a far-reaching influence on ancient China.

I. Impact of foreign invasions on China's traditional social system

Invasions by the Western capitalism in modern times made it impossible for China's traditional political system to develop and evolve along its own tracks. The Western powers had bombarded open the rusty gates of the Qing Empire by cannons and warships. The ancient Chinese nation was challenged by "a fierce enemy that had not been seen for several thousand years" and "a situation that had not been up for several thousand years". The stagnant Chinese Empire was strongly impacted by the Western civilization. The Western powers showed their strong military power and provided a more advanced system model which presented a reference substance that could be used to be comparable to the traditional system. On one hand, this accelerated its decline and collapse, and on the other hand, this made transplant of the modern Western political system by the traditional China an inevitable choice.

a. Impact of foreign invasions on traditional political system

The political system's evolution to modern development experienced Taiping Heavenly Kingdom, Reform Movement of 1898, Late Qing Dynasty New Policies and Revolution of 1911. This development was represented in two aspects:

(1) Modernization of leadership class in the political evolution movement. Modernization is capitalization, which decides the main role that capitalist class should have played during the modernization process. The movement leadership class tended increasingly toward modernization from peasants class during Taiping Heavenly Kingdom, capitalist class reformists during Reform Movement of 1898 to capitalist class revolutionaries during Revolution of 1911. Even though the Late Qing New Policies was led by the Qing imperial court, this would not change the mainstream in the entire political system evolution development. Capitalist class became increasingly the nucleus in the political evolution movement, which made the modern class nature more apparent in the political evolution movement and the movement nature more modern.

(2) Modernization of the movements' contents, propositions and the impact produced. Even if Taiping Heavenly Kingdom primarily represented peasants' interests in its entirety under the impact of the progressive wave in the world, this military administration also showed specific modernization program, namely, Hong Rengan's *A New Treatise on Political Counsel*. This was the first relatively complete capitalist administrative program in modern China because it emphasized both military construction and imitating the West to develop the national industry in economy. However, owing to the limitation of peasants class Hong Rengan and others failed to genuinely realize what the key was to achieve these modernization goals. During Reform Movement of 1898, capitalist class reformists' ideology had seen a great improvement because they not only realized the importance of learning Western science and technology and developing the national industry but also realized the importance of adopting Western political system. Therefore, they proposed to absorb strengths in the Western capitalist system and replace autocratic monarchy system with constitutional monarchy system and proposed the idea to establish System Bureau. However, owing to their weakness, they did not achieve their ideas during this movement. But these ideas moved China's modernization process from ideological aspect to political aspect and made politics develop toward

modernization. The Late Qing New Policies shared similarities with Reform Movement of 1898 in their form but the former surpassed the latter in their reform dynamics. For example, its "preparations for a constitution", *Constitutional Outline Made by the Imperial Order* and establishment of Responsible Cabinet and so on were all outstanding representations of political modernization. Especially, modernization reform such as in the military and education and so on in the New Policies trained a group of young military officers and intellectuals with a modernization revolution tendency who were the very people that pushed the modernization of modern political system to its height. Revolution of 1911 led by Dr. Sun Yat-sen had a clear goal of political modernization, namely, overthrowing the feudal rule of the Qing Dynasty and establishing a capitalist democratic republic. He clearly pointed out that "Domestically we need to examine our own people's desires and internationally we need to examine the world trends. We can only save China by establishing a republic system and we can only achieve this goal by overthrowing the imperial Qing government." Revolution of 1911 indeed attained this goal and overthrew the feudal rule of the Qing Dynasty and planted a seed of democratic republic ideology in the mind of the Chinese people. This revolution far surpassed all the previous movements in the aspect of pursuit and practice of a modern democratic system. The capitalist republic established as a result of Revolution of 1911 negated the autocratic monarchy system and was the richest fruit of modernization of politics in China.

From all of the above, from Taiping Heavenly Kingdom to Reform Movement of 1898 and to Late Qing Dynasty New Policies and finally to Revolution of 1911, political evolution movements not only permeated the entire modern history, but also showed the trend toward modernization development. They allowed China to march step by step on the path of modernization of capitalist democratic politics and established the political modernization as the core contents in China's modernization.

b. Impact of foreign invasions on traditional economic system

Like most developing countries, China's modern industry and commerce organizations were not established spontaneously inside the traditional society but instead under the influence of external factors and they were actually transplanted from developed capitalist countries. The leading content in traditional Chinese culture and its economic ideology with its nucleus of "inhibiting business" were completely out of tune with the innovation enterprise spirit that is based on the private ownership in the West. This incompatibility made the change from China's traditional industry and commerce system to modern industry and commerce system difficult and it would cost much more than that in the West. Introduction of the Western industry and commerce system was a major progress in the Chinese society. However, its hysteretic and incomplete nature was a main reason for obstructing China's modern economic development.

(1) The relatively early appearance of modern market and the backwardness in its system change. In the late medieval times successful economic growth was first realized in Western Europe with the Netherlands and England as its models. Changes in the market played a decisive role. Their common experience was to advocate free international trade, gradually reduce and then eliminate exclusivist and monopolistic system and acts under guild-controlled markets, encourage flow of production factors, advocate fair competition, and encourage merchants and financiers from all over Europe and even the world to freely enter their domestic markets to engage in trade. After the Song Dynasty in China, with abolishment of square-market system and weakened government control, domestic markets started to change from traditional style to modern style. This type of market had the basic characteristics of a modern market in terms of free entry, fair competition and absence of monopoly by the country and guilds and so on. However, till the Opium Wars, China still remained a closed domestic market and lacked the stimulus from international trade which was full of revolutionary factors. China had very few contacts with the outside world and its market expansion scale progressed very slowly. China lagged behind the West in establishment of the modern market system. The prohibitively high transaction cost inhibited the commercialization process, which in turn restricted the market expansion.

(2) Increase in market on resource allocation function and initial formation of production factors market. Through observation of history of economic development in the peoples in the world, we can see that a major indicator in a country or region's economy shifting from traditional society to modern society is that natural economy

changes to commodity economy and that economy where resources are allocated by customs and decrees changes to free market economy. These two processes are both intertwined and distinguished. The former is the basis for the latter and the latter is development of the former but only the realization of the latter can mark the completion of this process.

In the feudal society in China, the function that the country played in resource allocation generally tended to decline but market played an increasingly expanded and strengthened role. This was reflected in development in free trade in land and lax personal subsidiary relations, weakened control by the country over land and people and gradual decrease in the country's ability to make redistribution of land and to order about people to engage in various kinds of corvee labor. Although the governments in the dynasties in China always wanted to control as many resources as possible, the result was that officially-run industry was declining with each passing day and they had to resort to the market forces as much as possible. These facts show that in the late period in China's feudal society market had played in resource allocation a role that could not be ignored. China's production factors market especially its capital and labor market did not initially form in some economically advanced areas till late 19th century and early 20th century but still they were not sufficiently developed. In view of the whole country, a marked inequality and inconsistency resulted.

(3) Formation of the comprador system and the modern commercial trade network with treaty ports as the center. After the Opium Wars, China was forced to open to the outside world. The Sino-foreign economic relations established under this situation were primarily arranged in system in the form of unequal treaties between China and foreign countries. Armed with various privileges obtained by unequal treaties, foreign invaders staged their invasion by exporting to China their commodities, which resulted in the initial formation of the new modern commercial trade structure with treaty ports as the center.

The flow direction of China's modern commodity market is different from the traditional market in that primarily industrial products flowed from the coastal cities to the hinterland and agricultural products and processed byproducts flowed from the hinterland to the coastal cities. Gradually, a commercial network with treaty ports like Shanghai and other cities as the center and toward the hinterland and the countryside was formed. This commercial network utilized traditional commercial channels but it reorganized and restructured them. China's traditional commerce changed as a result of foreign businessmen's impact. While the national commerce maintained in varying degrees the previous capitalist commercial capital nature, it was added upon with the comprador capital nature and its activities were gradually incorporated into the world market.

After the signing of Nanking Treaty, the hong merchants system was abolished and foreign merchants were allowed to freely employ those who worked for them to trade. The first change caused by the resultant comprador system was that the privileged feudal monopoly was broken and an employment relationship characterized by voluntary combination of foreign trading firms and their Chinese employees was thus formed. This was a contract relationship. We can say that the primary indicator of the start of China's modern commerce after the Opium Wars was the establishment of a new free trade system, especially that markets in the coastal cities became competitive markets with free entry and exit, basically free from government intervention and also free from monopoly by any people and groups.

Another fundamental difference between China's modern commerce and its traditional commerce is that there was a change in the commodities exchanged. After the Opium Wars, commodity exchange by modern businesses operated by compradors and new-type import and export merchants first focused on exchange between large industrial products from the West and products made by China's peasants and handicraftsmen. Later, in addition to import commodities, China's modern industry products were added. It is substantially different from the exchange made between small-scale manufacturers in China's traditional commerce.

In the second half of the 19th century, China's new-type commerce introduced many modern operation modes such as combination of new-type insurance and banking industry with commerce, shift from clans to social credit in financing, expansion of credit trade, and progress in telecommunications, transport and storage, which led to decreased transaction cost.

(4) Change in business organization-establishment and expansion of

share-holding company system. Development of business organizations experienced a history from sole proprietorship to joint venture and then to company and from limitless liability system to limited liability system. Share-holding companies in the modern sense developed speedily after the mid-19th century in Western Europe. By the end of the 19th century, it became a dominant business organization form in the capitalist economy, which marked a great reform in industry system. Share-holding system can accelerate accumulation of capital, which makes capital more socialized and leads to dissemination of shares and sharing of risks, and separation of right of ownership from right of management.

Establishment of modern business system represented by share-holding companies allows replacement of business coordination management system for market coordination system to develop further, thus reducing transaction cost substantially.

After the early 20th century, a large number of multinational companies invaded China. These companies were all in the form of share-holding system for their management. We may say that they were share-holding system capital from all over the world. Faced with this challenge, the Chinese government successively promulgated a series of laws and decrees that aimed at learning from the Western model to protect and encourage share-holding system companies. Under this incentive, China saw its company system grow rapidly and share-holding system became gradually the guiding form in the industry businesses in major coastal cities. However, in comparison with the developed countries in the West, these share-holding companies were generally relatively small in scale and kinship still played a dominant role in many companies.

(5) Silver standard and currency system reform. The most fundamental question in currency system is standard system. As the industrialization leader, England was the first to adopt the gold standard in 1816. After the 1870s major industrialized countries in the world abolished the silver standard one after another, leaving China as the only country still in the silver standard. When the currency reform was made in 1935, China was the only major country in the world that was still in the silver standard. This long-term denial to dock with the world economy showed stubbornness in China's national economy. Its reaction in the national economic

policy was China's indifference to participation in the international economic cycle and its best efforts to maintain its economic closeness. The old currency system's influence on China's economy had both gains and losses. This influence's complexity and uncertainty made successive Chinese governments torn between ideas in their currency reforms. But the disadvantage of this policy eventually forced China to abandon its silver standard and adopt the currency system that was popular among all the modern countries.

(6) Rapid expansion of banking system and rise and decline of old-fashioned financial organizations. As a credit organization to specially trade in currency capital, modern banks emerged in the 16th century in Italy. However, banking system was only introduced to China after the Opium Wars. Under the model influence of foreign banks and incentive offered by higher profits, and in order to meet the demand of modern China's financing in its industry and commerce, modern banks in China were born at the end of the 19th century and saw an unprecedentedly rapid growth in the early 20th century, which was an event that greatly attracted people's attention in China's modernization process. One of the major businesses of China's banking industry was to facilitate financing for merchants and relations between banks and modern industry became closer in the 1920s and 1930s.

Old-style Chinese private banks and draft banks are old-fashioned financial organizations that traded in various technical business related to currency circulation. Once they had a complete credit and loan business and this became their main business, their business changed to include basic functions in modern banking industry. In order to meet the demand of the new situation, old-style Chinese private banks made adjustments in a timely manner from currency conversion to savings and loan business. They made short-term loans from foreign banks and provided financing in their own bills to Chinese merchants, especially importers and exporters. They changed from old-fashioned financial organizations to new ones and expanded their business greatly in the early 20th century. Owing to routinism draft banks failed to change their business in a timely manner to savings and loans but instead they attached themselves more closely to the soon-to-be-collapsed feudal financial needs and officials and noblemen's private credit, they rapidly declined in the second half of the 19th century.

(7) Reform in the industry and commerce administration and modernization of administration modes. Modern Western countries and their industry and commerce administrations were created to meet the demand of protecting capitalist ownership and they gained their right of existence by providing services to private industry and commerce and guaranteeing ownership practice. Since late Qing Dynasty, Chinese industry and commerce administrations gradually changed their administration from mandatory taxation to providing services to private industry and commerce for their property ownership and the relevant systems were formed. This shows modernization of industry and commerce administration modes. Specifically, special organizations were established to replace original administration in escrow or concurrent administration and a group of new industry and commerce administrations were created; newly established and existing industry and commerce administrations kept expanding, new staff were added and their organizations were becoming more and more specialized and knowledgeable; a vertical industry and commerce administration system from the central government to the local governments was established and the control power was upgraded to the central government and economic centralization system in the modern sense was strengthened; departments' responsibilities were clarified with specific division of jobs and their work was performed in accordance with the laws and management efficiency was raised; decision-making processes tended to be scientific and democratic. After the responsible departments in the industry and commerce administrations submitted their proposals, the cabinet examined and decided on them and the relevant organizations would execute these decisions.

(8) From restriction to promotion—change in the national industry and commerce policy. In the traditional society, China always adopted the policy of restricting their development toward private industry and commerce. This situation only started to change in late Qing Dynasty.

Since the late 19th century, the Qing government allowed private people to set up manufactories. After the early 20th century, the Qing court, the Provisional Government of the Republic of China and the Peiyang government modelled after the West and Japan to successively draft a series of policies and measures to promote, reward and protect industry and commerce and to promulgate laws and decrees to protect private ownership. This change in the national policy promoted prosperity of the national industry and commerce and provided guarantee for economic modernization. However, this change was preliminary and the laws and decrees were not perfect and they were even branded with the feudal system. In particular, legislation in the private ownership failed to shake off the tradition of being subject to the political power and showed marked incompleteness.

In ancient Chinese society, although private ownership emerged at a very early stage, it remained weak. Property ownership was instable and lacked legal protection and it was subject to the political power. This was similar to the medieval times in the West. One of the most fundamental characteristics in the change from the traditional society to the modern society in the West was establishment of private ownership which was gradually achieved in the long struggles between the capitalist class and the feudal political privileges. As China did not have this process in its history, its property ownership failed to shake off its attaching to the political power from the beginning to the end.

(9) Establishment of modern taxation system. After the Opium Wars, as the Qing government lost its taxation autonomy, it started to levy likin to offset the shortage in finance. In fact, this added to the domestic taxes. These practices were very detrimental to the development in industry and commerce.

During the late medieval times or early modern times, the Western countries generally abolished their domestic taxes after they collected the frontier customs dues. Collection of the domestic taxes yielded to the demand of protecting their own industrial development.

After the establishment of the Provisional Government of the Republic of China, through negotiations with the various powers, it gained taxation autonomy and started to collect consolidated tax and abolished likin and salt monopoly. It ended its long practice of commercial taxes with transit duties at its heart, established the direct taxation system with income tax at its center, clarified division of central government's finance and local governments' finance and centralized the lion's share to the central government and achieved its goal of changing the traditional taxation system to the modern taxation system.

II. Impact of foreign invasions on traditional Chinese culture

The 1850s and 1860s was a period when the modern Chinese society was experiencing a tumultuous history and an important period when the traditional Chinese society saw a fundamental change. After the severe shocks of the Opium Wars and under the strong impact of the Western capitalism, the stable structure in the Chinese society was subject to a tremendous shock and underwent constant turmoil and reforms. When the traditional Chinese economic structure was facing the Western impact and tended to disintegrate, those social values that were rooted in the traditional economic structure lost the social reality that matched them. Under the impact and influence of the Western capitalist values, the traditional concept of "respecting doctrines and despising techniques" was smashed and the ancient customs during the feudal times received varying degrees of shocks and "mercantilist ideas" in the modern sense started to emerge. The updating in the social values inevitably resulted in the shifts in the general mood of society, which provided a good atmosphere for China's early modernization.

a. break of the traditional value of "respecting doctrines and despising techniques" and reform in the educational system

The bias of "respecting doctrines and despising techniques" was a major content in the Sino-Western cultural difference, which was a closely-connected social value with the eight-part essay imperial examination strictly safeguarding the border of "those who work with their brains rule; those who labor with their physical strength are ruled." As a result, the low status of science and technology in the Chinese society was destined. Although traditional Chinese society did not deny that the society needed skills and workmanship, its disdainful attitude toward them was apparent.

After the Opium Wars, most Chinese people including a large number of scholars still adhered to this traditional value. (1) The concept of not seeking actual effect and doggedly observing doctrines was apparently detrimental to modern China that was surrounded by the various powers. Just as Prince Yixin pointed out, "All the cabinet members and officials at the time did not make their best efforts to assist the emperor with designing a practical strategy. Instead they only used empty words to perform their duties perfunctorily. And this resulted in the outbreak of the Second Opium War." (2) Under the strong impact of the Western influence upon China, some enlightened officials started to break away from constraint of the traditional concept of "respecting doctrines and despising techniques" and opposed doggedly observing doctrines and sought actual effect and they paid attention to the Western science and technology that were previously called "the lower techniques" such as handicraft and commerce. In Zuo Zongtang's memorial to the throne entitled "The First Outline on Proposing to Purchase Machines, Employ Foreign Technicians and Test-manufacture Steamships", he made a systematic description and analysis of the relationship between "doctrines" and "techniques" by stating that "The Chinese people's wisdom emphasizes ideology while foreigners' intelligence bases itself on practical work. The Chinese people view doctrines as primary and techniques as secondary. Foreigners view techniques as primary and doctrines as secondary. Doctrines and techniques serve their respective goals and they do not contradict with each other. So we need to put them aside now. If one says that our strength is not better than foreign countries, we can allow them to take the lead for a while, this is fine with us. If one says that our strength is not better than foreign countries, we can allow them to maintain their lead forever, this is not acceptable to us. This is where the matter needs to be taken seriously." (3) While he proposed that the Chinese people and foreigners treated the primary and the secondary differently but the two did not contradict with each another, he hinted his praise for the Western way that "foreigners' intelligence bases itself on practical work" and "foreigners view techniques as primary". He opposed the view of completely separating "doctrines" from "techniques" and believed that those who emphasized doctrines should specialize in techniques. He admitted that China had lagged behind the West. As a result, the most important thing to do now is that "we can allow them to take the lead for a while" but we need to prevent them to "maintain their lead forever". His argument forcefully hit the vital part of the value of "respecting doctrines and despising techniques" and paved the way in theory to some extent for the large-scale introduction of Western science and technology.

    Meanwhile, challenged by domestic troubles and foreign invasions, more and more scholars were no longer willing to bury themselves in empty doctrines and instead they shifted their attention to practical knowledge to seek practical strategies. As a result, some "techniques study" outside the orthodox "doctrines study" gained a beneficial development atmosphere. Some scholars and students then focused on doing research on astronomy, mathematics, geography, medicine and so on, which presented a somewhat rosy picture for the "techniques study" that was once considered "the variety knowledge".

Xue Fucheng "planned with deep feeling to engage in the study of practical strategies so that he someday would use them for the country. Then he discarded almost everything in order to study them … He started to conduct research on the vicissitudes of the situation over the past two thousand years, the ever-changing opportunities to use military stratagems and also studied an outline of astronomy, yinyang, traditional Chinese secret magical art of Qimen, divination and general history of strategic forts, mountains, and rivers in China. He was very diligent and thorough in all these studies."[1] A famous scientist Xu Shou "thought what he learned at a very young age was not practically useful, he then specialized in the natural sciences and… was particularly skillful in making machines."[2] They sought practical "techniques study" and pursued extensive reading and knowledge, which generally represented trends in changes in the mental state and value of those scholars and students who were talented and ambitious when they were facing radical changes in the situations. Under the influence of this idea, during several decades after the Opium Wars, a group of famous scholars with relative achievements in natural sciences such as mathematics, astronomy, chemistry, physics, geography and so on appeared successively in culturally developed areas such as Jiangsu, Zhejiang, Hunan, Hubei, Fujian, Guangdong and so on. These people helped greatly promote the change in the intellectual circle from "respecting doctrines and despising techniques" to actively paying attention to "techniques study" in style of study.

From the above, during the 1850s and 1860s when the Chinese and Western cultures began to cross which was a particular historical period, those who were the

---

[1] *Westernization Movement (Book VIII)*: 10.

[2] Li Changli. "Fashions and Folk Life's Ethics in Shanghai's Foreign Concessions During the Mid-19th Century". *The Scholarly Monthly*, No. 2, 1955.

first to break away from the value of "respecting doctrines and despising techniques" were the middle- and lower-ranked people that were influenced by the practical learning of the practical strategies. They went with the stream of the world, changed their course and deviated from the tradition by first paying attention to the "techniques study" and then accepting the new knowledge. They either suggested ways and means or directed themselves in scientific and technological work in the modern enterprises that were operated by the Modernization Movement officials. Their expertise and attitude toward the "techniques study" were instrumental to some extent in prompting the presiding officials' shift in their traditional value of "respecting doctrines and despising techniques" and thus made a beginning for the entire society's attitude shift toward the "techniques study". In 1896 Yan Fu translated *Evolution and Ethics*, which made a beginning for China's advocacy for the natural sciences. As products of the reforms, 1895 saw the founding of China's first university, Peiyang University in Tianjin; Imperial University of Peking (predecessor of today's Peking University) was founded in Beijing in 1898; and in 1911 Tsinghua Xuetang (Tsing Hua Imperial College) was established as a preparatory school for those students who were sent by the government to study in the United States; all these marked the emergence of China's modern education with a main focus on education in the natural sciences. With the rise of new industry, many educational forms and systems such as vocational education were introduced to China, which replaced the traditional educational system that concentrated on the eight-part essay imperial examination and Confucian classics and ceremonies.

b. development of mercantilist ideas

While the traditional concepts of "stressing agriculture and restraining commerce" and "agriculture first and commerce second" that were rooted in the feudal economic agricultural basis stabilized the agricultural economic structure and maintained the normal operation of the feudal country state ruling machine, it restrained the normal development of commodity economy inside the country and resulted in the entire society the formation of deep-rooted concept of "despising commerce and self-care".

After the Opium Wars, the situation changed suddenly. As the ban on maritime trade was lifted, Western products bombarded China like a flood and glutted the various trading ports. The increase in Sino-foreign trade expanded the sales market and also produced prosperity in trading in the cities and the countryside, which propelled development in the entire commerce. This was particularly obvious in the trading ports. Take only Tianjin for instance, it claimed a number one status in more than one hundred aspects such as postal service, railroad, education, finance, military, urban construction, industry, science and technology, commerce and trade, and so on. After the mid-1850s in Shanghai, trading companies and stores established by the Chinese people sprang up like bamboo shoots after a spring rain. These were foreign and Cantonese goods stores that specialized in importing foreign products, foreign fabric stores, hardware stores, Western pharmacies and so on; silk, tea and various dry goods warehouses that specialized in exporting business; old-style Chinese private banks, banking houses, telecommunications and transport business, moving business, rice stores and fabrics stores and so on, to name only a few.[1] With this development, appeared a large number of people who were engaged in commerce. The source of this group was really rich in variety. Some were directly employed by foreign trading companies like compradors and tongshi (interpreters); some were original old-style business people; but more were those who abandoned farm work, education or even government jobs in order to engage in commerce. As a result, an upsurge in becoming business people occurred during the reign of Emperor Xianfeng and Emperor Tongzhi. Although this upsurge in engaging in commerce had something to do with certain objective factors such as poverty-driven job hunting in cities so as to earn a livelihood, change in people's social value led to this upsurge too, which is a factor that cannot be ignored. The traditional concept of "stressing agriculture and restraining commerce" ranked merchants as the bottom of "scholar, farmer, artisan and merchant". People always viewed merchants as coveting wealth and profits, forgetting one's integrity when tempted by personal gain and having low morality. As a result, the social mentality in the society was generally "despising commerce". However, the radical changes in the post-modern social situation made people's livelihood worsen generally. Because money and property appealed more to people than reputation and social status alone and

---

[1] Duan Guangqing. *Jinghu's Self-written Chronicle*. Beijing: Zhonghua Book Company, 1984.

merchants with much capital and property enjoyed higher social status accordingly, people gradually gave up their discrimination against merchants. A local Qing Dynasty official by the name of Duan Guangqing once went to Shanghai to raise military expenditures. To his pleasant surprise, he enjoyed great support from merchants from Jiangsu and Zhejiang. This made him realize that not all merchants were those who coveted wealth and had low morality. He exclaimed that "There are a large number of merchants in Shanghai that are originally from Ningbo. In view of the situation in Southeastern China, we both had to raise military expenditures in Shanghai for our needs in Zhejiang and Jiangsu. We are fortunate that Ningbo natives here all take care of the official needs in their home provinces and contribute greatly to our needs." The disdain and contempt that shrouded merchants were fading. After the reign of Emperor Xianfeng and Emperor Tongzhi, merchants' social status continued to improve. What can be cited for this improvement is that at the time in the imperial edicts, memorials to the throne and official correspondence, "members of gentry" that referred to scholar-bureaucrats and "merchants" that referred to business people were used together and equally as leaders of the common people, namely, the social elite.

In view of the above, since the reign of Emperor Xianfeng and Emperor Tongzhi, mercantilist ideas in the society gradually developed and provided the advantage for the rise of mercantilism at a later time.

Meanwhile, faced with the grave fact that the Western powers used commercial exchange as a means to plunder China economically, some enlightened scholars and officials started to consider the current situation in the best interests of their country and from the political and economic perspectives and began to look for countermeasures. The idea of mercantilism appeared in their brainstorming. Zeng Guofan realized in the first year of the reign of Emperor Tongzhi that "China is founded on 'agriculture and war' while countries in the West base themselves on 'commerce and war'."[①] He had an initial knowledge of the difference in Sino-foreign ways to found their countries. As regards the many layers of exploitation that merchants were subject to, Zuo Zongtang stated that "The annual revenue is half

---

[①] *The Complete Works of Zuowenxianggong · Drafts of Memorials to the Throne (Volume XVIII).*

wasted on requests by outdated rules and half pressured by the efficiency of their hard work. How can merchants stand such layered exploitation?"① He advocated reforms in old habits and bad customs so as to "relax merchants' burden to maintain their strength and protect their profits earned". As regards traditional scholars' proposal of "weakening merchants", Guo Songtao fought it with his advocacy that "Farmers engage in agriculture to harvest just enough to earn their livelihood and merchants engage in commerce but to make huge profits. Whose work is more important is not difficult to know." He believed that "It does not contradict itself to protect merchants and enrich the country at the same time because these two goals benefit and suit themselves well." On the fact that merchants had little capital and small influence and were hard to compete with foreign merchants, they proposed to actively support merchants and strengthen Chinese merchants' competitiveness. Ding Richang wrote to Li Hongzhang in the third year of the reign of Emperor Tongzhi suggesting that Chinese merchants should be encouraged to purchase and construct steamships and once they were equipped with modern ocean-going means of transport they would win in their competition with foreign merchants because they were more familiar with the Chinese markets.② Zeng Guofan made similar proposals. From the above proposals to "relax merchants' burden", "protect merchants" and "support merchants financially", it is not hard to find that these proposals aimed to retrieve rights to make profits and compete with foreign merchants for profits.

In addition, at the same time when some enlightened people proposed "supporting merchants financially", they further proposed to set up large-scale modern enterprises and consolidate separate merchants' powers so as to strengthen competitiveness in commerce and trade. In the fifth year of the reign of Emperor Tongzhi, Guo Songtao realized that "in order for the Chinese people to win over foreigners, it is not proper to simply rely on officially-run businesses", instead we "should allow merchants to manufacture steamships so as to gain profits from foreigners and for them to be able to compete with foreigners for profits. That is to say they should be able to win over foreigners." As a result, he suggested that

---

① *Guo Songtao's Drafts of Memorials to the Throne*. Changsha: Yuelu Publishing House, 1983.
② *Guo Songtao's Diary (Volume II)*. Changsha: Hunan People's Publishing House, 1981: 56-57.

merchants should elect "Department of Steamship Trading" and "officially-run steamships should be under the jurisdiction of this department and to put these steamships to merchants for cargoes shipping with some payment for labor's meals and annual maintenance and repair fees."[①] His proposal was obviously featured with setting up commercial steamship companies. Rong Hong, who was full of commercial nationalist ideas, under the support of Tsungli Yamen, tried in 1868 to set up one share-holding steamship company in Shanghai. While this plan failed to succeed owing to various reasons, it made a beginning of establishing large-scale enterprises. With this influence, Li Hongzhang finally set up China Merchants Steam Navigation Company Limited in 1872 which completed Rong Hong's unfinished job. In view of the above, ideas and thoughts from proposals to "relax merchants' burden", "protect merchants" and "support merchants financially" to establishing modern privately-run large-scale enterprises provided ideological preparedness and social environment which are indispensable for modernization shift in China's traditional economy. Despite the fact that this ideological preparedness had apparent restrictions and defects, it is just under the influence of it that after the mid-1870s a large number of modern privately-run industrial and mining enterprises were founded, which promoted the ever deepening of China's modernization. As a result, this trailblazing achievement cannot be denied.

It is proper to say that development of mercantilism during the reign of Emperor Xianfeng and Emperor Tongzhi first originated from the strong impact on China's traditional economic structure by Western products. Among the common people, in order to make a livelihood and seek profits, an upsurge in engaging in commerce happened. Among the officials, "retrieving right to profits" and "competing with foreigners for profits" became the focus. "Supporting merchants financially" and "relaxing merchants' burden" and ideas to establish modern industrial and mining enterprises were proposed. The merging of these two trends resulted inevitably in change in traditional ideas of "despising merchants" and "merchants are ranked the lowest" and creation of the proper soil for existence of the modern trend of "commerce first" idea. During the reign of Emperor Xianfeng and

---

[①] Hao Yanping. *China's Modern Commercial Revolution*. Shanghai: Shanghai People's Publishing House, 1991: 668.

Emperor Tongzhi, the emergence of "commerce first" idea finally formed a trend in the 1870s and 1880s and gained partial acknowledgment and response in the society and greatly promoted the traditional society's modernization shift.

c. budding of modern China's reform ideas

Invasions by the Western powers brought severe impact on China's traditional political and economic systems. Meanwhile, the Western system's advancement promoted Chinese people with lofty ideals to think about how to change China's backwardness. As a result, many reform ideas made their first appearance.

(1) China's wide-open borders and proposal of "learning advanced techniques from foreign countries in order to defeat them"

The imperial Qing government was extremely shocked at the "strong military attacks" of the Western colonialists. Inside the ruling class a group of people still adhered to the ignorant idea that the Celestial Empire has "all kinds of things and they are in abundance" and "we do not need to rely on foreign products". Another group of people, represented by Lin Zexu, started to think that the Celestial Empire was not advanced in all the aspects compared with foreign countries and instead there were things in China that were less advanced than foreign countries. Lin Zexu was anxiously thinking about one question: how to make China stronger in order to defeat Western invaders' attacks? Lin Zexu was new to the large machinery industry in the West and his knowledge of capitalist economy, politics, culture and other aspects was almost blank. Preliminary contacts with the Western invaders and reading on the relevant materials on the West allowed Lin Zexu to be in the stage of "knowing them" on England and other Western powers, especially in their weaponry. He acknowledged the strengths of capitalist countries and thought that "China's warships and cannons are no match for their foreign counterparts". In order to "defeat foreign countries", he proposed that China "manufacture cannons and warships" and make the best efforts in manufacturing warships, cannons and other new weaponry to catch up with or surpass capitalist countries in the West and to achieve the goal of "the cannons manufactured need to be perfectly strong and warships to be perfectly solid". Lin Zexu's such proposal to catch up with the West in manufacture of cannons and warships in terms of "strong" and "solid" embodies itself his idea of learning from the West. From this perspective, it is not an overstated praise for the people to call Lin Zexu "the first person to view the world with open eyes" in modern China.

Wei Yuan further developed Lin Zexu's idea of "making China stronger and repelling foreign aggression". In the same year when the First Opium War ended, he wrote *Illustrated Treatise on the Maritime Kingdoms*. In the preface, he made it very clear that the goal of writing this book was "learning advanced techniques from foreign countries in order to defeat them". This is the first time that Wei Yuan proposed such an idea after the First Opium War. In a certain sense, Wei Yuan inherited the past and ushered in the future in the matter of how the Chinese people viewed the West. *Illustrated Treatise on the Maritime Kingdoms* was the trendsetter of the time and made a beginning of "seeking from the West both material and spiritual weaponry". The essence of "learning advanced techniques from foreign countries in order to defeat them" in this book can be summarized in four main aspects. (i) introduce Western technology, equipment and technicians, construct a shipyard and an arsenal at Guangdong, employ foreign engineers to teach marine navigation and weapons operation, and select skillful craftsmen and intelligent soldiers from Fujian and Guangdong to be students in the above training programs. (ii) imitate the Western practices of maintaining military forces, train them and add naval courses. (iii) allow "merchants and the common people in the coastal areas to voluntarily engage in setting up manufactories and shipyards to build ships for their own use or for sale". At wartime, lease these commercial ships to be warships. (iv) establish privately-run enterprises. Wei Yuan believed that "exquisite techniques" were not equal to "exquisite but useless techniques" and that we should learn from the West in taking advantage of wind power, hydraulic power and coal power so as to win over the natural creation, connect with the mental activity and use them for our people's benefits.

Proposal of the above ideas showed that a group of forward-looking Chinese people were greatly shocked by the military power of the Opium Wars. Lenin once said that "wars are a school". It is owing to the Opium Wars that the forerunners in modern China, through comparison and knowledge of weapons, realized China's weakness in weaponry and the necessity for the Chinese people to yield to foreigners in this respect. As a result, a dream to industrialize and strengthen China by "learning unnoticeably foreigners' techniques" began to take shape. The core of this industrialization idea is modernization in the military industry, which is in line with the contemporary history and reality. And the defeat in the Second Opium War following the defeat in the First Opium War forced the imperial Qing government to bring this ideology to practice on its agenda. The outcome was the establishment of the General Bureau of Machine Manufacture of Jiangnan, the Tientsin Arsenal, the Foochow Arsenal, the Nanjing Jinling Arsenal and other Modernization Movement industrial enterprises. We can see from the above that from the very beginning of China's industrial modernization, strengthening the country's military power occupied a major role.

(2) "industrialization of China through manufacturing" in the Hundred Days' Reform

The First Sino-Japanese War in 1894 destroyed the entire Beiyang Fleet and the ruling class' "Westernized Chinese style" in industrial modernization was declared a failure and "pursuing strength" and "pursuing wealth" came to naught. There was a shift in China's modern industrial modernization idea. "Industrialization of China through manufacturing" proposal represented by Kang Youwei took its place. In the entire process of the Hundred Days' Reform, Kang Youwei and others placed development of capitalist economy in the top priority and clearly proposed "industrialization of China through manufacturing", namely, China changed from an agricultural country into an industrialized one. They believed that establishing and developing a large machinery industry was the primary path to "strengthen the country" and "strengthen the military" and they made their best efforts in demonstrating large-scale industry played an important role in making "intelligent people" and development in large-scale industry was an important prerequisite to promoting citizens' cultural level, overcoming the ignorant and fogyish mentality and changing social ethos. They opposed "emphasizing agriculture and restraining commerce" and "building up the country with agriculture" advocated by the diehards and believed that "if a country adheres to agriculture, it will be conservative and ignorant with each passing day; if a country advocates industry, it will make progress and become more intelligent with each passing day" and that we would make our best efforts in developing industry which is the only way that China can shake off poverty, backwardness, conservatism and ignorance so as to become stronger and free from threats from the enemy. On the basis of this view, Kang Youwei proposed to Emperor Guangxu that "Your majesty really care about the major trends in the world by evaluating the vicissitudes of the ancient and modern times and making clear the national affairs, reforming the people's mind, eliminating ignorance and upholding wisdom, parting with conservatism, embracing making daily progress and making a decision on China to become an industrialized country. If we only pursue materialist goals, China will not become a power. That is why we need to guide our people with our rules and this is really the way to achieve our goal." Although capitalist thinkers before Kang Youwei like Xue Fucheng also emphasized the importance of establishing and developing large machinery industry, they only demonstrated this question from the perspectives of "strengthening the country" and "making the people wealthier" and they failed to recognize the huge revolutionary role that large machinery industry played in destroying old habits and traditions. But Kang Youwei was able to propose industrialization from the perspective of changing traditional ideas and customs, which is indeed a great progress compared with the capitalist reformists in the 1860s and 1870s. In his memorial to the throne, Kang Youwei also made an in-depth demonstration of the importance of "positioning China as an industrialized country". He mentioned that the area of European countries was only the size of a province or even a county in China and their population was only one tenth or even one percent of ours, however, their wealth status was ten times more than ours. The reason was that "their techniques were exquisite and advanced" and they were "in pursuit of materialistic goals" and the industrial revolution marked by invention of steam engine and its wide application created unprecedented social productivity and material wealth. This really shows that at that time Kang Youwei actually proposed that China needs to be industrialized in accordance with the Western capitalist path and China needs to be transformed from an agricultural country to an industrialized one.

During the Hundred Days' Reform, an important figure that followed Kang Youwei closely to advocate "industrialization of China through manufacturing" was Liang Qichao whose speeches on preaching capitalist industrialization were also clear and penetrating. He not only opposed "building up the country with agriculture" but also was not satisfied with "building up the country with commerce". He proposed in a straightforward manner "industrialization of China through manufacturing". He believed that "machinery is the most important tenet in a power" and once you have all kinds of machines you will be able to achieve the goal that "one tiller can feed one hundred people" and "one person's daily output can provide food supply for one hundred days", which would promote social productivity greatly.

Although Kang Youwei and Liang Qichao's proposals of "positioning China as an industrialized country" and "industrialization of China through manufacturing" differ in names, these two proposals are basically the same in meaning and they both aim to make China on the path to capitalist industrial modernization as soon as possible. In comparison with other people ahead of them, we can say that they surpassed them regarding their industrialization idea of establishing and developing large machinery industry and transforming China from an agricultural country to an industrialized one. So far, their understanding of the West transcended from the materialistic component to the system component and elevated the partial understanding held by the people before them to a more complete idea of industrial modernization. In view of this, Kang Youwei and Liang Qichao should be pioneers of modern China's national industrialization.

(3) Dr. Sun Yat-sen's *The International Development of China* and Industrial Modernization Construction

Although Kang Youwei and Liang Qichao's ideas of national industrialization touched the surface of the system component, they did not want and were unable to make thorough reforms in the system. With the failure of the Hundred Days' Reform, they faded away from China's political stage, and their ideas influenced less with the time. Later, it is Dr. Sun Yat-sen who elevated China's modern industrialization idea to its summit.

It took Dr. Sun Yat-sen about 25 years for his China industrialization idea from its initial thoughts to perfection, namely, from *Petition to Li Hongzhang* in 1894 to *The International Development of China* when he proposed the grand construction and plan on China's industrialization path in 1919. In *The International Development of China*, regarding his idea of China's industrialization path, in addition to the general features of European and American capitalist industrialization, it also reflected China particular basic condition and fully expressed his unique views on China's industrialization. First, he based China's industrialization on shaking off completely poverty and backwardness and took the path to wealth and strength taken by European and American capitalist countries. He had huge criticism on the fact that in Europe and America monopoly capitalists controlled the lifeline of their countries and only a handful of capitalists were benefited while a great number of people were harmed. He said that most of the large Western companies were privately owned with the aim of profiting as much as possible and "when all the small manufacturers were wiped out by them and owing to no competition they could raise their products' prices and the entire society would suffer from them invisibly". However, "it is the result of evolution that resulted in these large companies and not by pressure from human beings". In order to solve this problem, we should make the best of the situation and "put all these large companies under the public ownership of the country's people". In this way, large companies were run by the country and the profits earned should belong to the people and then all the people in the country would not subject themselves to the harm of capital. Obviously, Dr. Sun Yat-sen's proposal on national industrialization plan focused not only on the country's wealth and strength but also on people's ability to lead a happy life. He not only proposed to replace machine production for outdated handicraft labor, but also emphasized reforms need to be made in the economic system to achieve nationalization of large industry. This proposition to firmly take the industrialization path and deny private monopoly showed that Dr. Sun Yat-sen detected the capitalist industrialization's defects and he hoped that China should blaze its own trail in industrialization and he had a presage that China's industrialization must take the path of people's industrialization. Second, China's industrialization must take a combined path of transport and telecommunications, heavy industry and light industry and agriculture and should not copy the West as they started with light industry. Dr. Sun Yat-sen believed that China's basic condition and social and historical conditions did not allow China's industrialization to chase the beaten path of the capitalist countries and instead we must catch up with the world power within a short period of time. Only in this way can China ensure its independence, wealth and strength. How to implement China's industrialization? From the entire China's industrialization, *The International Development of China* highlighted the special roles of sea ports, sea transport and railroads and emphasized a combined development of heavy and light industry such as iron and steel, power industry and so on and agriculture. This indeed pointed out a special path for China's industrialization that is different from the Western powers. Third, Dr. Sun Yat-sen actively advocated that China's economic construction and industrialization must adopt the policy of opening up to the outside world. He pointed out that there were many countries in the world that were successful in realizing industrialization by utilizing foreign capital and technology. Dr. Sun Yat-sen believed that in the course of utilizing foreign capital and technology we need to do a good job regarding our economic and political relationships with foreign countries and we should not allow excessive exploitation by foreign capital to say nothing of damaging our country's sovereignty. Under the then historical conditions, Dr. Sun Yat-sen's proposition on introducing foreign capital was indeed a result of his deliberations and strategic foresight.

From the above demonstrations, we may see that China's modern industrialization ideas originated from Lin Zexu and Wei Yuan and culminated with Dr. Sun Yat-sen. China's modern industrial modernization ideas were an ideological process full of pains. With the Opium Wars came Lin Zexu and Wei Yuan's military industrial modernization. Then with the First Sino-Japanese War came the proposal of "industrialization of China through manufacturing". Finally, with the First World War, came *The International Development of China*, which is a grand blueprint of industrial modernization. In a semi-colonial and semi-feudal society, it is impossible to promote China's industrial modernization process. It is imperative for China to establish a brand-new and stable social structure in order to allow taking the industrial development path. It is not practical to retake the beaten path of development in the early period of capitalism about two hundred years ago. Owing to class and historical limitations, our forerunners' ideas on industrial modernization had defects of one sort or another, but these ideas remain very precious historical heritage of the Chinese people. Later generations can obtain many beneficial revelations from them, especially from the many propositions in Dr. Sun Yat-sen's

The International Development of China, which serve as lessons and references.

Section Three   Slow Development of Industrialization in Modern China

Starting with the Modernization Movement, China embarked on its own path to industrial modernization. This process is roughly divided into two periods. One is the budding period from rise of the Modernization Movement to pre-World War I. The other is development period from World War I to the period before the start of the War of Chinese People's Resistance Against Japanese Aggression.

I. The Modernization Movement and budding of modernization of China's economy

At the modern times, China's industrial sectors started from scratch and began its difficult take-off process. From Chart 5-1, we can see that from 1850 to 1887, rise of the Modernization Movement made national income of China's industry and mining and communications industry from nothing to RMB 2.48 billion in 1914.

Chart 5-1   Changes in growth and weight in China's modern manufacturing and old-fashioned manufacturing (1887-1936)

Currency value in 1936: RMB 100 million

		modern manufacturing	old-fashioned manufacturing	total
1887	output value	0	114.34	114.34
	weight (%)	0	100.00	100.00
1914	output value	2.90	149.91	152.81
	weight (%)	1.89	98.11	100.00
1936	output value	13.12	193.35	206.47
	weight (%)	6.35	93.65	100.00
1914-1936 annual growth rate		7.10	1.16	—

Sources: 1887 and 1914: based on calculations from *Modern China's Economic Development* (First Edition), Chapter V, Appendixes 3 and 4; 1936: in accordance with Wu Baosan. *China's National Income, 1933*, and *China's National Income Adjustments*.

While the industry developed in its entirety, the internal structure inside the industry also underwent a profound change. Development in the industry occurred after disintegration of the natural economy. As a result, emergence of the industry was a huge attack on China's traditional handicraft industry in the modern times. The internal change in the industry's structure was also reflected in the process of the decline of the handicraft industry and development in the machinery industry. In manufacturing, old-fashioned manual operation was gradually replaced by the new method of machine manufacturing. As a result, development in the industry and changes in its structure can also be seen in the comparison between new method of manufacturing and old-fashioned method of manufacturing.

As we can see from Chart 5-1, owing to the rise of the Modernization Movement, till the early 20th century, modern industry had produced some profits. Although its share in the national income was less than 2%, this is still a historical step.

In the industry and mining, before 1914 output value of China's modern industry and mining increased by RMB 157 million. Although the traditional handicraft industry had seen some growth, its weight share inside industry and mining started a decline trend. From 1887 to 1914, modern industry showed a rapid development and its output value increased by more than four times and its weight share had risen to 28.93%. Meanwhile, modern handicraft industry grew somewhat, but in view of modern industry's rapid development, its weight share declined markedly from 91% to 71.07%. In 1878, the fourth year during the reign of Emperor Guangxu, Tang Tingshu, Administrator of Tianjin China Merchants Steamship Navigation Company, acted under orders to raise capital of 1.21 million taels of silver to found the Kaiping Mines (later renamed to Kailuan (Kailan) Mining Administration). This coal mine was put into operation in 1881 and called externally as Chinese Engineering and Mining Company, which is China's first modern coal mine that was mechanized. This shows that in modern Chinese economic history there was a very marked trend in using machine manufacturing industry to replace traditional manual operation in industry and mining.

At the same time with industry and mining development, both new transport industry and old-fashioned transport industry enjoyed growth. However, new communications industry's weight had seen a clear growth. During the period between 1887 and 1914, old-fashioned transport industry developed at a relatively faster speed with an annual growth of 5.1%. During this period, new transport industry emerged but its output value in 1914 was only RMB 133 million.

In addition, according to the customs statistics, during the period between 1864 and 1903, the total import and export of sailing boats grew at an annual rate of 6.3%. Its growth rate slowed down with an annual rate of 2.4% between 1904 and 1914. In 1887, the total tonnage of China's ships was only 25,398 tons. In 1914, this grew to 92,549 tons. In 27 years, it grew by 2.64 times.

At the same time during the development in transport industry, postal service and telecommunications also started to take shape in China. Since 1878, the fourth year of the reign of Emperor Guangxu, Li Hongzhang entrusted Robert Hart, an Englishman, Detring, a German, to copy the European model to launch Tianjin Maritime Customs Postal Service and started to handle international postal service. Tianjin Maritime Customs entrusted Shanghai Maritime Customs Statistical Department to design and print a set of large dragon stamps in three dominations, which is China's first set of stamps. This marks the take-off of modern postal service. It is not until March, 1896 that the Imperial Chinese Post was established. The steady development in postal service was after the founding of the Republic of China. In 1912, post offices increased to 6,816 and mail routes' distance increased to 229,800 kilometers.

Before introduction of the Chinese national machine cotton spinning, China's traditional cotton spinning was impacted to some extent by foreign cloths. As a result, after introduction of the Chinese national machine cotton spinning, it replaced very quickly China's traditional cotton spinning. In 1894, output of spinning was only 342,000 official dan and hand-spinning's output was 4.69 million official dan. In 1913, machine spinning's output increased to 1.68 million official dan while hand-spinning's output decreased to 1.43 million official dan. Machine-spinning had already surpassed hand-spinning in absolute number.

II. National industry's rise and China's modern industry's development

After World War I, China's national industry started to rise. This brought the real golden age in China's modern industry development. From 1914 to 1936, industry and mining and communications industry rapidly increased by RMB 1.526 billion. In comparison, the share of industry and mining and communications industry in the total industrial and agricultural output also had a clear reflection in this aspect.

Take extractive industry for example, the total output of coal in China rose from 9.067 million tons in 1912 to 24.172 million tons in 1927 with an annual growth output of over 1 million tons. After 1928, it again rose from 25.092 million tons to 39.903 million tons in 1936.[①] During this period, coal mining's mechanization degree also increased. In 1914, the coal output by mechanized mining in China was 7.974 million tons. Up to 1936, this grew to 33.794 million tons. During these 22 years, it increased by more than three times. Its share in the total coal output rose from 56.2% to 84.7%. But coal output by indigenous method did not rise and instead it decreased by about 100,000 tons and its share in the total output also declined to 15.3%. From the above, we can see that there was a marked increase in mechanization degree in coal mining industry. At the same time, iron ores mined by mechanized method rose by 4.8 times and its share in the total output grew from 50.1% to 87%. However, iron ores mined by indigenous method showed an obvious decrease both in relative share and absolute quantity.

In metallurgy, output of smelted iron ores by new method rose from 130,000 tons to 669,700 tons and increased by more than four times. Its share in the total output rose from 43.3% to 82.7% while output by indigenous method during the same period decreased by 300,000 tons. Its share in the total raw iron output declined by 17.3%.[②] From the above, we can see that mechanized manufacturing in mining iron ores and smelting of raw iron occupied a clear advantage. For the annual total output of iron ores and pig iron in China and the share changes in the two different manufacturing methods, please refer to Chart 5-2.

These statistics show that owing to the denial of old-fashioned manufacturing method one part of manufacturing turned to machines and power. With the establishment of new-style mining manufactories, up till the War of Chinese People's Resistance Against Japanese Aggression, new-style coal mining industry and new-style metallurgy had commanded an absolute advantage and in most heavy

---

[①] Yan Zhongping et al. *Selected Archives of Statistical Materials on Modern Chinese Economic History*. Beijing: Science Publishing Company, 1955: Chart 8.

[②] Ibid., 102-104.

industry sectors, modern manufacturing was already at an absolute advantageous position.

Chart 5-2   Iron mining and raw iron annual output of China (1912-1937)

Unit: 1,000 tons

year	iron mining			pig iron		
	mechanized mining	indigenous method mining	weight of mechanized mining (%)	mechanized smelting	indigenous method smelting	weight of mechanized smelting (%)
1912	221.3	502.2	30.6	8.0	170.0	4.5
1927	1181.2	528.9	69.1	257.9	178.9	59.1
1937	3410.0	409.7	89.3	831.1	127.5	86.7

Source: Xu Dixin, Wu Chengming. *History of China's Capitalist Development (Volume III)*. Beijing: People's Publishing House, 1993: 120.

Chart 5-3   Growth and weight changes in China's new-style and old-fashioned transport and communications industry (1887-1936)

Currency value in 1936: RMB 100 million

period		new-style transport	old-fashioned transport	total
1887	net income value	0	1.36	1.36
	weight (%)	0	100.00	100.00
1914	net income value	1.33	5.22	6.55
	weight (%)	20.31	79.69	100.00
1936	net income value	3.16	7.26	10.42
	weight (%)	30.37	69.63	100.00
1914-1936 annual growth rate		4.00	1.50	—

Source: Xu Dixin, Wu Chengming. *History of China's Capitalist Development (Volume III)*. Beijing: People's Publishing House, 1993: 120.

During the period between 1914 and 1936, modern transport industry saw a rapid growth and its output value increased by 1.38 times with an annual growth rate of 4%. Up till 1936, its weight in the total transport value exceeded 30%. However, old-fashioned transport industry's growth speed slowed down and during these 22 years it grew by only 39% with an annual growth rate of 1.5%. Till 1936, its weight in the total transport value also decreased to less than 70%.

During the period between 1914 and 1930, sailing boats decreased with an annual rate of 4.4%.[①] After 1914, steamship transport developed rapidly. Till 1936, its tonnage increased to 576,875 tons and witnessed a 5.2 times increase during these 22 years.[②] In the keen competition, replacement of sailing boat transport by steamship transport accelerated. Take transport on Sichuan rivers for example, in 1919 sailing boat transport occupied more than half but in 1926 all transport was replaced by steamship transport. Another example is that transport of salt from Anhui along the middle and lower reaches of the Yangtze River used to be mostly by sailing boat. However, it was just during this period that steamship transport dispelled old-fashioned transport in an irresistible manner (Please see Chart 5-3).

Chart 5-4   Railroad construction situation of China (1887-1944)

Unit: kilometer

period	construction distance	annual construction distance
1887-1919	11,142.64	337.66
1919-1937	10,274.56	540.77
1937-1944	2,697.47	337.18

Source: calculations based on statistics from Yan Zhongping et al. *Selected Archives of Statistical Materials on Modern Chinese Economic History* (172-179). In the cases where no specific information on the actual years when the railroads were constructed, such railroads were not included. The overlapping of connecting years is for the convenience of categorizing jurisdiction of certain railroads when they were constructed.

Rise of railroad transport is one of the obvious changes in transport and communications industry during this period. We can see from Chart 5-4 the period between 1919 and 1937 is the period that had the most constructed railroad on average in history in old China. During this period, 540.77 kilometers of railroad were constructed annually on average, which is more than the periods before and after that (during the periods between 1887 and 1919 and between 1937 and 1944, about 337 kilometers of railroad were constructed annually on average). Volume of freight traffic by railroad during this period kept rising. In 1917, China's total volume by railroad was about 4.89517 billion tons/kilometers. In 1925, this

---

① Hou Jiming. *Foreign Investment and China's Economic Development, 1840-1937*: 171.

② Yan Zhongping et al. *Selected Archives of Statistical Materials on Modern Chinese Economic History.* Beijing: Science Publishing Company, 1955: 227, 234.

increased to 7.87244 billion tons/kilometers, with a growth rate of 60.8%. Till 1935, it reached 10.83765 billion tons/kilometers, again an increase of 37.3%. Among them, freight volume rose by 57.83% and passenger volume rose by 15.62%.[1] During this period, railroad carrying capacity also rose quickly, the number of engines rose from 600 in 1912 to 1,243 in 1935, engine's hauling capacity rose from 5,340 tons to 13,535 tons.[2]

The rapid growth in new-style transport was also represented in highway transport and civil aviation transport. These two forms of transport were from nothing to development and growth during this period. In 1913, China actually had no new-style highways at all. Since 1923, highways were constructed in a large scale. In 1928, China only had 29,127 kilometers of highways. In 1930, highways developed to 45,000 kilometers. In 1936, China's open traffic distance was about 121,300 kilometers.[3] China's first civil aviation company was founded in 1929. Till 1935, three civil aviation companies established 10 routes covering China and the miles connected by air exceeded 1.68 million miles.[4] But before the War of Chinese People's Resistance Against Japanese Aggression, China's civil aviation's main business was passenger transport and its postal items freight was simply negligible. As a result, civil aviation's contribution to the social economic development was primarily shortening the interval for long-distance postal items and strengthening Sino-foreign telecommunications.

As far as postal service is concerned, in 1927, post bureaus and offices increased to 12,126 and postal routes increased to 462,200 kilometers.[5] In 1936, excluding Northeastern China, post bureaus and offices totaled 12,619 and postal routes totaled 584,800 kilometers. During the period between 1920 and 1929, there

---

[1] Yan Zhongping et al. *Selected Archives of Statistical Materials on Modern Chinese Economic History*. Beijing: Science Publishing Company, 1955: 198, 207.

[2] Xu Dixin, Wu Chengming. *History of China's Capitalist Development (Volume II)*. Beijing: People's Publishing House, 1993: 829.

[3] Ning Ke. *History of China's Economic Development (Volume IV)*. Beijing: China Economy Publishing House, 1999: 2262.

[4] Zheng Youkui. *China's Foreign Trade and Industrial Development*. Shanghai: Shanghai Social Sciences Publishing Company, 1984: 39.

[5] *China Communications and its Development and Trend*: 317, cited from Ning Ke. *History of China's Economic Development (Volume IV)*. Beijing: China Economy Publishing House, 1999: 2282.

was an average annual progressive increase of 536,000,000 postal items. During the period between 1930 and 1936, postal items rose to 783,000,000. Meanwhile, postal service's average annual revenue grew from RMB 24,000,000 to RMB 40,700,000.[①] China's earliest telegraph service occurred in Taiwan. In 1882, Imperial Chinese Telegraph Administration, a government-controlled company, was changed to one that was government-supervised and merchant-managed. Later, China's telegraph service witnessed a rapid growth period. According to incomplete statistics, in 1895, China had 30,462 kilometers of telegraph lines in total. In 1912, this grew to 62,000 kilometers with 565 telegraph bureaus and offices and with a transmittal of 1.9 million telegraphs. Till 1922, the telegraph lines rose to 90,000 kilometers with 928 telegraph bureaus and offices and with a transmittal of 2.5 million telegraphs.[②] However, later there was little development in wire telegraphy. But wireless telegraphy and phone service started to develop.

Generally speaking, during the period between 1914 and 1936, transport industry developed at about one time faster than agricultural and industrial production. Particularly, modern transport means such as railroad, highways, steamships, civil aviation and so on developed in a faster manner. Expansion in the transport capability developed in a coordinated manner with development in other material production sectors and promoted the expansion in domestic commodity exchange and import and export trade. Communications and transport industry played an extremely important role in development of modern Chinese economy. In modern Chinese industry capital, communications and transport industry occupied a sizeable share, which is true in both Chinese capital and foreign capital. From Chart 5-5, although capital and output value in China's communications and transport industry during the Republic of China period had a sizeable share in development of modern industry capital, the role it played is not confined to this only and instead its role lies in its function as the main artery of economy. Lack of modern communications means not only affected industry and commerce, but also

---

[①] Xu Dixin, Wu Chengming. *History of China's Capitalist Development (Volume III)*. Beijing: People's Publishing House, 1993: 99.

[②] Xu Dixin, Wu Chengming. *History of China's Capitalist Development (Volume II)*. Beijing: People's Publishing House, 1993: 833.

constrained dissemination of agricultural technology and commercialization of agricultural production and in reverse it would affect social division of labor and specialization development.

Chart 5-5 Estimate of modern China's industry capital

Unit: RMB million

	1894	1911	1920	1936 (inside Shanhaiguan Pass)
total value of industry capital	12,155	178,673	257,929	544,593
among it, China capital:	6,749	76,548	112,022	358,669
communications and transport industry capital	4,410	112,051	151,445	230,592
among it, China capital:	1,795	47,616	68,445	179,796
value of communications and transport industry capital in total industry capital value (%)	36.28	62.71	58.72	41.58
value of China communications and transport industry capital in total China industry capital value (%)	26.60	62.20	61.10	50.13

Source: Xu Dixin, Wu Chengming. *History of China's Capitalist Development (Volume III)*. Beijing: People's Publishing House, 1993: 722-723, Chart 1.

In addition to heavy industry, in light industry, machine industry replaced traditional handicraft industry in some degree. This is especially true in filature industry, cotton spinning industry and flour-making industry. In the first half of the 1880s, hand-made filature basically prevailed with an average total annual production of 155,200 dan. Till 1936, machine-made filature industry came into existence from scratch with an output value of 141,900 dan. China's total export of filature silk increased from 89,000 dan in 1922 to 133,000 dan in 1929. From 1894 to 1929, China's total export of filature silk rose by 4.9 times and the numbers of mills and silk spinners (Shanghai, Jiangsu and Guangdong) increased by 2.4 times and

2.6 times respectively.① However, hand-made filature did not exit the market completely and it had an annual output of 91,700 dan.

In 1936, China's machine-spun cotton output reached 8.58 million official dan and cotton spun with indigenous method further decreased to 880,000 official dan. In comparison with cotton spinning industry, machine-spun cloth industry developed relatively slowly. In 1894, China's machine-spun cloth was only 5.39 million blots, which occupied 0.79% in China's total cotton cloth manufactured quantity. In 1913, China's total machine-spun cloth output rose to 17.56 million blots, which occupied only 2.26% in the total cotton cloth output. Till 1936, it increased to 40.97 billion blots, which was 45% of the total cotton cloth output.②

Chart 5-6 Summary of cotton mills during the period between 1921 and 1936

Unit: %

annual average growth rate	spindles	cloth spinners	cotton yarn output	cotton cloth output
1921-1930	7.58	10.44	2.37	16.21
1931-1936	1.19	6.32	0.25	5.92

Source: Xu Dixin, Wu Chengming. *History of China's Capitalist Development (Volume III)*. Beijing: People's Publishing House, 1993: 120.

In flour industry, mechanized flour industry, after its first appearance, also enjoyed a relatively faster development. Chart 5-7 records the quantity and share of various flour from 1913 to 1936. Among them, output value in Chinese national mechanized flour mills rose from 20.36 million bags in 1913 to 109.17 million bags in 1936 and its share in total mechanized flour output rose from 4.35% to 16.30%. During World War I in particular, flour industry saw a very robust development period. Export of China-made mechanized flour to foreign countries exceeded imports seven years in a row from 1915 to 1921. Owing to decline in imports and increase in exports only, Chinese domestic mills' annual sales expanded by 9.43

---

① Statistics on the numbers of mills and silk spinners comes from *History of China Modern Filature Industry*: 611-613; export volume: 660-661. For the number of silk spinners in Guangdong in 1920, refer to Xu Dixin, Wu Chengming. *History of China's Capitalist Development (Volume III)*. Beijing: People's Publishing House, 1993: 148.

② Xu Dixin, Wu Chengming. *History of China's Capitalist Development (Volume II)*. Beijing: People's Publishing House, 1993: 319, 320, B Chart 4 and B Chart 5.

million bags.① Despite the fast growth rate of mechanized flour, share of hand-made flour was still dominant at 81.60% of total flour output.

Chart 5-7 Production situation of flour in 1913 and 1936

Unit: 10,000 bags

category	1913	percentage in total flour output (%)	1936	percentage in total flour output (%)
mechanized flour mills	4,702	10.05	12,322	18.40
Chinese national capital	2,036	4.35	10,917	16.30
foreign capital	2,666	5.70	1,405	2.10
hand-made production	42,104	89.95	54,635	86.10
total	46,806	100.00	66,957	100.00

Source: Shanghai Municipal Foodstuff Bureau, Shanghai Municipal Industry and Commerce Administration, and Shanghai Academy of Social Sciences. *History of China's Modern Flour Industry*. Beijing: Zhonghua Book Company, 1987: 91, 94, 106, 111. Cited from Peng Nansheng. *Intermediary Economy: China's Modern Handicraft Industry Between Tradition and Modern Times (1840-1936)*: 120.

During the period between 1914 and 1936, China's industry enjoyed a relatively faster development, which resulted in some beneficial changes in the structure of foreign trade products. During this period, modern coal mining industry grew at an annual rate of more than 5%. Till the period before the War of the Chinese People's Resistance Against Japanese Aggression, coal import was very limited and its share in China's coal market decreased to about 2% then from 55% in the early 20th century. In comparison, coal export rose to 4.3 million tons in 1936 from the annual average of 1.16 million tons during the period between 1911 and 1915.② In order to meet the rapid development demand of modern industry and communications and transport industry, during this period, import value of production materials such as machines, pig iron, steel, other building hardware, chemical products, industrial dyestuff, communications equipment, liquid fuel and so on experienced an obvious increase. Statistics showed that share of production materials in import products increased to 44.5% in 1936 from 17.6% in 1910 and at

---

① Shanghai Municipal Foodstuff Bureau. *History of China's Modern Flour Industry*. Beijing: Zhonghua Book Company, 1987: 37-39.

② Lai Te. *Coal Industry in China's Economy and Society*. Beijing: Oriental Publishing House, 1991: 49, 71.

the same time share of consumption materials decreased from 82.4% to 55.5%.[1] Meanwhile, there was an increase in both the absolute value and relative value in finished products in export products; and in particular, the increase in machine finished products was more obvious. In 1913, the No. 1 cotton products and No. 2 cotton yarn in imports were as high as 182 million haikwan tael and commanded 32% in the total import value. Owing to development in the cotton spinning industry, till 1936 and before the War of the Chinese People's Resistance Against Japanese Aggression, import of cotton products and cotton yarns was only slightly more than 10 million haikwan tael and was less than 1/18 of the import value in 1913, and its share in the total import value also decreased to only 1.7%. In order to meet the demand of Chinese domestic mills, import of raw cotton increased and in 1913 such import was as high as 4.69 million dan. Meanwhile, export hardly had any increase and was 790,000 dan. In parallel, export of spun cotton rose. In 1916, China's export of spun cotton was only 13,000 dan which accounted for 5% of that year's import of cotton yarns. Later, it only took about ten years for export of cotton yarns to exceed its import. In 1931, this reached 618,000 dan and increased by nearly 47 times than in 1916. Export of cotton yarns reached its peak in 1928 and was valued at 16 million haikwan tael and was almost seven times than the 1913 export value. After World War I, especially starting in the mid-1920s, China's spun cotton export gradually took over markets in Southeastern Asia and then established itself in some countries' markets in Near East, Africa and South and Central America.[2] After 1931, owing to impact from the world economic crisis, export of cotton yarns and cotton cloth saw somewhat a decline.

III. Modernization of economy and Sino-foreign cultural integration

The country will be strong forever if people's popular feelings are followed and what is going on among the people is understood. This is where the Confucianist "people-based" ideology started. In Chinese history, although many progressive thinkers cared greatly about people's benefits and their livelihood hardships, they

---

[1] Yan Zhongping et al. *Selected Archives of Statistical Materials on Modern Chinese Economic History*: 73.

[2] Zheng Youkui. *China's Foreign Trade and Industrial Development*. Shanghai: Shanghai Social Sciences Publishing Company, 1984: 41-42.

failed to understand the essence of civil rights. People-based does not equal to civil rights. There is a material difference between the Confucianist "people-based" ideology and the civil rights value in the Western culture. Civil rights and human rights are unique concepts in the Western culture. In comparison, it is easier for Chinese culture to accept civil rights. The Confucianist "people-based" tradition is both the inexhaustible cultural source of progressive people in modern China to draw upon and also the cultural pivot of the first group of forerunners in modern China to accept the Western civil rights concept.

Since modern times in China, traditional society gradually evolved into a modern one. In this course, there was an ever-increasing pursuit for political democracy. And the word "democracy" was an imported commodity from the West to China. After defeats in the Opium Wars, some people with lofty ideals started to think about the reason that Western powers were so strong. Their conclusion was "democracy" and they believed that in order for China to shake off its oppressed status and become a power, it needs to introduce democracy. However, the Enlightenment scholars based their understanding of democracy on China's traditional cultural sources. They used "people-based" to explain "democracy" and "attention to the people" to expound "civil rights". As a result, they simply introduced the concept of "democracy" as a tool to China and married it with traditional Chinese culture to create unique democratic thoughts.

In the late 19th century, modern Chinese Enlightenment scholars led by Liang Qichao and Yan Fu gradually understood and accepted the democratic thoughts. They interpreted the Western democracy through the lens of Chinese culture and developed it on the basis of traditional Chinese culture.

First, a parliament is a collective representation of democracy. Liang Qichao believed that in order for China to survive and prosper, it must move close to parliamentary politics. He pointed out that the most severe problem in China was that governments at various levels did not communicate with one another. The ruling classes in the imperial Qing government vied for rights by defending and fighting among themselves and stopping communications; high-ranking officials even protected their own turfs and cliques by holding firmly to their powers and distributing profits among themselves; provinces fortified themselves as individual countries by protecting themselves only and failing to work together; grassroots governments worked for themselves only by failing to hear correct opinions and becoming ill-informed; senior and senile officers refused to retire and fresh blood were denied and the entire country was just like a pool of stagnant water. Liang Qichao believed that a parliament must be established in order to facilitate communications. His thinking logic was that "the weakness and strength of a country results entirely from democracy". Liang Qichao believed that a parliament is a collective representation of democracy. After a parliament was established, the top decision makers can amass the collective wisdom of the officials, the middle decision makers can listen to people's opinions and the bottom decision makers can opine their political views on how to build the country. In this way, the entire country can achieve the goal of reasons being heard and information being up to date and then "people's feelings" will guide the country's directions.

Second, replace monarchial power with civil rights. Liang Qichao proposed civil rights ideology before the Hundred Days' Reform, viewed civil rights and parliament as the two magic weapons to solve China's problems and thought that replacing monarchial power with civil rights was inevitable in history's development. He combined the human rights ideology in the West with the Gongyang Commentary's three periods and proposed the evolution rule of the period of many monarchs' ruling—the period of the only monarch ruling—the period of people ruling and demonstrated with historical evidence that this is an evolutionary process "from hardship to happiness, from evils to benevolence, from chaos to order and from brutality to civilization".[①] In the early 20th century, Liang Qichao further developed his civil rights ideology and proposed "the doctrine of new people". He introduced important concepts such as "nationals", "rights", "duty" and so on into "new people". The so-called "nationals" means people in the constitutional monarchy that enjoy democratic rights. Liang Qichao explained that "nationals are those people whose country is public property of the people. The country is composed of the people. Without these people, the country does not exist. One country's people take care of their own matters, promulgate their own laws, pursue

---

① Xiong Yuezhi. *History of Ideology in Modern China*. Shanghai: Shanghai People's Publishing House, 1986: 269.

their own benefits, and defend their own country against invasions. Without the people, the country will be humiliated and the country will perish. This is what I call the nationals".[1] The country is composed of its people. The people should be masters of their country. At the same time, he emphasized that Chinese people should become nationals that enjoy sovereignty and must establish the concepts of rights and duties and these rights and duties should be safeguarded by laws.

Third, "freedom as the form, democracy as the essence". Yan Fu relied on "On Evolution" as the theory and believed that the reason that China lagged behind the West was that China had no freedom. If China would like to catch up with and surpass the West, China must achieve individual freedom. He realized that Western democracy was nothing but a representation of freedom and the necessary means to achieve freedom. Freedom can lead the energy to achieve a country's wealth and strength and democracy can form the public spirit. And a democratic system must start with civil rights. Whether its people enjoy freedom and civil rights and whether they have autonomous capability determine the fundamentals that whether a country can implement a democratic system. Freedom must connect with a democratic system via the medium of civil rights, namely, a democratic system is a safeguard mechanism of autonomy and through autonomy political freedom can be made possible. In Yan Fu's views, autonomy is not only a buffer between people's freedom and the governmental power, but also a prerequisite for people to voluntarily obey the government. Autonomy already exists in social life that is "neither people's desires and nor other's orders". It is "related to public interest and people promise to each other and with these promises there is no difference as if they are initiated by ourselves".[2] If there is no autonomous system, territory that entirely belongs to individuals cannot be guaranteed and political freedom cannot be achieved either.

---

[1] Liang Qichao. "On the Great Trends in Modern Nationals' Competition and China's Future". *Selected Works of Liang Qichao*. Beijing: People's Literature Publishing House, 2004: 116.

[2] *Collections of Yan Fu's Works*. Beijing: Zhonghua Book Company, 1986: 1300.

Section Four Ideology of Political Independence and Economic Self-reliance

The founding of the People's Republic of China in 1949 ended its humiliating modern history and achieved its political independence. Its political independence determined its economic independence. Ever since then China has embarked on its way featured with economic development as its main goal and has made great achievements after scores of years and has formed preliminarily its own economic development path.

I. Maintaining independence and keeping the initiative and being self-reliance —International environment and choice of historical tradition

The period between 1949 and 1978 is the first period of PRC's industrialization, namely, purely relying on China's national strength to implement planned economy and preferential development of the heavy industry. In order to establish an independent industrial system and for the sake of national security, China adopted the strategy of catching up with and surpassing to preferentially develop the heavy industry and implementing high-accumulation and high-input to pursue the extension-type industrialization path that is characterized with quantity expansion.

This economic development strategy has the following characteristics: (1) its primary goal is to achieve high-speed development, (2) preferential development of heavy industry, (3) primary reliance on extension-type economic development, which means the main path to economic growth lies in increase in input of production factors, (4) start from war preparations and efficiency, speed up development of the inland and improve productivity, and (5) with the goal of establishing an independent industrial system in mind, implement import substitution.

Formation of the above economic development strategy is obviously not scientific and complete if it is simply viewed from the subjective cognition of the Chinese Communist Party and the government in the 1950s. Formation of such a strategy in the 1950s has its profound economic reasons and social background.

First, formation of this economic development strategy is indispensable from the economic development level and characteristic during the early period after the founding of PRC. In the early days of PRC, what had been left was a national economy with accumulated poverty and accumulated weakness and the bitter lessons of being bullied when China was backward. China was a country with a population of 500 million people. In terms of sheer population, China ranked first in the world; in terms of total area of the country, China ranked third in the world. However, China lagged far behind in terms of per capita national income. Just as Chairman Mao said, now what can we manufacture? We are able to make tables and chairs, tea bowls and tea pots, plant grains and also grind grains to powder and make paper. However, we are unable to make even one car, one plane, one tank and one tractor. This economic backwardness that did not match China's large country status at all was the root cause of PRC's choice of strategy of catching up with and surpassing to preferentially develop the heavy industry.

Second, formation of this economic development strategy is closely related to Soviet Union's model. As we know, success of China's democratic revolution is the result of China's learning from Soviet Union and accepting Marxism. Along the same vein, after China's success in revolution, on the question of how China can achieve industrialization China was similar to Soviet Union's contemporary situation. China could not rely on invading and plundering other countries to accumulate funds necessary for industrialization and China was facing the economic blockade and military threats imposed by the imperialists. Before Soviet Union's internal problems were "exposed" in 1955, its industrialization path was a success model of the strategy of catching up with and surpassing. The Soviet Union's path was proved by its victory during World War II and received worldwide admiration and was also the role model of the then socialism. As a result, its strategy was also a role model that China learned from in its own socialist economic construction.

Third, formation of this economic development strategy is somewhat related to the contemporary international situation. On one hand, in the early days of PRC, all the neglected tasks needed to be done and China had not recovered from the wars. In 1950, the Korean War broke out and China was dragged to this war, which led to its direct confrontation with the United States. On the other hand, after World War II, the world was divided into two camps, the socialists and the capitalists. Confrontation of these two camps resulted in the economic blockade imposed on socialist PRC by the capitalist countries. PRC needed to stand proudly in the nations of the world. Under this international environment, China could only rely on itself to develop its own economy and strengthen its national defense. As a result, China decided to adopt its basic guideline of maintaining independence and keeping the initiative to develop its economy and adopt the basic economic policy of preferentially developing the heavy industry and establishing the soonest possible an independent industrial system, strengthening its national defense power and safeguarding its national security.

Fourth, constraints such as China's economic development level and international environment and so on made PRC to be in the closed development which was independent from the world economic cycle for 28 years. Formation of the strategy of maintaining independence and keeping the initiative and being self-reliance, if analyzed from the perspective of ideology and culture, has also the support of traditional Chinese cultural background. To some extent, it is return of the traditional culture of the great unification of the Chinese nation formed by China's long history and culture and its resource endowment. China's independent development during a certain period is possible by relying on the intelligence and wisdom of the Chinese nation and its rich resources.

In summary from the above, post-1949 industrialization in China not only started from the bitter lessons of the imperialist invasions and oppression of China owing to China's backwardness in the past one hundred years or so, but also proceeded against the international backdrop of the confrontations between the two camps of the socialist countries and capitalist countries in the world and their fierce economic competition in economy. As a result, it is not strange that the Chinese Communist Party and the Chinese people put high-speed development as the first prerequisite to economic system and policy choice.

Formation of the economic development strategy in the 1950s can be marked as "the first Five-Year Plan". This strategy can be simply summarized as: primarily rely on accumulated construction funds inside China; start from establishment and preferential development of the heavy industry and high-speed development of the national economy; implement "import substitution" strategy, import the production materials for heavy industry development through export of some quantity of primary products and light-industry products such as agricultural products, mining products and so on and gradually replace the imports with the production materials manufactured in China; improve the distorted situation of extremely unreasonable industrial layout and the extremely unbalanced regional economic development; with the establishment and preferential development of the heavy industry, gradually equip agriculture, light industry and other industrial sectors with the production materials manufactured by the heavy industry; and with the development of the heavy industry, light industry, agriculture and other industrial sectors, gradually establish an independent and complete industrial system and the national economy system, and gradually improve people's life.

II. Maintaining independence and keeping the initiative and being self-reliance is the basis of China's economic development.

During the 29 years from the founding of the People's Republic of China to the Third Plenary Session of the 11th National Conference of the CPC, in accordance with the strategic economic development goals designed by the CPC Central Committee, all the Chinese people worked very hard and made the undeniable achievements in socialist economic development: relatively faster development in the total economic output level; marked improvement in people's living standards; increase in the agricultural production rate provided a forceful safeguard for the industrialization process; the national economic structure tended to be more reasonable; and a relatively large increase in the national defense and scientific and technological strength.

a. The economy experienced an enormous growth.

As regards the economic development during the period from 1949 till 1978, except the big economic decline during the period between 1959 and 1962 (i.e., the second Five-Year Plan) as a result of the Great Leap Forward, all the indicators in Chinese economy had experienced a very fast development. Till 1977, mainland China had joined Chinese Taipei and other 26 regions and countries to be listed in the group of growth rate of 4% to 6% and became one of the fastest-developing economies in the world. As far as the total economic output is concerned, the total gross domestic product during the period between 1952 and 1978 grew from RMB 67.9 billion to RMB 362.41 billion, with an annual growth rate of 6.1%. Very few of the developed and underdeveloped capitalist countries in the world could achieve this long-term average annual economic growth indicator. Calculated with unchangeable prices, in 1952, China's per capita gross domestic product was RMB 119; and in 1978, this number reached RMB 379. In 1952, the balance of the savings by the urban and rural people was RMB 860 million, and in 1978 this number was RMB 21.06 billion. People's consumption level saw a great increase; in 1952, average per capita consumption was only RMB 80, while in 1980, this number reached RMB 184. The living standard of the urban and rural people improved greatly and the comprehensive national power had a relative great increase.

In comparison with India that had similar national conditions to those in China, China's achievements made between 1949 to the period before the reform and opening up were even more marked. The annual average growth rate in India's agriculture from 1950 to 1956 was 2.5%, but this indicator in China from 1953 to 1979 was 3.4%. The annual average growth rate in India's industry from 1949 to 1978 was 6%, but this indicator in China from 1953 to 1979 was 11.1%. The founding of PRC government was the root cause for this great achievement. Just owing to the forceful leadership and administration of the new government, China's savings rate rose quickly from about 5% to about 30% and most of these funds were used in economic construction and played an important role.

b. Agricultural production conditions had improved greatly and the industrial foundation necessary for economic development was initially established.

During the period between 1952 and 1978, China's agricultural production conditions had a relatively great improvement. After the founding of PRC, land returned to the tillers all over China. After establishment of cooperatives and communalization, collective efforts in the expansive countryside were utilized to construct irrigation facilities during the winter slack seasons all over China to form a network of agricultural field irrigation construction that enabled the countryside and agricultural production and living conditions to improve greatly. The irrigable area in 1952 was 19.959 million hectares. The irrigable area in 1978 reached 44.965

million hectares. Large plots of wasteland in Northeastern China, and Northwestern China (Xinjiang) were turned to arable land. All these efforts laid a solid foundation for the agricultural growth. The total mechanical power in agriculture rose sharply from 118,000 kilowatt in 1952 to 8.84 million kilowatt in 1978. During this period, power consumption rose by over 1,000 times. The total arable area in 1949 for grains and cotton was 104 million hectares. Till 1976, this number reached 142 million hectares. Just owing to the improved conditions in agricultural production, increase in agricultural production rate allowed China's grain output to rise from 163.92 million tons in 1952 to 304.77 million tons in 1978 despite certain decline in China's arable land area. Feeding of a quarter of the world population was solved basically, which was a wonder in human history. While construction of agricultural infrastructure improved the production conditions, it also made it possible to alleviate the damage brought by natural disasters. The affected areas during 1972, 1978 and 1980 drought and flood disasters were 17.20 million hectares, 21.80 hectares and 22.30 million hectares respectively. It is hard to estimate the value of agricultural infrastructure constructed and its significance is also far-reaching. A Nobel laureate and American econometric historian Robert William Fogel once demonstrated that if in the late 19th century the US spent more money to construct ditches and tunnels and excavate canals, its economy would have developed more quickly. In addition, increase in agricultural products output and agricultural development also provided ample raw materials for industrial manufacture.

During the early days of PRC, China's industrial foundation was very weak. In 1949, industrial output value's percentage in the total economic value was very small and China's industrial system was not completely constructed for a long time. The idea of "building China with industry" or "industry as the foundation and commerce as the guideline" was proposed by some progressive thinkers in the 19th century. Numerous revolutionary forerunners and industrialists made all sorts of attempts. However, in China, "only after 1949 when China achieved unification and stability could the government have made up its mind to devote itself to developing the economy and was able to amass the necessary resources for this goal", this was made possible. After the founding of PRC, under the guidance of the strategy of "preferential development of the heavy industry", industry had a rapid development.

During the 26 years between 1952 and 1978, the total industrial output rose from RMB 11.98 billion in 1952 to RMB 160.7 billion in 1978, an increase of nearly 13 times. Its share in the gross domestic product increased from 17.55% in 1952 to 44.3% in 1978, a hike of nearly 27 percentage points. In the early days of the industrialization, England saw its industrial share increase by 11% during the period between 1801 and 1841; Japan saw an increase of only 22% during the periods between 1878 and 1882 and between 1923 and 1924. Within a short period of time, China's industrialization level had a relatively faster growth. In addition, basic industries such as coal, petroleum, machinery, chemicals and so on were established in the coastal and major cities. After the 1960s, in order to make war preparations, the Third Front construction was made to build basic industry such as heavy and chemical industry in the inland. Meanwhile, light industry also enjoyed relative growth, which laid a preliminary industrial foundation for regional layout for industrialization and industrialization materialization. An independent and relatively complete industrial system was about to emerge. Although tertiary industry developed relatively slowly, its share in the gross domestic product also saw a relatively greater growth and a relatively reasonable national economic system was initially established.

c. National defense power was enhanced tremendously and scientific and technological level was lifted greatly.

Just before and after the founding of PRC, a group of scientists with great achievements returned from overseas to China to participate in its economic construction. In order for China to achieve modernization, China had drafted the 1956-1967 science and technology development plan and started its 12-year process of key science and technology program. In June, 1956, China's first experimental atomic reactor started to operate; meanwhile, the first cyclotron was constructed. On November 28, 1956, the first ocean-going freighter that was designed by Soviet Union and built by China "Yuejin" with a displacement of 22,100 tons proceeded down the river. In the early 1960s, although Sino-Soviet relations deteriorated and Soviet specialists withdrew from China, Chinese scientists relied on their own efforts to independently complete 257 scientific research projects. On October 10, 1964, the first atomic bomb that China independently designed and built was detonated successfully. Following this success were the successful testing of China's first hydrogen bomb, and successful launching of China's first man-made satellite. China's research and testing of the atomic and hydrogen bombs and satellites were completed successfully. All this proved that China's science and technology had a huge lift and China's national defense power was extremely increased.

In general, the Chinese government fully utilized the national power and conducted a large-scale economic construction. This is something that various governments before 1949 were impossible or unable to accomplish. China's economic construction was an epoch-making and unprecedented event in Chinese history.

However, PRC was in a different world situation compared with old China before the Opium Wars. After the two world wars, science and technology in the West had achieved a galloping development. Under the high material civilization in the capitalist economy, its social system continues to be perfected and shows a robust vitality. However, as China was isolated from the West, China was lagging behind the developed countries in the world in its science and technology, productivity level, economic management, social welfare and so on. China's next round of opening up was a historical trend.

Chapter Six   Globalization of Cultures Moving toward Globalization of Economies

Section One   Influence of Cultural Dissemination and Globalization of Cultures on China

Globalization of economies is one of the main characteristics of the 20th century. With the increasing deepening of globalization of economies, it is predictable that globalization of cultures will be one of the main characteristics of the 21st century. In the course of the globalization of economies, many economic activities are inseparable from or closely connected with cultures. Cultures, as the social superstructure, inevitably reflect changes in the society and economy and changes and developments in economy will also impact cultures so as to cause corresponding changes to development in cultures. As a result, globalization of economies will no doubt bring globalization of cultures and cultural openness will further promote globalization of economies. What needs to be emphasized is that in the course of our continued absorption of advanced Western civilization, Chinese civilization has never lost its own independence status. At present and in the future, Chinese civilization should not and will not vanish in the global trends but instead it will develop in a healthier and more mature manner in its collision and combination with other cultures.

I. Areas under impact of globalization of cultures

Globalization of cultures brings crisis for national cultures but it also brings opportunities for them. We should not simply treat conflict with weak cultures as a result of invasion of national cultures by strong cultures. Human being's cultures have always been diversified. But diversity does not preclude mutual learning, absorption, loaning and even reform among national cultures in the world. Development in modern mass media technologies and exchange means greatly elevates speed of collision and intensity of mutual influence among global cultures. Different cultures need to be complemented and isolated cultures are unimaginable and singular cultures are also unimaginable. As a result, what comes with globalization of economies is neither globalization of cultures nor civilization conflicts but instead prosperity of diversified cultures. Emergence and establishment of this new type of cultural ecology is an important indicator of a higher stage of human being's evolution.

Globalization has involved all the countries and their people in the world in the course of modernization. In an open world, any country and people cannot exist in isolation with the outside world. Exchanges and blending of economy and trade and interpersonal exchanges will doubtlessly bring mutual influence in aspects such as social customs, ways of thinking, values and so on. In other words, without loaning and absorbing advanced cultures from other countries or peoples, one country or people will be swept outside the world development process and will find them difficult to further develop. Therefore, we should welcome more extensive and deeper cultural exchanges that are brought with globalization of economies. History has proven that Chinese civilization is good at absorbing outside civilization to enrich itself. Since late Ming Dynasty, Western civilization was gradually introduced to China. After the Opium Wars, Western civilization had bombarded China and influenced China's historical process for more than one hundred years. With the deepening of China's reform and opening up to the outside world, it is even more inevitable for China to stand aloof from globalization of cultures. Areas of its influence on China will be broadening. We would like to give the following examples.

a. Information area

Strictly speaking, since World War II, "information revolution" with information technology at its core has lifted the curtain of information society and knowledge age. Capital and labor, as the main foundation of economic development, have been dispelled by knowledge and information and "knowledge is power" has replaced the material productivity. During this process, cultural exchanges have become closer and cultural exchanges and cooperation have intensified mutual understanding of people. In particular, after collapse of the Soviet Union and end of the Cold War, cultural exchanges have indeed made countries without boundaries.

If we can say that globalization of cultures and globalization of economies are twins, the information technology revolution that has changed human being's way of life in the 21st century has resulted in the speedy arrival of globalization of mass media. In a certain sense, globalization of cultures is a result of globalization of economies and a direct result of technology revolution and globalization of mass media. The direct and obvious function of information revolution lies in: it not only changes tools of telecommunications and means of mass media, but also initiates a new age of cultural dissemination and exchanges. What is more important is that it enriches the cultural connotations, and presents a scene of globalization of cultures for cultural dissemination and exchanges. Just as some scholars believe, among the various representations of globalization, nothing is more important than international brands, mass cultural idols as well as live coverage of major events by satellites to millions of people all over the continents that are so direct, extensive and penetrating. With the rapid development of modern telecommunications, broadcasting and communications infrastructure, cultural exchanges have reached an unprecedented degree of global coverage of areas and quantity of exchanges. The Chinese people have never before than nowadays been able to obtain the latest information in the world with such fastest speed and broadest horizons and have never before independently analyzed world changes based on our "own" information obtained and have never before compared differences among cultural ways of the world civilization and have never before felt impact by modern civilization on traditional ways of life in such an intense manner. Country's administrators are becoming more and more cognizant of the importance of transparence, objectiveness and fairness in the information age and that isolated, uniform and planned information feeding way is no longer possible to exist effectively. Probably we can say that owing to highly advanced information technology, the form of globalization that people feel and experience most directly is globalization of cultures.

b. Corporate culture

In the most recent 20 years or so, it is fair to say that Chinese enterprises have undergone revolutionary and profound changes. From marketing to management and then to product design and so on, they are deeply impacted and heavily influenced by corporate culture of the world developed countries and these enterprises have gradually shaped their corporate cultures that are full of variety and in line with international ideas. Among them, the most important indicator is completion of the shift from mandatory plan to independent and innovative and gradual acknowledgement of corporate culture with a people-based idea core. In another development, China's admission to World Trade Organization is not simply openness among the markets, but also a gradual reform of its entire economic system in an in-depth sense. That is to change the top-side-down economic management mode with mandatory administrative plans that many Chinese enterprises were accustomed to since the founding of PRC to an economic management mode that is oriented by market economy rules. In this economic management mode, decision makers in enterprises should have a clear mind and comprehensive understanding of the market and design development plans in strict compliance with market economy rules and discard traditional work thinking and conventional working methods and weed through the old to bring forth the new in marketing ideas, enterprise management, conduction mechanism and so on. The change in enterprises from a simplified and politicalized human resources management to a "cultural" management with ever enriching connotations, especially the establishment of people-based ideas, is closely related to the enormous shock wave from globalization of cultures. More and more enterprises have realized that human resources are the driving force behind their business development and employers should always put human resources first and emphasize people-based, full respect for them, correct tapping of them so as to make these enterprises prosper. A good corporate culture will no doubt include the following: (1) respect all talented people, (2) care about all things on talented people, (3) a complete and candid two-way communication, (4) reward and praise all efforts and contributions, (5) continuous training and development and create opportunities for talented people, and (6) continuous development of enterprises on the base of corporate spirit with high cohesion.

  Previously, those elite talented people who were trained in Western management ideas in large multinational corporations/enterprises have found their most disturbing discord with Chinese domestic enterprises is that they have mastered a complete set of modern and excellent management modes but they were not allowed to go one step beyond the limit to put their new management modes into practice. They hope to find new challenges and more space for their self-realization. Now more and more Chinese domestic enterprises have realized this issue. Talented people have found more and more space for their skills and the "official" nature of these Chinese domestic enterprises is fading away and "people-based" nature is increasing.

c. Values

Promotion of globalization of cultures has challenged the traditional values with increasing influence over time. Consumption culture's rise and popular culture's popularity have strongly impacted people's traditional values and caused new changes to Chinese people's way of life, consumption habits and aesthetic taste.

Nowadays, Chinese people's consumption is not entirely for the use value of the commodities bought; not a small number of people have focused on other added and virtual values such as payment capability, social status, emotional embodiment and so on. People's consumption target is usually not the commodities themselves, instead what they value is personal taste, style, potential energy or latent energy that the advertisements represent and hint. This type of aesthetic taste is again rendered by mass media to become vogue and popular, which not only determines sale trends in the market but also guides manufacturers' choice and then influences way of life for people in the modern society and choice of their aesthetic taste. This phenomenon that personal taste, style and latent energy provided by product packaging and product advertising determine product value and manufacture and sales process has become modern consumption society's leading culture form and has induced people to be similar in their aesthetic taste, way of life as well as values.

Advanced and new mass media technologies especially emergence of international mass media tycoons have integrated global cultural exchanges. As a result, current cultural exchanges have far exceeded previous cultural exchanges in terms of scope, intensity, speed as well as diversity and are unprecedented. In comparison, importance of national culture and cultural recognition and its system has no doubt been discounted. The contemporary Chinese youth's appreciation and recognition of European, American, Japanese and Korean popular cultures simply proves this point.

In another development, as regards values, under the background of globalization, every union or country must rely as a prerequisite on other union or country's security for its own existence in terms of economic resources, ecological environment and territorial security. Their relationship must be established on a culture that is closely connected internally and with mutually constructed factors—mutually interdependent. In other words, today's human activities have been connected as a mutually interactive entirety. This requires that people's way of behavior and mode of thinking must break away from that fighting symbiotic mode of binary opposition and either A or B and discard that type of "zero sum" game rule from the mode of thinking and adopt instead a "win-win" rule.

In the past, Chinese and Western values were two cultural models of different quality. The two cultures' opposition is very obvious. For example, Chinese traditional values emphasize implicitness and courtesy while Western culture stresses directness, openness and self-recognition. Under the influence of globalization of cultures, more and more cultures have embarked on the path of mutual tolerance and blending. The concept of "agree to disagree" is fast taking root. People of different nationalities and countries have different cultures and values. As long as they do not oppose each other they will add new colors and energy to the modern world. Diversity is something indispensable even for a moment for the large system of human beings and the specific people that live and work in this large system.

d. Festival culture

Globalization of cultures has brought unprecedented impact and influence on festival culture of the Chinese people. Whether people approve or disapprove it, more and more foreign festivals such as Valentine's Day, Mother's Day, April Fool's Day, Halloween and so on have penetrated the Chinese society, especially Chinese young people's life. Some people predicted with worries that popularity of Western festivals would endanger our own traditional festivals and space of culture. However, if we pin our hope of saving our own culture on resisting and isolating foreign cultures, will this be viewed as weak and powerless? One partial reason that foreign festivals such as Christmas can take root in China or even become mainstay festivals is difference in spirit between Chinese and foreign festivals. In the Eastern and Chinese culture, implicitness and reservedness are the mainstay spirit. But Western festivals emphasize more on humanistic sentiment and childish plot in addition to commemoration and memorial just as Valentine's Day, April Fool's Day, Christmas and so on. These festivals fit more nicely Chinese people's pursuit of leisure after more than 20 years' reform and opening up to the outside world. Some people are nervous about popularity of foreign festivals in China and its impact on our national festival culture. Although this national suffering consciousness is very valuable, those people nevertheless have groundless worries or anxieties. Eastern and Western festivals would not probably have such either A or B conflicts. Moreover, as far as Chinese people's sentiment of the falling leaves settling on the roots is concerned, status of Spring Festival is absolutely well respected and cannot be shaken loose. The less popularity of major ancient Chinese festivals such as Lantern Festival and Mid-Autumn Festival is due to the fact that the Chinese government has played a major role. Over the dynasties, it was a topside-down transmission for worshipping Confucianism and Buddhism. It needs to be taken into account whether the government and officials emphasize these festivals has an influence on Chinese people's negligence of Chinese national festivals.

Although cultural arena is not a direct representation of a country's comprehensive power, it relates to a nation's moral ideal, values and ideology and consists of a country's "belief system" and provides legality for social actions. Culture plays an important construction role in forming population's uniform will, establishing collective goals and achieving goals. Therefore, considering from a country's benefits and long-term development plan, we must actively participate in international cultural activities just as we do in international economic competition and adhere to our own cultural position, strengthen international cultural exchanges and cooperation, learn from others' strong points to offset our own weakness, promote changing any traditional values that obstruct social development so as to further develop the excellent culture of the Chinese nation.

II. Influence mechanism of globalization of cultures

Globalization of cultures means all cultures in the world in various forms flow globally under mutual influence of "blending" and "inequality". Its influence mechanism should be mutual. Cultures of the countries and nations gradually formed an exchange mechanism that has complementary advantages and ever-changing concepts in the course of mutual influence and mutual penetration. This is a very complex process. The process of globalization of cultures has formed "globalized cultures", which promotes the ever-progressing of human civilization.

First, globalization of cultures is not one type of culture's expansion and monopoly as Americanization or Sinification that people are concerned about; it is not a main culture in the world such as "Confucianism" or "Western culture". Instead it is an integration of all cultures. In today's world, various groups of cultures exist. In the course of world blending, they inevitably conflict with one another so as to safeguard their own characteristics, self-affirmation and self-recognition. These contradiction and conflicts do not represent confrontation between two certain cultures and do not mean in the course of globalization the eventual formation of one singular world culture. If viewed from cultures, globalization represents one type of process of mutual transmission and mutual blending of inhomogeneous cultures, namely, a process of formation of one rich, vivid and diversified global culture. This is a two-way movement process that is composed of two vectors of global cultures' unity and national cultures' diversity and is ever-reciprocating. As far as every nation and country is concerned, here is a question on correct handling of the relationship between global cultures' unity and national cultures' diversity and the key is to maintain dynamic balance between the two.

Second, globalization of cultures is not a phenomenon established on the basis of land territorial division but instead a cultural process established on cultural main body—human beings. A famous British historian Arnold Joseph Toynbee proposed his theory of "challenge-and-response" in order to explain emergence and development of cultures of the nations in the world. This theory holds that every nation's culture is just a response to the challenge of the creation environment this nation faced. That is to say that every nation's living environment plays an important role in its culture's creation and development. We should realize that on one hand owing to differences in geographical living environment and national development history, cultural differences exist among different regions and different nations and on the other hand owing to ever progressive society and formation of the global village, people in different nations and countries and different territories are able to have the same cultural views. Just owing to existence of mutual differences and interdependence relationship, human being's divine nature and general human nature are the uniform cultural ideas that maintain human being's uniformity. An example is that "democracy" and "freedom" are accepted globally. As a result, seeking common ground while maintaining differences and agreeing to disagree become the most important principles in influence mechanism in globalization of cultures.

Third, globalization of cultures is a dynamic fluidity instead of a static cultural form. It is primarily represented by the mutual combination among individual cultural groups in the world in terms of personnel, technology, capital and ideology. Among this fluidity, what people care most is penetration of ideology. This global ideology fluidity is not a simple input and output of ideas. Instead it must be achieved by way of "cross-culture" translation. For example, ways of advertising and tastes offered in China by Pizza Hut and McDonald's are more Chinese.

Fourth, globalization of cultures does not negate differences between strong cultures and weak cultures in the world and does not ignore confrontation in cultures between developed countries and developing countries. It relies on diverse and multiple combination forms caused by multidirectional cultural fluidity to bring about imperceptible influence. Different ways of fluidity lead to different cultural presence locations. In the course of this mutual exchanges, status of various cultures is equal. What is different is that the degree of communication capacities and degree of receptivity of nation states determine the degree and scope of such influence. For example, with the deepening of "cultural commercialization", influence scope of cultures of various large commercial countries is increasing with the increase of shares of their products in the world market. However, the goal of global cultural promotion lies in fully combining and absorbing local cultural strengths and creating a harmonious situation in the course of cultural exchange.[1]

III. Globalization of cultures and its relationship with China's economic development

Globalization of cultures that comes with globalization of economies has been on the horizon. As the relationship between today's world cultures and its economies is becoming closer, and even some cultural disseminations themselves are economic acts, as a result, globalization of cultures will inevitably have a very important impact on China's economic development.

a. Globalization of cultures has brought new energy to China's economic development.

Nowadays, globalization of world economies is an inevitable outcome of advanced development of human society's productivity and world exchange. As an objective natural history process, it keeps showing its characteristic of surpassing nation-states' boundaries with passing of time. Globalization of economies is an outcome of new scientific and technological revolution in the 20th century. The new scientific and technological revolution with electronic information technology at its core has created a "magic power" that can almost be omnipotent in human being's conquering and reforming of the nature. With new scientific and technological revolution as its power and foundation, globalization of economies has completely broken the natural and social boundaries among various countries and has expanded this type of unlimited power of creativity to a global scope. In the course of increasingly expanded globalization of economies, its new management ideas, new economic development models, new values thinking cores and so on are actually rapidly disseminated mostly by globalization of cultures. These hormones in new ideology and culture have extremely changed our views of the world and changed our ways of thinking and behavior and then infused new energy factors into China's economic development.

b. Globalization of cultures has provided China's economic system reform with new factors.

---

[1] Jiang Hua. "On the Six Challenges of Globalization to China's Culture". *Journal of China University of Petroleum*, March, 2002.

Objectively, globalization of economies requires that China must expand opening up to the outside world and participate fully in international competition and cooperation. Especially after China's admission to the World Trade Organization, China's economic system reform not only has to satisfy our demand of domestic economic and social development, but also has to comply with requirements of the legal system of the WTO. It needs to adapt to the development and changes of globalization of economies, participate in international competition and cooperation under condition of freedom of multilateral trade, and achieve beneficial operation. Otherwise, it will probably lose the opportunity to develop with the world in tandem. Meanwhile, harmony, balance and stability in economic and social development between China and the world must be achieved. New challenges are raised in China's efforts in transforming its government administration functions, improving management capabilities, perfecting economic and legal system, and standardizing governmental administration process. Currently, China is very much in need of the experience in handling international affairs and high-caliber professionals in this area, factors and conditions in risk aversion mechanism, political and cultural support and so on. In particular, sharp contrasts exist between huge risks hidden in future development in global economy, environment, and society and China's capabilities in meeting these challenges. Globalization of cultures has no doubt provided us with various facilities in easily and comfortably grasping the latest economic management knowledge in the world in a speedy manner and extensively exchanging and studying them. This will make fundamental factors in our economic system development reform richer.

c. Globalization of cultures has brought new forms to Chinese people's economic life.

Globalization of economies primarily influences directly and fully in-depth development in our economy and society through market economy mechanism. Foundation of globalization of economies is globalization of world market. In accordance with freedom of competition principle, world market spontaneously regulates relationship between countries' economic development and world economy. Globalization of economies is not only globalization of material civilization but also globalization of spiritual civilization. Globalization of economies has brought us not only advanced material civilization in today's world but also advanced spiritual civilization (of course, including negative cultural products; the key is our own capabilities in identifying, absorbing and attracting them). Influence of advanced spiritual civilization on economy has brought generalization in international exchanges and internationalization of ways of life. Since reform and opening up to the outside world, through various types of international exchanges, the Chinese people have formed increasingly closer economic and social connections with people in the world. Both in its width and depth, this has become very extensive. Public way of life in our society also shows a trend to constantly become more international and global.

d. Globalization of cultures has brought new challenges to China's mass media.

Composition of a modern society primarily has three aspects: democratic politics, market economy and mass media. In modern society construction, mass media has played one of the three most important roles, which indicates its significance. As Chinese society now becomes more and more economized, quite a number of mass media have indeed become part of the market economy. It admits of no doubt that relationship between mass media and globalization of cultures is closer. Influence of globalization of cultures on mass media is omnipresent and brings both challenges and opportunities. The WTO specifically stipulates that its members shall abide by rules in their host countries and follow principle of negotiations when they conduct non-goods trades (service industry and intellectual property rights). In their admission agreements to join the WTO applicant members shall pledge in a timetable on when to open up a certain industry, and degree of such opening up. In China's agreement signed with the WTO there was no mention on media industry. The WTO acknowledges that within 15 years China is a non-market-economy country and it is up to China in its guidelines and policies to decide whether to open up its media industry and degree of such opening up. Despite this fact, China's admission agreement with the WTO has indirect stipulations on its media industry. For example, opening up of the retail industry three years after China's admission to the WTO, there would be impact on metropolitan advertising with commodity retail industry advertising as its main income. In addition, tariffs on paper products would be reduced. Since 2005, implementation of such pledges such as zero tariffs on all information technology products and so on would impact China's media industry. China conditionally pledged to open up its public telecommunications industry. In telecommunications industry, large foreign enterprise groups must enter China in large numbers and through their control of online communication of information they would have a significant impact on the current media industry. Moreover, we also allowed extensive opening up of banking, insurance and transport industry and pledged to open up various industries in repair and maintenance, storage and warehouse and advertising. As various service industries have similarities in their business, and we have allowed foreign investors to establish cultural communication companies and advertising companies in China, we would certainly not restrict their cultural communication and advertising business that target media. In this way, they may use various kinds of legal acts to actually integrate with media industry.

China's opening up of its telecommunications and advertising industry would promote significant changes in development in China's media forms and media capital. If we treat telecommunications and advertising as the two edge points in China's media, these significant changes would happen in an expansive area between these two points. With arrival of digitalization age, information in any forms, after digitalization process, would be integrated into uniform digital information. This would break existing barriers among various kinds of media and promote integration of these media. Technological advancements, especially in continued digitalization of telecommunications network, advancements in video compression technology, application of optical fibers and new-generation radio technology and so on, not only expand new productivity but also reduce entry barriers by other industries into telecommunications services. As a new productivity, this would inevitably impact old production relationship. As a result, it would be likely for different industries such as telecommunications, media, computer and so on to take their own paths toward integration.

In summary, globalization of cultures has the following influence on China's media: First, globalization will promote a new media form in China's media and this new media form's characteristics are: maintain its personality, dilute its edges, and mutual blending; second, globalization will promote a new operation mechanism in China's media and this mechanism's characteristics are: diversified business, market operation, and economies of scale; third, globalization will promote a new management thinking in China's media and this management thinking's characteristics are cross-industry, cross-region, cross-media and breaking monopoly.

In general, influence of cultural communications and globalization of cultures on China is multifaceted and omnidirectional. Direction of influence is bidirectional interaction between international and domestic. Globalization has direct influence on China's economic and social development and China's economic and social development also has positive influence on stable development in international society. In its influence content, this bidirectional interaction is an integration development status that features cross-penetration among economy, politics and culture, transformation among themselves and comprehensive expansion. Globalization directly promotes integration among various countries' economies, politics and cultures, which is not only integrated development in economies, politics and cultures among countries, but also integrated development of one country's internal economy, politics and culture. Culturally, civilization conflicts co-exist with cultural integration. Chinese culture and Western culture are still in the process of blending. Globalization's influence on China's economy and society is both functional and structural and is a process of entire interaction of a structural function relationship or standardization development. The general representation is with market adjustment as its basis, with governmental control as its core and with cultural integration as its attribution and is to make relationship between globalization and China's economy and society gradually attain standardization development pattern. The influence trend is alternating development of mutual blending and maintaining characteristics. Globalization's influence on China's stability in its politics, economy and society is an objective and real existence that is independent from people's will. As a result, it is an inevitable choice to take a new stand to promote reforms, expand opening up and maintain sustainable and stable development so as to tackle various challenges that globalization brings about. This is a mutual interaction of "impact-reaction" and its movement orbit and outcome are in general a process of "absorption-blending-maintaining characteristics" and constant cyclic development toward infinity.

Under globalization of economies, development in world economy, politics and culture is already very closely connected to become an integrated development process. Each country's economy, politics and culture have already become an organic integrity that cannot be separated from world economy, politics and culture. As a result, in order to achieve synchronous development of Chinese society with the world, we must fully utilize the opportunities that globalization of economies and globalization of cultures have brought, with economic development as its basis, with political civilization as its core and with cultural exchanges as its link, connect with all the parties concerned and interact with them and transform interchangeably to achieve a comprehensive and coordinated development in economy, politics and culture.

Section Two Empirical Analysis of Reform and Opening up to the Outside World and Influence of Globalization of Cultures

I. Demonstration of reform and opening up to the outside world being accompanied with foreign cultural influence

China's economic opening up and cultural opening up are mutually blended to absorb the beneficial elements from foreign cultures, which has played an important role in the miraculous rise of China's economy over the 20 years or so since reform and opening up to the outside world. Since the late1970s China's opening up has gradually exceeded the economic realm and shown new scenes in such areas as politics, culture and so on. In such cultural surface structure areas as costume, social life, entertainment and so on, jeans hit, disco hit, sightseeing hit and so on appeared. In such deep structure areas as normative culture, value culture and so on, modern Western theories such as control theory, system theory, information theory and existentialist ethics and social teachings and ideological trend of romanticism of the Frankfurt School have caused many Chinese people especially young people to think about. In the economic area, nowadays a great majority of the Chinese entrepreneurs have attached great significance to the study and absorption of commercial ideas from their international counterparts, and the management standards and accounting systems that domestic enterprises have adopted have been drawing close to international standards at an extremely high speed. During the past 20 years that China has adopted reform and opening up to the outside world, the traditional culture of this ancient civilized country with a history of over several thousand years has been in conflicts and blending with contemporary Western culture in multiple directions. China's wonderful new birth journey, based on in-depth reforms and self-perfection, has benefited from the support of global capital, technology, management expertise and resources and actively adapted itself to blending and absorption of Sino-foreign cultures. This has resulted in the speedy rise of China's comprehensive national strength in its economy and has become the focus of the world attention.

Analyzed from contemporary economic development locus, modern economy is a knowledge economy with marriage between "high technology" and "high culture" but it is more of a highly "humanistic" economy. From product design to manufacture flow design, from corporate strategic management to corporate brand management, from humanistic service to customer's needs to construction of corporate teamwork spirit, all these are full of modern humanistic spirit. Traditional "liberal arts" has penetrated all aspects of economic life through "humanistic design". Now it is very hard to find products without cultural indicators, sales without assistance of cultural influence and consumption without experience of cultural significance. In this sense, modern economy has based itself on culture to a great extent and with the benefit of cultural spread to form globalization of economies.

Foreign cultural influence in Tianjin's foreign-invested enterprises is very marked. For example, a Japanese investor, Tianjin Mitsumi Electric Co., Ltd., is a well-known manufactory of computer and telecommunications peripheral equipment. Its main products are satellite receivers, cellular phone chargers and so on that enjoy a very high market share both in Chinese and Japanese markets. Thirteen years ago when this company started to invest in Tianjin, it brought to China its strict and detailed performance evaluation method of Japanese style. At first, many of its employees in Tianjin found this method hard to adapt to. The company adopted the practice of sending its key employees overseas for rotation training and has accumulatively trained more than 200 person-times. Through this type of international training, its local employees gradually adapted to its strict corporate evaluation method and the company has found continued strengthening of its various work flow management both in its strict and detailed degrees. Its corporate management level has seen constant improvement. Internally, the company has established a cultural spirit of pursuit of quality and the attitude of "no detail is overlooked". The company has seen its corporate management level constantly improving and its product quality winning extensive market recognition. In the recent years, its annual sales revenue has reached over USD 200 million.

The guideline that Tianjin Mitsumi Electric Co., Ltd. adopted to establish the cultural construction is primarily to combine the best parts on moral sentiment in the Japanese culture and Chinese culture. The company proposes an idea of cultural construction that centers on people and believes that its most fundamental product is not electronic products but people with lofty moral sentiment. Only people with noble minds are able to manufacture the best products. To its employees, the company is not only a place to earn their livelihood, but also an environment that can chasten and develop them. The company has drafted a year-long education and training plan for implementation and holds a great number of various types of competitive and entertaining activities as well as a variety of arts festivals, photo shows, Chinese calligraphy exhibitions and theatrical performances. In order for more employees to be involved for training purposes, these events are sponsored in rotation by the dozen or so departments in the company. Its trade union and comprehensive department assist these departments with those events so that departmental ordinary and key employees are practically trained from a corporate perspective. In order to create a family environment, every year the company hosts sightseeing tours for all the employees. Every time scores of high-class coaches are arranged for these tours with the assistance from the governmental traffic control department. Its vast fleet is the most impressive one and a legend in its development area.

While managers at Tianjin Mitsumi Electric Co., Ltd. have been responsible for its investors and shareholders, it attaches more significance to its employees and does not advocate an image of strict internal hierarchy system that some foreign-invested enterprises have adopted. Instead it makes its best efforts in creating internally one cultural atmosphere that is responsible for its employees by advocating close and harmonious relationship between its superiors and their subordinates and encouraging its employees to suggest different opinions to their superiors. A bottom to top method is used in its performance evaluation for its employees. The company has attached great importance to giving full play to the initiative of self-management of its employees. It requires that all employees wear corporate uniforms. The general manager appointed by the Japanese party insists on having meals inside the employee cafeteria with Chinese employees so as to be close and communicative with them. For those employees that are unfit for their positions, the company never terminates them easily. The company does not adopt to "leverage the assets of other cultures" and to "get rid of employees". Instead, the company makes its best efforts in assigning those employees to more suitable positions based on education and training. After more than ten years of hard work, Tianjin Mitsumi Electric Co., Ltd. has formed a family-style relationship internally. Its employees' identification and sense of belonging continue to increase, which has played a very significant role in stimulating their creativity and responsibility and has become an important driving force for this successful company over time.

Practice of Tianjin Mitsumi Electric Co., Ltd. has proven that creation of corporate culture in accordance with modern enterprise management models is an important source for Western enterprises to improve cohesion and build up teamwork spirit. What this company has been doing is to bring this Western company's corporate culture to China and to achieve high-efficiency corporate manufacture and operation through cultural spread and influence.

Generally, there are two reasons that today cultural questions have caused extensive attention: one is that economic system reform has formed a strong impact on original culture and values, and the other is that some original culture and values have become barriers to in-depth reform and materialization of modernization. As a result, to absorb the essence of foreign cultures, accept their beneficial influence and remove their dregs has become the trend of the times.

China's admission to the WTO means acceptance of a new system pattern, legal culture and policy system. This is not a passive acceptance but one after meticulous deliberation and repeated trade-offs as well as a strategic choice for its own development. This is not only a choice of economic and trade system but also a profound choice of culture. As a full member of the WTO, the Chinese government would conduct its business in strict compliance with the internationally-accepted rules and abide by multilateral trade principles, implement market entry rules, increase transparency of trade policies and administration, implement national treatment of foreign companies and enterprises, implement non-discriminatory policies, and reform its own rules, systems and interaction ideas that are not acceptable to the WTO principles. China would base itself on system innovations, and integrate and establish its own cultural administration ideas and achieve development and coordination among different values and life styles on the new platform of the WTO rules.

"Inter-blending of culture and economy" reveals one important phenomenon in the nature of a trend in today's social development. Some data show that the US cultural industry export is about 70% of the world total export and is 38.5% of its foreign trade. With the development of the times and science and technology, new cultural industrial sectors keep increasing. For example, television industry, event planning industry, network companies, translation and interpretation companies, job-hunters, various types of intermediary companies, promotion, packaging and advertising industries and so on and so forth. Share of cultural elements in product design, manufacture, marketing (promotion and packaging) and the transaction process or in other words cultural content and cultural value added in traditional manufacturing industry, for example, cultural connotation such as product's style, colors, symbolic meanings and so on, timing to launch products and their promotional modes, scope, strategies, namely, "marketing planning", has been increasing over time. Sometimes, they are taking the lead. Support from knowledge and science and technology for economic development is rising with each passing day. In comparison with farming and nomadic cultivation age, industrial economy age and knowledge economy age are marked with a change process from more reliance on laborer's personal skills to more reliance on technological science, theoretical science or even liberal arts science. Meanwhile, as a result of changes in people's ideas, new product development, industrial structure adjustments as well as economic structure changes are also increasing over time. For example, green industry brought by "green culture", environmental protection industry and restraint and substitution of traditional polluting industries, removal of lands from cultivation to afforestation and grassland and retrieving grassland from grazing brought by the idea of nature and harmony, sightseeing agriculture brought by modern humanistic ideas, social folk customs, history and culture, root-seeking culture and so on and so forth. It is well known that corporate culture such as laborer's spirit and will power, moral sentiment, cultural making, management styles and levels of managers, and so on are blended into economy and influence economic benefits. All this shows that in social reality culture and economy are closely intertwined and blended.

There are various benefits in international exchanges among different cultures and value systems, especially for our country that was in isolation with the outside world for such a long time because we can obtain greater interest from these exchanges. In the process of renewing traditional culture and opening up to the outside world we have a dual task: while we modestly learn the advanced parts in foreign cultures we need to try to maintain the valuable treasures in our national culture. Globalization of cultures is a trend that is beyond our individual will and we should adhere to emancipation of the mind, seeking truth from facts, keeping pace with the times and conscientiously freeing our ideological cognition from those ideas, practices and system restraints that are no longer in line with modern economic and social development.

It is almost everyone's consensus that integrating with the world economy is a huge driving force for China's rapid economic development. Meanwhile, another important reason is what the 16th National Conference of the CPC called "inter-blending of culture and economy". In the report of the 16th National Conference of the CPC, "In today's world, culture and economy are inter-blended and the role and function of this feature are becoming more and more obvious in the competition of the comprehensive national power. The power of culture is deeply embedded in the vitality, creativity and cohesion of our nation. All the members in CPC should profoundly recognize the strategic significance of cultural construction and promote development and prosperity of the socialist culture." The discussions in the 16th National Conference of the CPC have profoundly elaborated the close and inner relationship between cultural and economic development and rise of our nation.

Comparative cultural theories are of the opinion that you cannot study economy independently from social culture. In economic activities, human behavior influences culture incessantly, including such elements as psychology, consciousness, ideas, ways of thinking, national character and so on. Once a social system opens its door to the outside world, no matter what your subjective consciousness is, foreign cultures will actually spread to all walks of social life.

How we evaluate the cultural effect of this type of conflicts and blending is relevant to the question on which attitude we have toward cultural opening up. Through the cultural opening up, with a clear mind and determination, we can introduce, absorb and blend the beneficial parts in foreign cultures so as to benefit infusing fresh blood into our national culture and speeding up process of cultural modernization in China. As a result, absorption of foreign cultures plays a decisive role in reform and opening up to the outside world. Opening up to the outside world is not only opening up in economy but also opening up in ideology and culture. We can even say that cultural opening up and then emancipation of mind is an important prerequisite to fully utilizing globalization of economies to promote economic development. Meanwhile, this is also an important content in further promoting opening up in the national economy.

II. Demonstration of reform and opening up to the outside world bringing cultural impacts

Reform and opening up to the outside world would inevitably bring cultural impacts. The impacts would first be shown in a narrow sense in cultural life, namely, people's spiritual and cultural life. Many people should recall in the early period of reform and opening up to the outside world Teresa Teng's songs made their way into mainland China and quite a number of people called them "decadent music". However, in the arts arena nowadays, it is commonly seen by the people to have cultures from other parts of the world. You can find classical music from Vienna, and modern rock and roll from the US, all of which have found extensive clientele in China. Young people, after experiencing Hong Kong and Taiwan music, TV shows and arts, welcomed "South Korea fad". In general, when China opened up its doors, with emancipation of mind movement one after another, the Chinese people no longer adopted a doubtless and resistant attitude but instead they embraced with open arms all valuable things in the world and opened up their eyes to look for all things that are beneficial to economic development and social progress in China. After their doubtful attitude on foreign cultural impact, the Chinese people quickly adopted a blending and absorbing approach.[①]

The cultural impact brought by reform and opening up to the outside world has been felt obviously internally in a large number of foreign-invested enterprises. Owing to differences in Sino-foreign cultural ideas, the original cultural ideas held by many Chinese employees are in conflict and friction with those held by foreign employees. At the same time when a huge amount of foreign investment was introduced since reform and opening up to the outside world, foreigners are more and more blended into the Chinese market. It is nothing new that Chinese employees are working together with foreign employees. Americans are viewed as passionate, Germans are precise and French are romantic ... However, owing to different cultural backgrounds, in some enterprises where Chinese employees and foreigners are co-workers, communication barriers and cultural conflicts often occurred. During the early days of reform and opening up to the outside world, some familiar scenes were certain Chinese employees who used to work in Chinese state-owned enterprises in the so-called "Common Rice Pot" found it very hard to adjust to their new employers' keen internal competition and ruthless elimination.

Another impact stemmed from the relationship between government agencies and enterprises as well as government's economic administration system and mode. During the almost 30 years of planned economy period in China, the resultant exclusive state-owned enterprises were the only economic system. This was reflected in the economic administration of the government in that enterprises were viewed as affiliates and subordinates of the government and enterprises often believed that their development was determined by the resources provided to them by the government. Inside these enterprises, many managers and employees believed

---

[①] Liu Dongchao. *Globalization Age and Contemporary Culture in China*. www.confucius2000.com.

that their own development was determined by their relationship with their superiors, the government. Cultural ideas formed under this system were inevitably characterized with "Common Rice Pot". Since reform and opening up to the outside world, with the in-depth marketization of the economic system, state-owned capital was withdrawn from a large number of downstream industries, which made them "industries with general competitiveness". In these industries, the players were not those state-owned enterprises anymore but instead were non-state-owned enterprises such as township and village-owned, collectively-owned, privately-owned, foreign-invested and "shareholding" ones. Inside these industries, what these enterprises faced was not only competition from similar enterprises in the regions, but actually indirect competition from enterprises all over China and the world. Enterprises without competitiveness were mercilessly eliminated. Employees without competitiveness often faced the risk of being eliminated from their positions. There was no room allowed in these enterprises for "Common Rice Pot" people who drifted along only and the space for exclusive reliance on government-provided resources for survival was quickly fading. Many enterprises had to face bankruptcy impact and many employees were threatened "being laid off". Market competitiveness gradually impacted the relationship between the government and enterprises and so was the case with interpersonal relationship inside these enterprises and it was obvious that original government administration ideas and administration culture were affected. Reaction to this impact in culture was that first some people were doubtful about reform and opening up to the outside world and some believed that foreign investment weakened the government's adjustment and control power of industries and some believed that foreign investors occupied the market and squeezed the development space that Chinese enterprises used to enjoy and some believed that rise in foreign-invested, township and village-owned, collectively-owned and privately-owned enterprises was liable for bankruptcy of state-owned enterprises. All these ideas were actually old-fashioned economic administration and economic development ones and were in conflict with new cultural ideas. Opening up brought development and maturity of the market economy and changes in the relationship between the government and enterprises. What today's China shows is that the party in power, if it fails to represent the interests of as many people as possible and fails to represent the development direction of the social productivity and fails to represent the progress direction of the advanced culture, will be discarded by the society and by the people.

During China's more than one decade negotiations with the WTO for China's admission, "wolf cry" lingered in our ears. In the midst of this surge, China's ship of reform and opening up to the outside world marched fearlessly onward and left all the complaints behind it. Now we can see that the root of this cultural shock resulted from the bang of two different economic systems. This cultural shock was inevitable as China was in a transition process from its closed planned economy to participation in globalization of economies. Nowadays, young people of the new generation are accustomed to the internationally-accepted thinking modes. Unlike their parents, they do not pin their hope of job security and livelihood and career development on the "Iron Rice Bowl" and "Common Rice Pot" provided by their enterprises. They are very clear that their own development only relies on competition and cooperation and their contribution to their society. It is the government and society's responsibility for their own safety, not their enterprises' responsibility anymore. These seemingly tiny changes are actually the conscious or unconscious adjustments in cultural ideas after the Chinese people withstood foreign cultural shocks. From this sense, the government is no longer director of the economy and initiator of economic development. Instead the government is a judge, guard and public servant who creates beneficial social environment for this development, system norms and game rules. Moreover, their power should also represent and safeguard the people's interests. The change in the relationship between enterprises and government and between government and its people is inevitable as a result of marketization of the market economy and also an important representation of the cultural change.

In some government agencies and functional departments where reform relatively lagged behind, certain old-fashioned administration styles and certain outdated policies and laws and regulations were often in conflict with foreign cultures. For example, some foreign-invested enterprises were often puzzled by the red-tape examination and approval procedures and longwinded waiting period in some departments. With the dual impact both from economy and culture, the government's administration culture is also undergoing a huge change. First, government's direct administration on enterprise matters, big and small, changed to indirect administration, from participation to intervention and service. The government's dual role originally as both a drafter of industry rules and operator of enterprise capital changed to one status, namely, guardian of a fair social competition environment. This change process is unfinished. In some upstream industries, this dual government role still lingers. Even in many downstream industries that are marketized government's influence over micro-economy is still kept to some extent through its administrative adjustment and control over resources. But, it is the trend for changes in government administration culture no matter how difficult the process of reform and opening up to the outside world is. This change will intensify till a brand-new socialist market economy system is established. The driving force behind this change comes from the function of the economic rules. In an open international competition, whoever cherishes the outmoded and preserves the outworn will be mercilessly eliminated. The state keeps promulgating one reform plan and policy after another and actively and step by step moves reform forward. Currently, in many upstream industries, a great number of large-scale state-managed enterprises, with the promotion of the state policies, laws and regulations, are undergoing extensive Sino-foreign investment and shareholding reforms. And in "industries with general competition", various administrative permissions and examinations and approvals by the government, also under the promotion of new administrative laws and regulations that the government keeps drafting, are undergoing one wave after another of quick and simplified processes. The direction of this trend is very clear. In the process of reform and opening up to the outside world, the government's administration culture will inevitably enter a uniform orbit with the requirements of the market economy.

With the cultural impact and blending, in Chinese enterprises, the "Common Rice Pot" that was popular lost its appeal too. Employees in enterprises are already accustomed to the competition both from the market and within their enterprises. However, owing to culture's profundity and stability, it is fair to say that in the future cultural shocks and frictions inside enterprises will continue to exist for a long time. This is especially true in foreign-invested enterprises where in many respects

Chinese and foreign employees differ in their values including differences in traditional cultures, religious beliefs, racial superiority, barriers in language and communication and so on. The differences and shocks in these areas will exist for a long time in China's process to be integrated with world economy and cultures. It is believed that as China blends with the world in a more in-depth manner, these shocks will be better solved gradually.

III. Demonstration of reform and opening up to the outside world and cultural blending

Collision and blending between foreign cultures and the Chinese traditional culture are mostly represented in the cross-culture management in multinational enterprises. Investors and managers from various places in the world and with all kinds of cultural ideas that are extremely different from the Chinese traditional culture come to China and work with many Chinese employees in groups. Everyday collision and blending between the two cultures occur here. Here cultures, values, modes of thinking, standards of behavior, languages, customs and beliefs have marked differences. People with different cultural backgrounds differ greatly in their management ideas and modes of management. This results in cultural frictions and conflicts. If these conflicts and contradiction cannot be satisfactorily resolved operation and development of multinational enterprises would encounter barriers or even failures. "Cultural conflict" is an objective process that multinational enterprises have to face when they are operating in different countries. How multinational enterprises adopt different "cross-cultural management" strategies with an aim at host countries with cultures completely different from their own becomes a critical question that means success or failure.

Edward Burnett Tylor, founder of cultural anthropology, defines culture as "Culture, or civilization, taken in its broad, ethnographic sense, is that complex whole which includes knowledge, belief, art, morals, law, custom, and any other capabilities and habits acquired by man as a member of society." And "cultural differences" mean differences among countries and peoples in culture.

If operators in multinational companies fail to successfully handle the "cultural differences" inside their companies the "cultural conflicts" would be bound to follow.

The so-called "cultural conflict" means a process of mutual opposition and rejection between different forms of cultures or cultural elements. It refers to conflicts as a result of cultural differences between multinational companies and their host countries when the former are operating in the latter. It also includes conflicts as a result of employees with different cultural backgrounds inside one enterprise.

Over the past two decades, almost all the multinational companies that are investing in China successfully, without any exception, have made huge investment in this area and made the correct choice.

Motorola, Inc., a world IT manufacturing and research and development giant, established its manufacturing base in Tianjin in 1992 with an initial investment of USD120 million. Since then, it increased its investment to USD3.5 billion and became one of the largest wholly-owned foreign-invested enterprises in one single industry in China. Its 2004 sales revenue reached USD7.73 billion, about RMB 60 billion and its 2004 growth rate was as high as 66%. In 2004 its cellular phones sales topped 33.9 million and commanded the largest market share in China. The achievements of this company, aside from its sales performance, are its pioneering success in making cultural blending possible, which makes people think deeply.

Once you are inside this company, what has caught your attention most is the internal corporate publications that are posted in its workshops. Among these posters, various kinds of CPC grassroots activities are the most eye-catching. This company was the first wholly-owned foreign-invested enterprise in China that established CPC grassroots organizations. Currently, its corporate CPC Committee is supplemented by five general branches and 12 sub-branches with a total of almost 300 members. The Party activities adhere to the principle of "Three Making Public"—making public Party organizations, making public Party memberships and making public various Party activities. The corporate CPC Committee launched "sticking to our own posts and adding glory to the Party" events and with the mode of "one test paper (Party member's study test paper) every quarter", it aimed to strengthen theoretical study and ideological education and hosted model roles events such as "Follow me" and "Look at me" contests to establish Party members' model roles with their best standards of conduct. Every year Party members were highly praised in their corporate performance evaluations and most Party members were promoted to important corporate positions. About 80% Party members hold various managerial and technological leadership positions. The corporate managers always highly support and pay important attention to the Party activities and allow them to play the Party's role in the corporate operations. When the company is working to solve its problems in manufacturing and operations, its managers rely not only on its technical experts, but also on giving full play to the function of the Party members. In their words, the advanced employees in the forefront are most of the time Party members and their role models need to be fully tapped in the manufacturing.

Motorola Inc. endeavors to establish among all of its employees the career virtue of "maintaining unchanged respect for people, unchangeable honesty and pursuit of perfection". Top leaders practice what they preach by actively engaging in about ten modes of communication such as communication with their employees and dialogs between senior executives and ordinary employees, "I suggest" events, internal newspapers and publications, dialogs by email and so on. Its general manager has established communication channels with every employee. Every employee has the authority to bypass its immediate supervisor to talk with supervisor one level up around the clock. Any matters that are related to employees' interests, no matter how trivial they are, receive top attention. When the company first established its presence in Tianjin Economic and Technological Development Area, details such as check-in and check-out time, breakfast arrangements, hanging of clocks inside workshops and so on, were all handled by the general manager on the basis of employees' opinions and requests and received his personal attention and instructions. In the early 1990s China had not yet offered housing collective reserve fund system. To solve its employees' housing problem, the company drafted employee housing plans and carefully selected sites in Tianjin and Beijing to construct housing for its employees in a large scale. The company provides preferential housing savings funds to ensure that employees, after certain years of service in the company, are able to buy their appropriate housing without spending their salaries. Its workers' union has organized activities actively and encouraged employees to make reasonable suggestions on the corporate management and personal life and their remuneration. It also organizes such cultural activities and celebrations as family day events, sports meets, karaoke contests, calligraphy and fine arts contests, talent shows and so on. These events make employees feel respected and warmth and a warm atmosphere like a family is formed inside the company.

Motorola Inc. holds extensive contests every year in its branches in the world such as quality contests, technology contests, TCS, TFE, EHS and so on. Contestants from Motorola (China) Electronics Co., Ltd. won prizes several times at these contests. After investing in China for ten years, Motorola Inc. had changed from sending its Chinese employees to study at its overseas branches to sending its employees from its branches in other parts of the world to study at Motorola (China) Electronics Co., Ltd. Currently, it is its practice to hold its worldwide CEO joint conference in China every year.

Another characteristic that Motorola Inc. adopted to integrate itself into the local culture is to draft and implement its "win-win"-based four "localization strategies". The first strategy is to localize investment and technology transfers. Through large-scale investment and constant added investments, Motorola (China) Electronics Co., Ltd. is now the largest market share holder in sales in the world in Motorola Inc. Meanwhile, its top research, development and design keep leaning to China. Currently, in China it has established 18 research and development organizations and founded its most advanced 3G (the third-generation telecommunications technology) research and development center that is responsible for Motorola Inc.'s global research and development of the 3G network. Its second strategy is to localize its talents. It has implemented its reinforced training programs, high-efficiency scholarship plans and recruitment plans for overseas Chinese students. It also founded Motorola University to offer advanced training classes for senior managers in China. Meanwhile, it sets up training centers to train technicians and employees as well as wholesalers and retailers with a total number of trainees of several thousand person-times. Its third strategy is to localize its parts and accessories manufacturing. Through its assistance to Chinese suppliers to improve their techniques and management, it has equipment upgrades and expands its purchases from Chinese companies for its raw materials and parts. In recent years its localization rate for its raw materials remains as high as over 65%. Its fourth strategy is to promote localization through joint ventures. It not only works closely with well-known Chinese colleges and universities for its research and development, but also partners with eight Chinese companies through joint ventures over time to jointly manufacture high-tech products.

Despite the considerable differences between Sino-American cultures such as political system, culture and traditions, beliefs, customs and so on, Motorola Inc.'s success and innovations reflect that such differences make these two cultural existence extremely complementary. One culture's existence may fully compensate for another culture's weakness and singularity. What is more important is that globalization of cultures does not only mean that "plateau culture" flows or spreads to "plain culture" or "lowland culture", but also means that plateau culture and plain culture can be mutually blended. This cultural blending process is also localization of some plateau culture or is a prerequisite to its survival and root-taking in new areas.

In the course of development of foreign-invested enterprises in China, cultural blending is always a critical question of success or failure. In the 1990s, a group of German equipment manufactories that enjoyed a reputation of world leaders almost came to Tianjin at the same time. They generally had the world-class technology and rich management experience and their products had enjoyed excellent reputation both in their home market and in the world. However, some of them were "acclimatized" for a long time. Despite their repeated changes of German managers, they failed to find the best way for them to penetrate the Chinese market. Although they had brought to China their products with the best quality and best technology, they had difficulty in taking a step in China. Among this group of German giants, SEW-EURODRIVE (Tianjin) Co., Ltd. excelled and achieved a huge success. This company is a world leader in reducers and its products have found extensive applications in oilfields, ports, iron and steel industry, automobiles, ocean-going vessels and so on. The total sales revues from all its global branches reached 1.5 billion euro. After eight years of investment in Tianjin, its sales revenue rose from RMB 50 million to RMB 2 billion with a per capita output value standing at RMB 1.5 million. Currently, its business in various sectors still keeps growing rapidly. This company has adopted the most advanced international equipment and techniques and their raw materials are custom-made in accordance with the most advanced international standards. However, its success does not only rely on its technological advancement and superior quality products. Instead this company has successfully blended into the local Chinese culture. As a family-run business, the general manager they hired is not a German but instead a Chinese who was trained and worked in Germany and Singapore and he was given full authority. With its in-depth understanding of the Chinese market, SEW-EURODRIVE (Tianjin) Co., Ltd. has established a complete set of client-oriented sales modes with a focus on the Chinese market's characteristics and has brought its German parent's technology edge into full play. This company believes that it must customize its services to each client's needs in response to their clients in various industries. First, they understand many Chinese clients have a general recognition of German products' quality but they are unfamiliar with their prices and after-sales services. While they adhere to the policy of ensuring international standards and best quality, they also have a tight control of their costs. In addition, their corporate mission is the close-to-customer service. They proposed that they need to treat clients' problems as their own and treat their clients as their family members. As regards its after-sales services to the clients, they not only solved these problems in a timely manner, but also fully understood their specific problems and emphasized their communication with the clients in a heart-to-heart manner. This treat-your-clients-as-your-family-members policy has earned this company the impression that the clients are not dealing with a foreign-invested company but with someone in their own family. Family members understand each other's problems and take care of them in a very thoughtful way. With this successful blending into the culture of the Chinese market, this company has achieved a huge success in its market promotion. Internally, the company has tried to dilute its nature of a foreign-invested enterprise and adopted a management style that suits the Chinese culture by emphasizing group honor among its employees and upholding good teamwork spirit as the most important standard for its employees. The company has made its best efforts to provide the best possible career development opportunities for each employee but it strongly encourages collectivism and discourages individualist ideas that are very popular in the Western culture. It requests its employees to be not only active and enterprising but also unselfish and oblivious of themselves and lenient with others. The company's basic evaluation and training requirement for its employees is to work with others in an amicable manner. The result is that the company's strategy to fully blend itself into the Chinese culture ensures its great development and huge success in the Chinese market.

Like foreign-invested enterprises that came to invest in China, when Chinese companies "go overseas" and invest in other parts of the world, they must blend their own culture with the local culture and endeavor to create a new corporate culture that suits the international market. Since reform and opening up to the outside world, with the rapid strengthening of the Chinese economic power, a group of Chinese companies have accumulated powerful strength in the Chinese domestic market and have already gone overseas for an investment adventure. Their host countries include not only developing countries but also developed ones. In these host countries where languages, cultures and customs are quite different, they must follow the policy of cultural blending.

Take Haier Group, China's leading home appliance manufacturer, for example. This company has invested in the US since the late 1990s and won general recognition and praise in the local American society. Haier America Inc. was recognized by the State of South Carolina as the model in promoting investment by trade and its factory there was awarded "Employment Achievement". The state not only provided this factory with the preferential treatment of salary tax refund but also named a street "Haier Boulevard", which is the first street in America that was named after a Chinese company. Kershaw County government where Camden is located also awarded Haier America Inc. its "2001 Community Contribution Award".

One important reason of success of Haier Group in the US is that it has attached great importance to the local American consumers' culture and psychological needs. While the company is expanding its market share, it also impresses its American consumers with its excellent reputation. The products that the company sells in America fully satisfy the individual needs of consumers in design. In 2003, Haier America Inc. won the Golden Hammer Award, an American design award. Its product lines developed from single small refrigerators and small freezers to an enormous group of products that compete with leading brand names.

On July 1, 2004, it cooperated with Target and made the astonishing achievement of selling 7,000 air conditioners within seven hours in New York City. Currently, Haier products have successfully become partners in the top ten American chain stores and won "Best Supplier Award", "Inspection-free Supplier Qualification" and other awards.

McKinsey Quarterly (No. 3, 2003) reported its exclusive interview with Haier Group's CEO Zhang Ruimin in an article entitled "China's Refrigerator Giant". Zhang Ruimin elaborated Haier Group's strategies such as operation by SBU and implementation of localization and so on to achieve creation of world brands. *McKinsey Quarterly* highly praised this strategy that "Haier expands gradually its market share by selling to a small group of consumers technologically advanced products to establish its brand image. This strategy allows the company to gain higher profits with its brand instead of engaging in a cut-throat competition with other suppliers of less expensive products to foreign companies."

Haier's process of creating local name brands is divided into three periods, namely, localization recognition period, localization root-taking period and localized name brand period. This is the trilogy that Haier is marching to the world.

First step: In accordance with its guideline of "create name brands" instead of "earn foreign exchange", export its products to explore the overseas market and earn its reputation;

Second step: In accordance with its principle of "first establish the market, then establish a factory", when sales revenue has reached its breakeven point of establishing a local factory, establish a factory overseas to offer "credibility reputation";

Third step: Implement the localization development strategy of "three in one" to earn "honor reputation".

The first step in this trilogy is to plant the seeds, the second step is to take roots and the third step is to gain results. The specifics of implementation are as follows:

(1) Rely on quality to earn recognition from the local consumers. Haier has avoided the error of the traditional concept of export only for foreign exchange. It affirmed its strategy to create a name brand instead of merely earning foreign exchange by adhering to "Haier—Made in China" for a name brand. Haier

refrigerators were placed inside Germany, its teacher, to compete with its German counterparts by removing Haier's labels and competing successfully in a performance contest to prove its superior quality.

(2) "Three in one" root-taking. Haier has established ten information centers overseas, six design sub-branches to specifically design home appliance products that suit the local consumers' characteristics as so to make its products more competitive. Since 1996, Haier has started to set up its overseas manufactories in the Philippines, Indonesia, Malaysia, America and other countries. In 1999, it established its manufacturing base in South Carolina, which marks the formation of Haier's first "three in one localization" overseas group, namely, its design center in Los Angeles, its marketing center in New York City and its manufacturing center in South Carolina. The company has based itself in the local communities for its intelligent fusion and financing needs and develops itself into a localized world name brand. They summarized this thinking process as "thinking globally, and acting locally". Its advertising strategies are highly localized too. For example, Haier America Inc.'s advertising jingle is "What the world comes home to" whereas in Europe it adopts "Haier and higher".

(3) Preemptive satisfaction of local consumers' request. Haier believes that in order to create a local name brand, only high quality is not enough and they must combine closely with the needs of local consumers and need to preemptively satisfy needs of the local consumers. Haier's super energy-saving and Freon-free refrigerators are a representative example because they have not only solved the environmental protection request from the international community but also taken into consideration the personal interests of consumers and combined development of Freon-free refrigerators with the goal of saving 50% energy. Haier's super energy-saving and Freon-free refrigerators have met the German standards of Class A Energy-saving. German consumers who bought this model are eligible for its government's subsidies.

Haier Group proposed that the key to achieving localization is intelligent fusion, making Haier culture recognized by Haier people. In America, Haier Group did not send its own senior executives to America but instead hired locals to manage and operate Haier America Inc. An American, Michael Jemal, was hired as President to lead Haier America Trading LLC. The rapid development of Haier products in America has made Mr. Jemal believe that Haier is a company that is full of vigor and great potential. As a result, he made Haier his life-long pursuit and turned Haier America Inc. to be the one third market share holder in Haier's global sales revenue within the shortest period possible. In order to explore the American market, he often worked overtime and worked on Sundays, which is unimaginable in the mind of American people. He often took home the software and his laptop for work. The practice proved well that first hiring a local as its president and then influencing other employees of Haier America Inc. by his role model is almost impossible for cadres sent from Haier Group's home office in China. Localization of senior executives conforms to American market characteristics and the American culture, which is an important safeguard of Haier's successful international development.

Internationalization of Haier's culture is also reflected in quality, finance and marketing. Quality needs to conform to international standards; financial operation data and operation rules need to conform to international financial system; and marketing ideas and network need to conform to international standards. In the course of the collision and blending of its corporate culture with the international culture, "Haier" is no longer Qingdao or China's Haier and its home office in China is no longer a manufacturing base to export its products to the world. Instead China's Haier has become part of the entire Haier International.

Haier's experience shows that after Chinese companies have learned or accepted world-advanced corporate culture and corporate operation strategies, they can bring these to a great height of development and success and achieve their own survival and development in America.

Now let us look at another Chinese company that has been successful in its efforts of march to the world—Huawei Technologies Co., Ltd. headquartered in Shenzhen, Guangdong Province.

In 1988, Huawei commenced an undertaking with only RMB 20,000 as start-up capital in an unnamed place in Shenzhen's Nanshan District. During a period of 17 years, it made a commercial miracle. In 2004, Huawei's global sales revenue reached RMB 46.2 billion with a growth rate of 45.7%. In the first half of 2005, its global sales revenue broke RMB 33 billion.

Up till now, Huawei has conducted research and development and marketing cooperation with many companies such as 3Com, Siemens, NEC, Matsushita, TI, Intel, Motorola, Lucent, SUN, IBM and others. It established COSMOBIC Technology Co., Ltd. with NEC and Matsushita and it formed a joint venture of TD-SCDMA with Siemens. Huawei's home office is with a carpet of green grass and flowers blooming like a piece of brocade; its industrial park is crisscrossed with roads named after sages of the past dynasties and scientists. All this makes you believe that you were entering an institution of higher learning by mistake. In the course of its internationalization, this business that was once called "a hyena" has now become an international company—a telecommunications giant regarded by the West with special esteem.

A report published by RHK, an international market research company, shows Huawei products' current market share in the global market. Its NGN and exchangers are No. 1; ADSL ranks No. 2; optical fiber and comprehensive access network is No. 3. Huawei's 3G has now been part of the global first camp and takes the lead in commercial use in UAE, Malaysia and Mauritius; it penetrates successfully the European market and establishes the 3G network in the Netherlands. In 2004 Huawei's business scope covered more than 300 operators in over 90 countries and regions. It not only has been triumphant in the developing countries but also continues to expand into the developed countries. In the top 50 world telecommunications operator giants, Huawei has now ranked 22nd and its international enterprise has taken an early form.

From its inception, this company has embraced and insisted on a full openness status. They believe that only by elimination of narrow-minded regional closeness can they achieve internationalization; only by elimination of narrow-minded ego of Huawei arrogance can they achieve career professionalism; and only by elimination of narrow-minded branding awareness can they achieve maturity. Chen Zhufang, a Huawei senior executive, said because Huawei is an international company, its senior executives pay special attention to international news on TV. Any sign of disturbance or trouble in the world would pluck the central nerves of Huawei, say tsunamis in Southeastern Asia, human bombs in Iraq, hurricanes in the US and air crashes in India. The reason is that Huawei's elite employees are all over the world and they are the cornerstone of Huawei's internationalization endeavor.

Huawei attaches great significance to finding the best connection point between the Eastern culture and the Western culture by making best use of the advantages and avoiding the disadvantages and creating a unique and vigorous corporate culture. Huawei has hired employees from different nationalities and regions all over the world and allowed them to be in complete harmony, bring out the best in each other and absorb the essence of different management cultures. Huawei's corporate culture is not only full of the flavor of Western multinational companies but also full of the Chinese culture charm, namely, creating the best values for its clients with the utmost enthusiasm. Huawei admires creating excellence, despises bureaucracy, and respects intelligent capital. Chen Zhufang analogizes Huawei's international culture strategy as "use impractical means to solve a problem"—change itself and blend both itself and others into one. Despite delivery pains, harmony will be achieved after these pains. Huawei summarizes this strategy as first passively adapting and obeying, then reforming and finally forming the uniform standards.

Huawei's management believes that it does not work if its employees' career is only designed by its HR Department and sustainable development should ultimately reflect people-orientation. At Huawei, all its positions come with qualifications. No matter which positions they are, software development or marketing promotion, managers or secretaries, all need to be affirmed by passing successfully qualifications for different index systems. At Huawei, the secretary's position alone has five grades and each employee has the right to design his own future. Ren Zhengfei, Huawei's President, often cites a famous quote "by winning the people over, your success is guaranteed" to emphasize that the company's future is secured by investing in its employees' future.

In Huawei's market development strategy, it treats its clients' dream as its utmost pursuit and assists them with increasing their competitiveness and profit-making capabilities as the starting point. In its cooperation with AIS in Thailand, Huawei quickly responded to AIS' needs by providing the products and solutions with the top quality and best service and made this client rise to be the largest operator in Thailand and the largest company with the most market value in Thailand's stock market. In 1997, Russian economy reached its lowest ebb and many international telecommunications giants such as NEC, Siemens and Alcatel left Moscow one after another. Huawei seized this opportunity to enter Russia at its lowest market point, made its structure and organization well and elaborately worked there. Eventually, Huawei started its harvest with its patience and hard work. When the Russian economy started to recover, Huawei people's great efforts had moved the Russian market and Huawei was able to catch the first bus with the new round of Russian government's purchasing plan. In 2001, Huawei signed a GSM equipment supply contract of a handsome amount with Russian national telecommunications department. At the end of 2002, Huawei again secured an order to construct the 3,797-kilometre Moscow-Siberia national optical transmission trunk line. In 2003, Huawei's sales revenue in the Commonwealth of Independent States had exceeded USD 300 million, which made international giants praise over its performance.

In its course to compete and cooperate with its overseas counterparts, Huawei insists on its joint development principle with its counterparts. Huawei has earned its clients' recognition by making its best efforts and providing high-quality products and superior service. It absolutely will not harm the entire industry's profits by making some more sales and be the destroyer of the market rules. It would rather give up some market shares and insist on working with their overseas counterparts sincerely. It refuses to be an opportunist, stage any price wars, and disturb markets and it insists on working with its counterparts for a peaceful co-existence and a win-win solution.

Through our analyses of the above success of both Chinese and foreign companies working in different countries with their investment and operations, we can find that all those companies with successful multinational investment, without any exception, have all adopted the basic strategy of promoting cross-culture blending. This is their key trump of achieving their success and is also the necessary requirement of globalization of economies in the world. This requirement means that in the course of globalization by multinational companies, they must combine closely their own advanced cultural ideas with the local culture's uniqueness, make their best efforts to adapt to or blend with the local culture and find the development space for their core corporate culture in the blending. Otherwise, if one multinational company failed to blend successfully its corporate culture with its host country's culture in its internationalization efforts to create a fair corporate operation environment, it would fail in its international competition. The reason may also be that if a multinational company blindly pushes for its own corporate culture and over-emphasizes its own culture's uniqueness, it may well be branded by the host country as invading the host country culturally, and such branding will affect its image in the host country. There is nothing new in failures such as this one.

IV. Carrying forward the fine cultural tradition and achieving blending and developing with all the advanced cultures in the world

At the turn of the century, globalization development that is propelled by knowledge economy has entered "post-industrial age". Non-material and spiritual exchange and consumption have become a typical growth area that surpasses nation-states. Cultural competition has become a focus area in the national comprehensive strength competition. It has become a fashion and trend to conscientiously adopt the necessary steps to synchronize cultural development and a country's economic construction. In April, 1998, in an international conference that was attended by 150 governments, the delegates reached a consensus to include for consideration "culture" in areas of economic policy-making. In the conference in Florence, Italy in October, 1999, the World Bank pointed out that culture is an important part of economic development and culture will also be an important element in terms of world economic operation and conditions, which is an indication that drawing close of economy and culture has started to be blended or even overlapped.

During China's reform and opening up to the outside world in the past two decades or more, China's economy has achieved long-term high-speed growth and China's national comprehensive strength has increased over time. With its continuous rapid economic growth, Chinese people have enjoyed a wealthier life and their consumption demand has also shown a trend of consistent rapid growth. This is especially true in the economically developed coastal areas because their market demand hierarchy has dramatically increased. Great development has happened to modern service industries such as tourism, consultancy, logistics, finance, insurance, franchise, community service and so on. In this process, an important condition to achieve this growth results from absorbing the world-advanced cultures and promoting China's economic and cultural development. Under the current globalization of economies, in order to achieve rapid development, any country or region must blend itself with the mainstream and maximize its use of all the possibly useful resources in the world such as economy, technology, culture and so on.

Despite so many hardships and dangers that the Chinese nation has suffered, it has still stood firmly in the world. This is inseparable from its lofty ethical sentiment and time-honored wisdom as well as its broad and profound traditional culture. While globalization of economies has brought more economic exchanges, it also brings cultural blending. Under the background of globalization of economies, we should reinforce and carry forward our excellent home culture but also recognize, absorb and blend with essence and fine elements of the world cultures to enrich and perfect our home culture. This is very significant for China's economy to speedily march to the world.

Construction of an advanced culture should carry out and tap strongly the fine parts of its own cultural details. Meanwhile, it should extensively absorb all the essence possible from cultures in the world. Currently, under the background of globalization of economies, an advanced culture should definitely be open, multiple and inclusive and must absorb and blend with all the beneficial cultures and fruits of civilization. The essence of blending the Eastern culture with the Western one is to first recognize the reasonable value of existence of the other culture and tap and recognize its cream inside its connotation and on this basis combine its own characteristics to achieve a joint development.

With China's admission to the WTO, globalization of economies speeds up. This will naturally bring further development of globalization of cultures. We should further strengthen communication and understanding with all civilizations in the world to absorb the advanced elements in world cultures and blend them with our own fine traditions to form a new type of advanced culture that is extensive and profound. This is the development direction of China's cultural construction and is also the shared direction of all the fine cultures in the world.

China should stand firmly in the world with its advanced economic development, democratic politics and a fair society and become the driving force in world peace and development in the 21st century. Whether China can achieve this goal lies in the key to seize the current beneficial international environment to develop itself. This requires us not to be "ignorant and boastful" but to absorb the essence of foreign cultures as much as possible, develop our communication with the outside world, maintain our economic openness and blend ourselves with the international economic system and international community.

People's behaviors are dictated by traditional culture all the time. Although social behaviors of individuals or social groups or certain social classes are shown in various forms, there are still marks left that are in the nature of such deep structure elements in traditional culture such as psychology, consciousness, ideas, modes of thinking, national characters and so on. As a result, while attempt in self-perfection by traditional culture to update is not impossible, its process is relatively slow and its scale is very tiny. In order to expedite reform in traditional culture, it needs to utilize cultural openness to the outside world and introduce, absorb and blend with advanced foreign cultures with a clear mind and bold steps to facilitate disintegration of inert elements inside traditional culture to infuse national culture with fresh blood so as to achieve cultural modernization. In the course of reform and opening up to the outside world of traditional culture, we shoulder the dual tasks: while learning the advanced parts in foreign cultures modestly, we should make our best efforts in maintaining the valuable treasures in our own national culture. History will eventually prove that we are bound to attain our grand goal we have craved with the hard work of the Chinese people.

Section Three   Relationship between Chinese Culture and Globalization of Cultures

China's reform and opening up to the outside world in the past two decades or more witnesses China's tremendous achievements in various sectors; economic development, social progress and cultural prosperity have commanded the attention of the world. While China speeds up its economic development, it also faces the question of cultural development. On one hand, China needs to strengthen and develop its own excellent home culture; on the other hand, China needs to absorb and blend its culture with the essence of the world cultures so as to benefit China's economic reform, develop its socialist culture and from the needs of its national economic development actively promote globalization of its home culture.

I. Globalization of cultures influences China's traditional culture.

With development of information technology and blending of different cultures, updating speed of cultures increases over time. Frequent updating of knowledge greatly shrinks shares and influence of traditional culture. This reality of update in culture that is faster and stronger than culture inheritance has caused crisis and loss of traditional culture. Some people believe loss of traditional culture will make culture grass without roots and it will be hard to form a systematic culture system in the new cultural elements that keep updating. Some other people believe cultural transmission and inheritance is the fundament and safeguard for a country to form its cohesion. We may say that globalization of cultures has now exerted a significant influence on China's traditional culture.

a. Globalization of cultures and globalization of economies

Globalization of cultures is driven by indefinite expansion of capital.[1] Capital's pursuit of profits makes it penetrate into the cultural sector from the economic sector. Global dumping of cultural commodities can not only bring high direct profits but also reshape and reinforce the world system that the West needs through spread of the Western way of life, mode of consumption and value ideas and will bring the West more long-term indirect interests in other areas. Development in information technology provides realistic information for globalization of cultures. And it is exactly development in information technology that makes possibility turn into reality. Modern duplicating technology and long-distance communications technology create modern media and promote mass production of cultural products and allow culture industry's rapid rise. Information highway also becomes the cultural expansion highway. However, culture is a dynamic, developmental, ever

---

[1] Ye Hong. *Formation of Globalization of Cultures and Its Consequence.* Cited from http://culstudies.com.

enriching and perfecting system. In the course of a culture's communication and exchange with different cultures, it will keep loaning and absorbing the fine parts of heterogeneous cultures and discarding its own disadvantages. This type of historical process of cultural exchanges is just the process of culture trending toward globalization. In globalization of cultures, owing to people's sacred nature and general human nature as well as human being's consciousness and recognition of cultural tendency, countries will surpass restrictions on regions, nationalities, nations and political systems to form extensive cultural recognition in the globe so as to promote the ever blending of their cultures in the world.

China's traditional culture and the Western culture are quite complementary. Globalization of cultures has promoted blending of China's traditional culture with other cultures. Viewed from the materialistic perspective, globalization of economies has increased variety of consumable commodities in various countries. At the same time of consumption of overseas commodities, the countries start to understand, familiarize with and accept foreign cultures embedded in these commodities. Viewed from the systematic perspective, globalization of economies is established on the basis of market economy. In order to suit the globalization trend, countries have seized the opportunity that globalization has brought to reform successively portions in their economic systems that are unfit for development of market economy so as to promote global spread of market economy spirit. In addition, frictions and conflicts in the course of economic development have promoted various types of international rules and customary practices. Viewed from the spiritual perspective, with expansion of globalization, cultures of various countries have shown a tendency of blending. Although the culture of each country and nationality maintains its peculiarity to a relative extent, they have completed some partial blending that has formed a global culture. This type of culture, as the common ingredient, exists in the culture of every country and nationality. Generation of this global culture means that a type of common value that surpassed national boundaries, social systems, and ideology has become reality.

Blending of global cultures has in turn further promoted development in globalization of economies. Acceptance of foreign cultures has expedited import of foreign commodities with the same cultural background. Expansion of market economy rules on the global arena has reduced barriers to flows of international trade and international capital, which has laid a system foundation for the global flow of the world resources. International rules and international customary practices have provided a uniform yardstick for international economic exchanges. Meanwhile, formation of globalization of cultures has reduced differences among cultures. A common cultural background is a prerequisite to successful operation in host countries of foreign marketing methods and operation and management ideas. As a result, decrease in differences among cultures is beneficial to reducing "cultural barriers" that cause multinational operation risks. More importantly, formation of the common value in the global culture leads to a uniform selection standard and behavior yardstick that people can use on a global basis and this reduces unpredictability of economic agent behaviors in multinational operation. Therefore, we can believe that globalization of economies and globalization of cultures are an in-depth reflection of the relationship between economy and culture on the global scope.

b. Globalization of cultures and national culture

No single culture will remain advanced all the time. Cultural development is a dynamic process. Globalization has involved all the countries and nationalities in the world in the modernization process. However, from the very beginning, this process is conducted under the condition of inequality and strong and weak extremes between the developed countries and the developing ones. Generally speaking, the developed countries are at the status of beneficiaries and their cultural spirit, values and so on are allowed to expand and their entity is to be given full play. Although globalization provides the developing countries with opportunities, faced with the advanced advantages of the developed countries, their national cultures are placed at the marginal status. Globalization of cultures has brought some changes and consequences to countries in the world. On one hand, they caused recognition crisis for cultures and on the other hand, they led to more cultural conflicts. While globalization of cultures has challenged cultures of the nations, they have also brought them development opportunities. The width and depth of mutual opening, mutual exchanging and blending among global cultural systems is unprecedented. This type of more extensive and more inclusive diversified space is beneficial to healthy development of cultures. We can say that in the course of the transition of foreign cultures into local cultures, globalization of cultures develops and promotes the national cultures. The first one is that after historical cleansing traditional national cultures have precipitated to form a relatively relevant system. This system will not be broken within a short period of time, especially in that the core part has a relative stability. In addition, in the interaction between economy and culture, evolution in culture is an advancing and continuing process. In the traditional cultures, although some elements that are not suitable to globalization of economies exist, some active elements that are excellent exist as well. These active elements should not be discarded in the wave of globalization of economies but instead should be inherited and carried forward. The second one is that one country or nation's very existence has its cultural foundation that is different from other cultures. Globalization of economies has not eliminated the political boundaries among countries. Every country still communicates with other countries from its own best interests. The presence of a country's national interests requires each country to act with its independence to advocate and support its home culture. The third one is that foreign cultures cannot completely shake off the home culture in their collisions, conflicts and blending with the home culture so as to entirely take roots in the home country. Foreign cultures must respect the fine elements in the home culture and while they impact the home culture they must adapt to the macro-environment of the home culture. In their breaking-in period the passive elements in the foreign cultures that are not beneficial to development of the home culture should be discarded and their active elements should be maintained. This precipitation process is also the process of localization of foreign cultures.

c. Coordination of culture and economy for large developing countries under globalization of economies

Development history of the developing countries for more than half of a century shows us that strategy of full substitution for imports does not work. Sufficient use of the global market, introduction of foreign technology and capital and development of export-oriented economy are the only way to faster economic development. The more blended the home culture is with foreign cultures, the more helpful it is to in-depth development of reform and opening up to the outside world.

The goal for economic system reform of large developing countries is to establish or perfect the market economy. Transition from a planned economy to a market economy and perfection of the market economy definitely lead to changes in social and economic structure and political structure. Either changes in the economic structure or changes in the political structure result in the process that the social in-depth structure and psychological structure of the people in society experience cultural updating. Cultural support will make the political environment more stable. By such means as education, science and technology, ideology and ethics, literature, arts and so on, people are encouraged to support reform in some links in the political superstructure so as to expand space for democracy and freedom and to coordinate and integrate various types of social relationships to promote economic reform and development. If the political environment lacks support from an excellent culture, old-fashioned thinking in ideology will definitely block reform in some links in the political superstructure and will lead to the absolutism in policies and strategies, which will obstruct the economic development. A harmonious ecological environment also requires cultural support. The mechanism of market in pursuit of profits makes people consider only the usefulness when they are viewing the question of environment and partially use the existing knowledge, experience and techniques to madly plunder at the nature, which causes human being to be challenged by such ecological environmental problems as environmental pollution, severe depletion of the natural resources and the ever decreasing of species. Imbalance in ecological environment will eventually lead to destruction of the economic development and also of people's development environment. As a result, cultural support for ecological environment is just to allow people, on the basis of correct understanding of the objective rules of the external environment, change their world view from human centralism to natural and harmonious co-existence between people and the nature in terms of human being's treatment of the nature; and to change the development view from conquering the nature and basing human being's progress on excessive demand from the nature and arbitrarily squandering to the development view of coordinating with the nature to achieve a balance and treasuring and protecting the resources and the environment in the course of development. Formation of a healthy psychological environment cannot be achieved without the cultural support. The market economy requires that its entity have a strong ability to bear and a healthy and active psychological environment. This is especially true when the market economy system is still at its establishment period when the market mechanism is not yet robust and the market competition is keen, under the strong temptation of material desire, people's value system is under a huge impact. As a result, the cultural support in psychological environment is to simply help people to build up a scientific and rational philosophy and values, have rational expectations of the market economy development, tap enthusiasm and creativity of the masses, correct and overcome hedonism resulting from over-emphasizing material interests in the industrial civilization and establish the human value standards that are required for modern market economy system.

Globalization of cultures has made requests to changes in cultures of large developing countries. Because while large developing countries are implementing economic system reforms, they are further expanding and deepening opening up to the outside world and attracting direct investments from multinational companies. Opening up to the outside world and attracting foreign investments by large developing countries cannot be achieved without the cultural support that is suitable to this goal. Currently, when multinational companies are making an investment decision in a foreign country, in addition to that country's hard investment environment, they must consider its soft investment environment which is more important. In the soft investment environment, the host country's culture is an extremely important variable. First, a host country's culture can affect a company's products and services provided. Multinational companies must make the necessary adjustments to their products and services provided in accordance with a host country's culture. Differences in a host country's culture and a home country's culture of multinational companies can increase the marketing costs associated with multinational companies in the host country. Second, degree of acceptance by a host country's culture for foreign-invested enterprises can be of significant impact on foreign-invested enterprises' production costs in the host country. It is well known that at the early time of China's reform and opening up to the outside world, most job seekers would prefer to work in government agencies and state-owned enterprises. This situation had forced foreign-invested enterprises to provide a salary that was much higher than that offered by public-owned enterprises so as to attract the employees they needed. This situation, however, was changing unconsciously as people became more familiar with and acceptable to foreign-invested enterprises. Even worse, differences between a host country's culture and a home country's culture would have various degrees of impact on the communication and understanding among employees with these two types of cultural backgrounds. Barriers to this communication and understanding can affect implementation of the enterprises' decisions and spread of innovative thinking. This would result in low efficiency in production, increase in production costs and loss of market opportunities. We can say that this type of impact sometimes can be fatal to operations of multinational companies in host countries.

When Mark Casson (2003) analyzed the question of "Culture and Economic Performance", he emphasized four elements of culture[①]: individualism versus collectivism, pragmatism versus proceduralism, the degree of trust, and the level of tension.

Individualism emphasizes personal autonomy, whilst collectivism asserts that it is natural for people to be socially embedded in a larger group. Pragmatism favours improvisation and flair in taking decisions, whilst proceduralism emphasizes reliance on rules. High trust reflects a belief that "other people are honest and hardworking, whether they are supervised or not", whilst low trust reflects a belief that "people will take every profitable opportunity to shirk and cheat". The level of tension reflects the level of achievement to which people aspire, and their determination to succeed. When major decisions are being made, corporate culture emphasizes practical value of improvisation and flair in taking decisions over routine procedures. Meanwhile, success achieved by many emerging countries when they engage in state-led export plans hints that practical but not procedural governments are more likely to make a huge success.

In addition, globalization of economies makes economies of countries especially developing countries more subject to outside impacts. Expansion in economic fluctuations strengthens the necessity for flexibility, which helps the

---

[①] Mark Casson. *Culture and Economic Performance*. March 2003, http://ecare.ulb.ac.be/ecare/Princeton/papers/29%20casson.pdf.

transition from collectivism to pursuit of individual values and from proceduralism to pragmatism. Globalization of economies destroys local trade network owing to outside impacts and in turn it lowers the trust among trade partners. Globalization of communications makes people in low-productivity countries realize the opportunities presented by innovations and growth led by export-orientation, which encourages transition from low-tension culture to high-tension culture. Comparison of successes and failures of different countries shows that the most promising are those people-oriented cultures emphasizing realistic development with high-trust and high-tension. As high-tension level can stimulate competition and competition tends to destroy trust, this type of contradiction makes no country maintain all these four culture elements at the same time. If a country's trust is quite popular, it is not naturally formed. Instead it is planned by the people. Then, simple competition is shown as a suboptimal choice. As a result, globalization of economies requires large developing countries to transform to a corporate culture that is competitive, showing its own values, practical, with low-trust and high-tension.

d. Globalization of cultures promotes China's traditional culture toward modernization.

China's culture enjoys a history of several thousand years with feudal society civilization as its background and has been gradually shaped over the long and ancient history. During the modern society where China's civilization and the Western civilization collided extensively, China's traditional culture was under impact and blending from multiple layers such as politics, economy, culture and so on. Looking back on each stage in development of China's traditional culture, at each stage something new was added and its contents were very rich and its ingredients very complex. Even though modernization of China's traditional culture has been going on for more than one hundred years, modernization of China's traditional culture has not yet completed. Modernization of China's traditional culture is a necessary requirement in the historical development. Despite its twists and turns, it will be finished in the end. With China's in-depth domestic reform and increased international exchanges, we should be more open-minded. We will have a better understanding of the rules in cultural development. Various barriers to modernization of China's traditional culture will be gradually removed and modernization process of China's traditional culture will be greatly expedited.

II. Globalization of cultures requires China's traditional culture be carried forward and brought to a great height of development.

Globalization of cultures brings China to an unprecedented age of opening up. Opening up to the outside world has shaped the interaction relationship between China and the outside world. This means China's culture is no longer a closed and self-sufficient system but instead a national culture that is inside the global network of opening and interaction.

a. Globalization of cultures requires China maintain an open cultural psychology.

In the interaction between China's home culture and foreign cultures, the Chinese people have gradually cultivated an open national cultural psychology toward foreign cultures. First, this is shown in the expansion in social psychological space. The Chinese people have shaken off the traditional cultural psychology to view China's culture as the only civilization of mankind which is narrow-minded, conservative and self-important and realized that diamond cut diamond. They not only have taken an objective attitude toward new things that have never been seen, learned all kinds of new knowledge with great enthusiasm, but also have actively introduced, imitated and learned advanced foreign things. With the expansion in social psychological space, the Chinese people have blended into the world modernization trend with open arms and marched onto an increasingly closely-connected world. Second, it is shown in the dialectical attitude toward foreign cultures. Through a twisted historical process, especially after reform and opening up to the outside world for the past two decades or so, people's attitude toward foreign cultures has become enlightened and dialectical and they are able to treat foreign cultures reasonably and not extremely. They have gradually learned to distinguish the advanced civilization fruit in foreign cultures that are shared, inherited and blended by all mankind from those that are negative and treat them separately instead of rejecting them in its entirety. Thirdly, this is shown in formation of sense of responsibility, sense of urgency and awareness of unexpected development. Since opening up to the outside world, the Chinese people have seen more and more clearly the gap between China and the developed countries, have realized the grave challenges posed by the scientific and technological revolution, have felt the huge pressure from struggles between market and national comprehensive strength and China is vulnerable to attack if lagging behind. They have also understood more and more profoundly that this fierce and long lasting competition relates to the future and fate of the Chinese nation and have formed a strong awareness of unexpected development and sense of responsibility. There is no doubt that formation of an open national cultural psychology toward foreign cultures is both the direct outcome of many years of success and failure in China's culture practice and an inevitable outcome from foreign cultures on the home culture. In an age where the world has ever become an entity of interaction, adoption of an open attitude toward foreign cultures is a necessary condition for the home culture to earn the space to survive and develop.

b. Globalization of cultures promotes blending of China's traditional culture with foreign cultures.

Since reform and opening up to the outside world, the Chinese society has realized the transition from the traditional people to the modern people in a relative degree.[①] This transition is obviously a result of the function of China's domestic social modernization process, and it is also a result of the outside world especially the modern influence. Under condition of opening up to the outside world, people have extensively used all kinds of imported and assembled products, have frequently interacted with foreign companies and foreign-invested enterprises, and have had frequent contacts with foreigners and foreign spiritual products, as a result, they are consistently and imperceptibly influenced by foreign cultures and have strengthened their competition concept, time concept, efficiency ideas, commodity consciousness and benefit consciousness. Consciousness of legal system of contemporary Chinese people is becoming stronger and stronger. They have learned from international legal systems, applied laws and regulations to adjust various kinds of complex social relationships and made the society on the path to legal management. Despite the fact that ancient Chinese society had quite a number of criminal articles and litigation procedures as well as corresponding legal principles, rule by man still had the

---

[①] Chen Lixu. "Function of Globalization of Cultures on China's Native Culture". *Journal of Chinese Communist Party School of Fujian Provincial Committee of Chinese Communist Party*, No. 1, 2000.

decisive role. We can say that traditional Chinese society's "rule of law" is actually characterized by "rule by man" and is simply an attachment to "rule by man". In the process of opening up to the outside world, introduction of legal spirit from overseas has no doubt strongly impacted China's tradition of rule by man and promoted strengthening of people's legal consciousness.

c. Globalization of cultures promotes synchronization of China's traditional culture and the world trend.

China's contemporary culture is a huge system that contains internally very complex ingredients and tension. From a time perspective, it contains elements precipitated from ancient civilization over several thousand years and also has fruits and hard lessons left by both domestic and foreign struggles and revolutionary construction and further it includes a great amount of fortune and a large number of ingredients that gushed into China from overseas after reform and opening up to the outside world. From the cultural entity perspective, it has both predominant culture derived from the state government and mass culture and elite culture. These ingredients have a relationship that is mutually inclusive and complementary and also a relationship that is mutually opposite and mutually conflicting. China's admission to the WTO has expedited China's steps to blend into the world economy. The ever-progressing information technology, popularization of telephones and electronic computers, and use of Internet service by tens of thousands of families have shortened the distance among peoples and among different cultures. This allows more frequent exchanges of different cultural values and provides conditions for understanding of different cultural systems. China's admission to the WTO marks deepening of its reform and opening up to the outside world. Cultures such as foreign values, life styles and so on have come all the way from overseas. This type of cultural trends that come with influx of economic products permeates various aspects of China's society and life and social consciousness with their extensive coverage and constantly impacts China's traditional culture. Meanwhile, globalization of cultures promotes synchronization of China's traditional culture and the world trend. Their relationship is changing in different forms.

In summary, nowadays the world culture has blended with economy and politics and its status and function in international competition have become more and more obvious. Cultural power is deeply embedded in the national vitality and creativity. Prosperity, strength and stable development can greatly stimulate the national self-confidence, self-respect and sense of pride.

III. Globalization of China's culture and Sinification of global cultures

Every society is an entity of economy, politics and culture. Simple and partial development in economy will only lead to social deformity and loss of economic goals and eventually result in economic deterioration. In the 21st century, cultural updating is faster and stronger than cultural inheritance and then this will cause crisis and loss of the traditional culture. Development in information technology and constant blending of different cultures will inevitably expedite speed of cultural updating. Frequent knowledge updating constantly squeezes cultural space and shrinks influence of the traditional culture and causes the traditional culture stay away from our daily life over time. Loss of the traditional culture will make culture rootless grass and this makes it hard to form a systematic cultural system before constantly updating new cultural elements. Absence of a systematic cultural system is a loss of a uniform value judgment standard and selection standard and the domestic consumption market will be divided by invisible trade barriers as a result of cultural differences and it will be hard for a country to form a cohesive and unified domestic market. In the age of economies of scale, the size of the domestic market is critically significant to enterprise competitiveness in the world market. In the same vein, if the home culture can penetrate overseas to assimilate cultures of other countries, this means expansion of international market by domestic manufacturers. As a result, in the age of knowledge, it is a critical matter to strengthen and develop the home culture and make it march to the world.

a. Sinification of global cultures

In view of the localization of cultures and diversity of world cultures, global operation strategies of multinational companies gradually shift to localization strategies. In China, with its achievements of reform and opening up to the outside world in the past 20 years or so, multinational companies from the world were introduced in a large number. With these companies, they have brought multinational corporate culture that is characterized by the world advanced technologies, advanced management and advanced culture. This has promoted Sinification of global cultures. First, multinational companies have to take into consideration the local cultural traditions when they are marketing in China. Cultural differences result in objective differences in people's cultural standards, ways of life, social customs and specific aesthetic standards. This type of differences directly determines people's consumption behavior modes. As a result, in the process of marketing their products, these foreign cultures are gradually Sinicized. Second, investment and production of multinational companies in China need to be combined with China's traditional culture. Many successful multinational companies such as IBM and Motorola are the most localized. It is a key to success for multinational companies on how to stimulate and give full play to the morale of their employees in localization of their purchasing, production, human resources and management. Success of multinational companies in China is indispensable of their understanding and grasp of China's home culture. Finally, operations of multinational companies in China are subject to China's economic system and laws and regulations. It is critical to their success or failure for multinational companies to fully understand and properly adapt themselves to local economic systems. Formation of China's economic systems and laws and regulations contains China's home culture. All these elements have promoted the localization trend in China of cultures of other countries.

Like the home culture, foreign cultures have both essence and trash. An American economist, Daniel Bell, believed that crisis of modernist culture is in essence a belief crisis and culture loses its cohesion and is unable to provide a set of complete utmost meaning in the daily life.[①] Culture has shown slackness. Since the 1980s, many scholars in the West bitterly criticized capitalist civilization that they all relied upon for their livelihood. They generally believed that modern industrial civilization is a kind of civilization form that is based on gratification of mankind's physiological desires. While this civilization brings huge fortune for mankind, it also brings a series of crises such as pollution, population issues and ecological issues. As a result, we must utilize Marxist cultural and world views to treat foreign

---

[①] Wang Shuzu. *Globalization of Economies and Economic Development Strategies in Large Developing Countries*. Beijing: China Financial and Economic Publishing House, 2003: 150.

cultures by being critical to discard the trash and maintain the essence and creatively utilize those beneficial elements that are in line with the demand of China's market economy and its productivity development.

b. Globalization of China's culture

In the great situation of China's opening up to the outside world, while China needs to introduce foreign commodities, capital, technology and management expertise, China's commodities and enterprises also need to go to the world. Culture that functions as the guide, moderator and control mechanism for economic development will naturally go overseas to provide the necessary support for march of China's economy to the world.

The more developed the society is, the more fully exposed the negative influence of capitalist ethical values and the market economy will become. While in the 20th century developed countries in the West had made huge achievements in science, technology and economic development, they also faced a series of problems such as ever-depleting energy, environmental pollution, ecological imbalance, deteriorating relationship between mankind and the nature, and so on. Meanwhile, they also faced grave social spiritual crises such as collectivism awareness weakening, values confusion, moral degeneration and so on. The "social diseases" in capitalism such as "the Beat Generation" that started in America and influenced the whole Western world in the 1950s, "the Hippies in the 1960s", "the Madonna phenomenon" in the 1980s, and so on show the decadence of the Western culture in a relatively extreme layer. These problems together with the emergence of the social spiritual crises made the Western scholars feel that the Western culture can no longer provide the power for Western economic development. Some Western scholars turned to the East, especially China, for their cultural support. In their comparison of the Eastern and Western spiritual values and ethical concepts, they have found that thought of "universal love", bosom of "statecraft and aid to the people", the natural view of "harmony between man and the nature", great significance of integrity, the courage to dedication and so on in China's traditional culture have unique cures for the negative influence brought by the Western culture and the market economy. For example, cultural spirits such as advocacy of the harmony among individuals, families, organizations and the society, restrictions on individual and personal interests and excessive desires, emphasis on personal loyalty, responsibility, restraint and so on can better suit demand of modernization. More importantly, life philosophy and world view of harmony and unity among body and mind, people to people, people to society, people to the nature that China's culture advocates have practical significance to the perfection of people's character and sentiment, to the blending and development among the material and the spirit, part and the whole, people, the natural ecological environment and so on in the material civilization construction and then to realization of sustainable development of material civilization. We can say that both demand by Western economic development for China's culture and globalization of China's economy require march of China's culture to the world. Active promotion of globalization of China's culture benefits not only march of China's economy to the world but also the long-term development of world economy. China's culture should contribute to the development of other parts of the world.

c. China's culture is on its way to maturity

Various cultures will have conflicts and rejections. History shows that flow of civilization and information is not of equal value. It always flows from the advanced to the backward. The ever-strengthening of China's economy promotes the spread of China's culture and increases influence of China's culture in the world.

Progress of any nation's civilization is indispensable of development in the world civilization. China is origin of the Confucianist culture. Since the ancient times, China's culture has always been at the vanguard in Eastern Asia and has always been the advanced culture and the mainstream culture and enjoys the cultural superiority. With improvement in communications and telecommunications conditions, the relative advancement of China's culture in the world has vanished. On the contrary, when the Western culture evolved into a scientific and rational culture in the industrial society, China's culture became a backward one. While China's reform and opening up to the outside world has brought more economic exchanges, it has also brought blending of the world culture. China needs to carry forward its home culture and China's home culture also needs to absorb the reasonable and excellent ingredients in foreign cultures to enrich and perfect itself. While we reinforce and develop our home culture, we need to cast our attention to the world and be good at gleaning the active elements from different heterogonous cultures.

Now China has joined the WTO, which requires China to protect intellectual property rights and allow cultural products from the West to enter its domestic market. Meanwhile, our government's ways to manage its culture need to be changed from administrative orders to service and directions and from direct administration to indirect administration. Under the prerequisite of respect for subject consciousness, we need to advocate rationalism as the dominant culture and need to sing aloud the theme. All this requires that the administration modes of China's culture be shifted and that China's culture on its way to maturity under the trend of globalization of cultures. Even though China's admission to the WTO increases foreign cultures' impact on China's traditional culture, the inclusiveness and unique characteristics in China's traditional culture make it rejuvenate when it is blended and collided with many other cultures.

We can say that as an important part of the global culture, it is not only an important question for China itself on how to develop China's culture in the age of globalization, but also an important question for the world cultural shifts. This will not only influence Chinese people's cultural life, but also influence development direction of the other aspects in the Chinese society and even the prospects of the world culture to a certain degree. As a result, China's culture needs to blend with the world's advanced culture in the great trend of globalization of cultures, and mature in such blending and grow in its maturity.

Conclusion

Whether you admit it or not, globalization of economies always accompanies globalization of cultures. Globalization of economies shows that some degree of advancement in culture or advancement in a certain part has special appeal to production modes, ways of life, social communication, blending modes and so on in a relatively backward economic entity. So generally speaking, an economic entity with some economic development advantage is always able to earn more recognition in its cultural area and then it becomes an important disseminator in globalization of cultures. In response to this, an advanced culture always has the attention of those countries or people with the hope of further economic development and catching up with and surpassing the advanced economies to learn, absorb and then carry forward it. In the process of national cultures' constant breaking through their own territorial boundaries and limitations of modes and marching to the world, under the simultaneous function of conflicts and blending, they have formed the world cultural ingredients, the dynamic evolution process or outcome of foreign cultures, home cultures and national cultures.

From the perspective of historical evolution, globalization of cultures started in the Renaissance in Europe. The Renaissance history shows that an advanced culture always appears in a specific historical condition. And formation of this type of advanced culture plays a critical role in development in science and technology and social economy. Just because of this, when people admire and learn modes of developed economic development, they always seek the cultural advancement in that country or economic entity to some extent. Likewise, one country's culture as well as its advancement in economy keeps absorbing the advanced and rational ingredients from other peoples or countries' cultures. Process of the Renaissance in Europe is a movement of ideological emancipation and is also a model in absorbing all the advanced contents in the world.

In the cultural blending and collision among countries, Japan's culture is of typical significance in terms of accepting advanced foreign cultures and improving its own culture. Japans' modern and contemporary economic development is a type of ideological emancipation to a great extent. It accepted the advanced foreign cultures first, accepted advanced Western technologies and then absorbed and re-created them. What we can see is a situation that one will be beaten when lagging behind economically. However, in order to break away from the disadvantageous position, while one must learn advanced foreign production technologies, one must learn or accept the advanced elements in foreign cultures so as to form new thinking and new ideas. Development and maturity in Japan's economy is to a large extent a model to achieve successfully globalization of cultures on the basis of globalization of economies.

In comparison with Japan's success, in modern times the reason that China's economy was lagging behind and at a stagnant or declining status lies in the fact that China not only closed its doors economically, but also closed its doors culturally and refused to accept advanced foreign technologies and refused to accept advanced foreign cultures, which is its biggest problem. This restrained people's ideological emancipation and restrained absorption and exertion of people's capabilities in changing the nature, and creating material fortune. The outcome is denying the advancement of other peoples' civilization or its advanced parts, being self-important and not enterprising. With this situation, China was assured of its lagging behind in its economy. Modern Chinese history proves that refusal of globalization of cultures, just like refusal of globalization of economies, would lead to obstruction of one country's development in its social economy.

After reform and opening up to the outside world, China has faced the world with a brand-new posture in order to rejuvenate China for all of its people's utmost interests. We pay attention to learning all the advanced material production technology, management methods and economic operation systems in the world and pay attention to absorbing and recognizing advanced cultures. Meanwhile, we pay attention to inheriting and carrying forward our own national culture and its core is that while we adapt to and take advantage of the trend of globalization of economies, we also gradually learn, digest and absorb the advanced cultures in the world that can promote economic development and social progress. Practice proves that globalization of economies inevitably accompanies globalization of cultures. The process of adapting to globalization of economies also contains adapting to or accepting globalization of cultures.

Naturally, globalization of cultures in the process of globalization of economies brings us the opportunities to learn advanced cultures, and it also brings us the shocks and impacts. Whether we admit it or not, the impacts on our national culture we face are basically the outcome of lagging behind economically and closed-door cultural policy. In view of this, we should not impute all faults and wrongs on others. Former CPC Secretary General Hu Jintao pointed out that we support countries select their development paths that suit their own conditions in accordance with their own national situations and complete their development modes from their own practice and meanwhile we should fully utilize the beneficial conditions and opportunities that globalization of economies has brought us to promote different development modes in the world to draw the strong points of others to offset their own weakness and jointly develop when seeking common ground while accepting the existing differences in their competition and comparison and to constantly infuse fresh energy in the world economic development. At the same time of economic progress, we should also glean the essence from all the advanced cultures in the world to enrich and develop our national culture. We believe that as long as we continue marching on our paths, the advancement in China's culture will definitely be recognized, learned, digested and absorbed in the global scope. The reason is that we have confidence that in the history of globalization of cultures, China's culture must be globalized.

References

Materials in English

1. Anton van Schaik. *Culture, Institutions, and Economic Development*. September, 2000, http://www.uvt.nl/faculteiten/few/economic/schaik/ecdev.pdf.

2. Buruna, Ian. *Voltaire's Coconuts, or Anglomania in Europe*. London: Weidenfield & Nicolson, 1999.

3. Greif, A. "Cultural beliefs and the organization of society: A historical and theoretical reflection on collectivist and individualist societies". *Journal of Political Economy*, 1994 (102): 912-950.

4. Landes, D. "Culture makes almost all the difference". In *Culture Matters*. L. E. Harrison and S. P. Huntington, eds. New York: Basic Books, 2000.

5. Landes, David S. *The Wealth and Poverty of Nations*. New York: W. W. Norton, 1998.

6. Mark Casson. *Culture and Economic Performance*. March, 2003, http://www.ecare.ulb.ac.be/ecare/Princeton/papers/29%20casson.pdf.

7. Rajan, R., and L. Zingales. "The great reversals: The politics of financial development in the 20th century" (unpublished working paper). Chicago: University of Chicago, 2000.

8. Stephen Nickell and Richard Layard. "Labour Market Institutions and Economic Performance". Discussion Paper Series, 23. Oxford: Center for Economic Performance, 1997.

9. Weber M. *The Protestant Ethic and the Spirit of Capitalism*. London: Allen & Unwin, 1930.

10. John F. H. New. *Renaissance and Reformation*. New York: John Wiley & Sons Inc., 1969.

11. Denys Hay. *The Renaissance 1493-1520*. Cambridge: Cambridge University Press, 1975.

12. Donald R. Kelley. *Renaissance Humanism*. Boston: Twayne Publishers, 1991.

13. Marie Boas. *The Scientific Renaissance 1450-1630*. New York: Harper & Brothers, 1962.

14. Harry A. Miskimin. *The Economy of Later Renaissance Europe 1460-1600*. Cambridge: Cambridge University Press, 1977.

中文参考文献 Materials in Chinese

1. 白津夫：《中国改革 20 年：经济理论前沿问题》，济南：济南出版社，1999 年。
Bai Jinfu. *China's 20-year Reform: Frontier Problems in Economic Theories*. Jinan: Jinan Publishing House, 1999.

2. 陈刚、李林河：《对文化全球化与本土化的辩证思考》，《江淮论坛》，2000 年第 5 期。
Chen Gang, Li Linhe. "Dialectical Thinking on Relationship Between Globalization of Cultures and Localization". *Jianghuai Forum*, No. 5, 2000.

3. 陈筠泉、李景源：《新世纪文化走向——论市场经济与文化、伦理建设》，北京：社会科学文献出版社，1999 年。
Chen Yunquan, Li Jingyuan. *Cultural Trends in the New Century—On Market Economy and Construction on Culture and Ethics*. Beijing: Social Sciences Academic Press, 1999.

4. 陈立旭：《论经济全球化对文化全球化的作用》，《唯实》，2001 年第 7 期。
Chen Lixu. "On Function of Globalization of Economies on Globalization of Cultures". *Weishi*, No. 7, 2001.

5. 陈立旭：《文化全球化对中国本土文化的作用》，《中共福建省委党校学报》，2000 年第 1 期。
Chen Lixu. "Function of Globalization of Cultures on China's Native Culture". *Journal of Chinese Communist Party School of Fujian Provincial Committee of Chinese Communist Party*, No. 1, 2000.

6. 但海剑：《"文化全球化"概念的界定》，《武汉教育学院学报》，第 18 卷第 4 期，1999 年 8 月。
Dan Haijian. "Definition of Concept of 'Globalization of Cultures'". *Journal of Wuhan Education College*, No. 4, Volume 18, August, 1999.

7. 丁立群：《文化全球化：价值断裂与融合》，《哲学研究》，2000 年第 12 期。
Ding Liqun. "Globalization of Cultures: Breaking and Blending in Value". *Philosophy Study*, No. 12, 2000.

8. 高波、张志鹏：《文化与经济发展：一个文献评述》，《江海学刊》，2004 年第 1 期。
Gao Bo, Zhang Zhipeng. "Culture and Economic Development: Comments on Literature". *Jianghai Journal*, No. 1, 2004.

9. 高永晨：《对文化全球化的几点理解》，《南京林业大学学报（人文社会科学版）》，第1卷第4期，2001年12月。

Gao Yongchen. "Some Understanding on Globalization of Cultures". *Journal of Nanjing Forestry University (Liberal Arts and Social Science Edition)*, No. 4, Volume 1, December, 2001.

10. 顾宁、张振：《传统文化的发展趋势——兼论传统文化与市场经济新理念的矛盾》，《社会科学论坛》，2004年第8期。

Gu Ning, Zhang Zhen. "Development Trends in Traditional Culture—On Contraction Between Traditional Culture and New Ideas in Market Economy". *Social Sciences Forum*, No. 8, 2004.

11. 郭建宁：《文化全球化的可能、现实与应对》，《社会科学》，2003年第4期。

Guo Jianning. "Possibility, Reality and Countermeasures of Globalization of Cultures". *Social Sciences*, No. 4, 2003.

12. 侯爱萍：《文化全球化背景下中共先进文化的建构与发展》，《山东农业大学学报（社会科学版）》，第5卷第2期，2003年6月。

Hou Aiping. "Construction and Development in China's Advanced Culture in the Background of Globalization of Cultures". *Journal of Shandong Agriculture University (Social Sciences Edition)*, No. 2, Volume 5, June, 2003.

13. 花建：《软权力之争：全球化视野中的文化潮流》，上海：上海社会科学院出版社，2001年。

Hua Jian. *Fighting for Soft Power: Cultural Trends in the Globalization Perspective*. Shanghai: Shanghai Academy of Social Sciences Publishing House, 2001.

14. 贾春峰：《文化力启动经济力——21世纪企业战略新思维》，北京：中国经济出版社，2001年。

Jia Chunfeng. *Cultural Power Activates Economic Power—Enterprise Strategic Thinking in the 21st Century*. Beijing: Economy Publishing House, 2001.

15. 江宁康：《文化全球化：一个需要探讨的命题》，《南京社会科学》，2003年第2期。

Jiang Ningkang. "Globalization of Cultures: A Proposition That Needs to be Discussed". *Nanjing Social Sciences*, No. 2, 2003.

16. 蒋兆平：《经济全球化的文化壁垒》，郑州大学硕士学位论文，2003年。

Jiang Zhaoping. "Cultural Barriers in Globalization of Economies". Master thesis, Zhengzhou University, 2003.

17. 赖纳·特茨拉夫：《全球化压力下的世界文化》，南昌：江西人民出版社，2001年。

Rainer Tetzlaff. *World Cultures Under Globalization Pressure*. Nanchang: Jiangxi People's Publishing House, 2001.

18. 黎德化:《论经济全球化与文化全球化的互动机制》,《河北学刊》, 第 21 卷第 4 期, 2001 年 7 月。

Li Dehua. "On Interactive Mechanism Between Globalization of Economies and Globalization of Cultures". *Hebei Journal*, No. 4, Volume 21, July, 2001.

19. 李舫:《我国文化产业已成为国民经济支柱产业》,《经济研究参考》, 2005 年第 15 期。

Li Fang. "Our Country's Culture Industry Has Become a Pillar Industry in the National Economy". *Economic Study Reference*, No. 15, 2005.

20. 李丽:《合而不同——关于文化全球化悖论的断想》,《长春师范学院学报》, 第 22 卷第 2 期, 2003 年 6 月。

Li Li. "Harmony in Diversity—Intermittent Ideas on Paradox of Globalization of Cultures". *Journal of Changchun Normal College*, No. 2, Volume 22, June, 2003.

21. 李艳秀:《经济全球化内涵辨析》,《农村经济》, 2003 年第 11 期。

Li Yanxiu. "Analysis of Connotation of Globalization of Cultures". *Countryside Economy*, No. 11, 2003.

22. 刘冬雪:《文化全球化与文化多样性》,《社会科学辑刊》, 2003 年第 1 期。

Liu Dongxue. "Globalization of Cultures and Cultural Diversity". *Journal of Social Sciences*, No. 1, 2003.

23. 龙太江:《对外开放的文化内涵》,《衡阳师专学报(社会科学)》, 第 19 卷第 1 期, 1998 年 2 月。

Long Taijiang. "Cultural Connotation of Opening Up to the Outside World". *Journal of Hengyang Teachers College (Social Sciences)*, No. 1, Volume 19, February, 1998.

24. 陆仁柱:《经济全球化与中国文化》,《世界经济与政治》, 1997 年第 11 期。

Lu Renzhu. "Globalization of Economies and China's Culture". *World Economy and Politics*, No. 11, 1997.

25. 孟宪云:《浅谈我国对外开放的选择》,《创造》, 2000 年 9 月。

Meng Xianyun. "A Preliminary Discussion on Our Country's Choice of Opening Up to the Outside World". *Chuangzao*, September, 2000.

26. 潘治富:《中共三代领导核心对外开放的战略思考》,《九江师专学报(哲学社会科学版)》, 2002 年第 3 期。

Pan Zhifu. "Strategic Thinking of Three Generations of Leaders of the Chinese Communist Party on Opening Up to the Outside World". *Jiujiang Teachers College (Philosophy and Social Sciences Edition)*, No. 3, 2002.

27. 史希平：《文化全球化对中国外向型企业文化建设的启示》,《企业经济》, 2004 年第 11 期。

Shi Xiping. "Revelation of Globalization of Cultures on Cultural Construction of China's Export-oriented Enterprises". *Enterprise Economy*, No. 11, 2004.

28. 孙景峰：《经济全球化对全球文化的影响——兼论中国文化发展战略》,《思想战线》, 2002 年第 3 期。

Sun Jingfeng. "Impact of Globalization of Economies on Global Cultures—On Development Strategy of China's Culture". *Ideology Front*, No. 3, 2002.

29. 万俊人：《经济全球化与文化多元论》,《中国社会科学》, 2001 年第 2 期。

Wan Junren. "Globalization of Economies and Theory of Cultural Diversity". *China Social Sciences*, No. 2, 2001.

30. 王埃亮：《文化全球化与中国传统文化的抉择》,《理论探讨》, 2005 年第 1 期。

Wang Ailiang. "Globalization of Cultures and Choice of China's Traditional Culture". *Theory Probe*, No. 1, 2005.

31. 王健：《论经济全球化与经济一体化的理论内涵》,《辽宁行政学院学报》, 2003 年第 1 期。

Wang Jian. "On Theoretical Connotation of Globalization of Economies and Economic Integration". *Journal of Liaoning Administrative College*, No. 1, 2003.

32. 王立宏：《文化演化与经济制度变迁》,《黑龙江社会科学》, 2005 年第 1 期。

Wang Lihong. "Cultural Evolution and Economic System Changes". *Heilongjiang Social Sciences*, No. 1, 2005.

33. 王升：《文化心理因素对东北亚国际经济合作的影响》,《东北亚论坛》, 2000 年第 1 期。

Wang Sheng. "Impact of Cultural Psychology Elements on International Cooperation in Northeastern Asia". *Northeastern Asia Forum*, No. 1, 2000.

34. 王学东：《文化全球化及其论争的再思考》,《社会科学辑刊》, 2003 年第 1 期。

Wang Xuedong. "Further Thinking on Globalization of Cultures and its Arguments". *Journal of Social Sciences*, No. 1, 2003.

35. 王艳华：《经济全球化时代中国当代文化精神的建构》, 东北师范大学硕士学位论文,

2003 年。

Wang Yanhua. "Construction of China's Contemporary Cultural Spirit in the Age of Globalization of Economies". Master thesis, Northeastern Normal University, 2003.

36. 王颖：《文化全球化的思考》,《山东社会科学》, 2004 年第 8 期。

Wang Ying. "Thinking on Globalization of Cultures". *Shandong Social Sciences*, No. 8, 2004.

37. 王振华：《经济发展的文化效应分析》,《唐都学刊》, 2003 年第 3 期。

Wang Zhenhua. "Analysis of Cultural Effect on Economic Development". *Tangdu Journal*, No. 3, 2003.

38. 吴永年：《印度传统文化与经济发展》,《当代亚太》, 2005 年第 2 期。

Wu Yongnian. "India's Traditional Culture and Economic Development". *Contemporary Asia Pacific*, No. 2, 2005.

39. 项歆妮、陈夜雨：《"文化全球化"是一种悖论》,《南昌大学学报（人社版）》, 2004 年第 3 期。

Xiang Xinni, Chen Yeyu. "'Globalization of Cultures' is a Paradox". *Journal of Nanchang University (Liberal Arts and Social Sciences Edition)*, No. 3, 2004.

40. 谢晓娟：《略论中国对外开放战略》,《辽宁教育学院学报》, 第 15 卷第 6 期, 1998 年 11 月。

Xie Xiaojuan. "On China's Strategy of Opening Up to the Outside World". *Journal of Liaoning Education College*, No. 6, Volume 15, November, 1998.

41. 薛敬孝、曾令波：《论经济全球化的内涵和表现形式》,《北华大学学报（社会科学版）》, 2000 年 3 月。

Xue Jingxiao, Zeng Lingbo. "On Connotation and Representation Forms of Globalization of Economies". *Journal of Beihua University (Social Sciences Edition)*, March, 2000.

42. 叶险明：《"文化全球化"辨析》,《河北学刊》, 第 21 卷第 4 期, 2001 年 7 月。

Ye Xianming. "Analysis of 'Globalization of Cultures'". *Hebei Journal*, No. 4, Volume 21, July, 2001.

43. 于沛：《反"文化全球化"——经济全球化背景下对文化多样性的思考》,《史学理论研究》, 2004 年第 4 期。

Yu Pei. "Anti-Globalization of Cultures—Thinking on Cultural Diversity in the Background of Globalization of Economies". *Historical Theory Study*, No. 4, 2004.

44. 张建华：《入世后再论中国面临的紧要问题》, 北京：经济日报出版社, 2001 年。

Zhang Jianhua. *Further Discussion on Important Questions That China Faces After Its WTO*

Admission. Beijing: The Economic Daily Press, 2001.

45. 张汝伦：《经济全球化和文化认同》，《哲学研究》，2001 年第 2 期。

Zhang Rulun. "Globalization of Economies and Cultural Recognition". *Philosophy Study*, No. 2, 2001.

46. 张晓：《经济全球化与当代中国先进文化的构建》，郑州大学硕士学位论文，2004 年。

Zhang Xiao. "Globalization of Economies and Construction of Contemporary Advanced Culture in China". Master thesis, Zhengzhou University, 2004.

47. 赵俊：《文化全球化分析——国际关系视角下的文化全球化》，《社会科学》，2003 年第 3 期。

Zhao Jun. "Analysis of Globalization of Cultures—Globalization of Cultures Under Perspective of International Relationship". *Social Sciences*, No. 3, 2003.

48. 周长城、何芳：《经济行为与文化：社会学视野下的跨国企业》，《武汉大学学报（社会科学版）》，第 56 卷第 1 期，2003 年 1 月。

Zhou Changcheng, He Fang. "Economic Behaviors and Culture—Multinational Enterprises Under Eyeshot of Social Sciences". *Journal of Wuhan University (Social Sciences Edition)*, No. 1, Volume 56, January, 2003.

49. 戴路：《关于文化全球化的几点思考》，《中国青年报》，2001 年 12 月 6 日。

Dai Lu. "Some Thoughts on Globalization of Cultures". *China Youth Daily*, December 6, 2001.

50. 刘东超：《全球化时代和当代中国文化》，www.confucius2000.com，2001-12-26。

Liu Dongchao. "Globalization Age and Contemporary Culture in China". www.confucius2000.com, 2001-12-26.

51. 商友敬：《中国文化与全球化》，南京：江苏教育出版社，2003 年。

Shang Youjing. *China's Culture and Globalization*. Nanjing: Jiangsu Education Publishing House, 2003.

52. 叶虹：《文化全球化的形成及其后果》，引自文化研究网（http://www.culstudies.com）。

Ye Hong. "Formation of Globalization of Cultures and Its Consequence". http://www.culstudies.com.

53. 马继迁：《文化全球化与当代中国文化探析》，《五邑大学学报（社会科学版）》，2004 年 4 月。

Ma Jiqian. "Probe on Globalization of Cultures and Contemporary Culture in China". *Journal of Wuyi University (Social Sciences Edition)*, April, 2004.

54. 吴廷璆：《日本史》，天津：南开大学出版社，1994 年。
Wu Tingqiu. *History of Japan*. Tianjin: Nankai University Press, 1994.

55. 速水融、宫本又郎：《日本经济史》第一卷，《经济社会的成立》（中译本），北京：三联书店，1997 年。
Hayami Akira, Matao Miyamoto. *The Economic History of Japan, Volume 1 (Establishment of Economic Society)*. Beijing: SDX Joint Publishing Company, 1997.

56. 斯塔夫里阿诺斯：《全球通史：1500 年以后的世界》，吴象婴、梁赤民译，上海：上海社会科学院出版社，1992 年。
Leften Stavros Stavrianos. *A Global History, World After 1500*. Trans. Wu Xiangying, Liang Chimin. Shanghai: Shanghai Social Sciences Publishing House, 1992.

57. 厉以宁：《资本主义的起源——比较经济史研究》，北京：商务印书馆，2003 年。
Li Yining. *The Origin of Capitalism—A Study on Comparative Economic History*. Beijing: The Commercial Press, 2003.

58. 鲁恩·本尼迪克特：《菊与刀——日本文化的类型》，吕万和等译，北京：商务印书馆，1990 年。
Ruth Fulton Benedict. *The Chrysanthemum and the Sword*. Trans. Lv Wanhe et al. Beijing: The Commercial Press, 1990.

59. 叶渭渠：《日本文化史》，南宁：广西师范大学出版社，2003 年。
Ye Weiqu. *History of Japan's Culture*. Nanning: Guangxi Normal University Publishing House, 2003.

60. 邵艳梅：《日本近代经济高速发展的历史文化原因》，《廊坊师范学院学报》，2001 年 1 月。
Shao Yanmei. "Historical and Cultural Reasons of Japan's Modern-time High-speed Development in Economy". *Journal of Langfang Normal College*, January, 2001.

61. 金仁淑、冯志：《强制性制度变迁与明治维新的二元效应》，《日本学论坛》，2004 年 4 月。
Jin Renshu, Feng Zhi. "Compulsory System Change and Meiji Restoration's Binary Effect". *Japanology Forum*, April, 2004.

62. 沈仁安：《明治维新新论》，《外国问题研究》，1986 年第 3 期。
Shen Ren'an. "Meiji Restoration, a New Study". *Foreign Questions Study*, No. 3, 1986.

63. 川岛武宣：《日本社会的家族构成》，东京：日本评论社，1955 年。
Takeyoshi Kawashima. *Family Structure of Japanese Society*. Tokyo: Nippon Hyoron Sha

Co., Ltd. Publishers, 1955.

64. 汤重南：《日本文化与现代化》，沈阳：辽海出版社，1999年。

Tang Zhongnan. *Japan's Culture and Modernization*. Shenyang: Liaohai Publishing House, 1999.

65.《马克思恩格斯选集》，北京：人民出版社，1972年。

Selected Works of Marx and Engels. Beijing: People's Publishing House, 1972.

66.《大美百科全书》第23卷，宜兰：光复书局，1991年。

Encyclopedia Americana (Volume XXIII). Yilan: Kwang Fu Book Enterprises Co., Ltd., 1991.

67. P. O. 克利斯特勒：《意大利文艺复兴时期八个哲学家》，姚鹏、陶建平译，上海：上海译文出版社，1987年。

Paul Oskar Kristeller. *Eight Philosophers of the Italian Renaissance*. Trans. Yao Peng, Tao Jianping. Shanghai: Shanghai Translation Publishing House, 1987.

68.《爱因斯坦文集》，许良英等，编译，北京：商务印书馆，1979年。

Collected Works of Einstein. Ed. & trans. Xu Liangying et al. Beijing: The Commercial Press, 1979.

69. 艾伦·G. 狄博斯：《文艺复兴时期的人与自然》，周雁翎译，上海：复旦大学出版社，2000年。

Allen G. Debus. *Man and Nature in the Renaissance*. Trans. Zhou Yanling. Shanghai: Fudan University Publishing House, 2000.

70. 保尔·芒图著：《十八世纪产业革命》，北京：商务印书馆，1991年。

Paul Mantoux. *The Industrial Revolution in the Eighteenth Century*. Beijing: The Commercial Press, 1991.

71. 朱孝远：《近代欧洲的兴起》，上海：学林出版社，1997年。

Zhu Xiaoyuan. *Rise of Modern Europe*. Shanghai: Academia Press, 1997.

72. 坚尼·布鲁克尔：《文艺复兴时期的佛罗伦萨》，朱龙华译，北京：三联书店，1985年。

Gene Adam Brucker. *Renaissance Florence*. Trans. Zhu Longhua. Beijing: SDX Joint Publishing Company, 1985.

73. 雅各布·布克哈特：《意大利文艺复兴时期的文化》，何新译，北京：商务印书馆，1996年。

Carl Jacob Christoph Burckhardt. *The Civilization of the Renaissance in Italy*. Trans. He Xin. Beijing: The Commercial Press, 1996.

74. R. J. 弗伯斯、E. J. 狄克斯特霍伊斯：《科学技术史》，北京：求实出版社，1985 年。
Robert Jacobus Forbes, Eduard Jan Dijksterhuis. *History of Science and Technology*. Beijing: Qiushi Press, 1985.

75. 希提：《阿拉伯通史》，北京：商务印书馆，1979 年。
Philip Khuri Hitti. *History of the Arabs*. Beijing: The Commercial Press, 1979.

76. 陈志强：《拜占廷学研究》，北京：人民出版社，2001 年。
Chen Zhiqiang. *Byzantine Study*. Beijing: People's Publishing House, 2001.

77. 徐善伟：《东学西渐与西方文化的复兴》，上海：上海人民出版社，2002 年。
Xu Shanwei. *The Introduction of Eastern Learning to the West and Revival of Western Culture*. Shanghai: Shanghai People's Publishing House, 2002.

78. 陈志强、徐家玲：《试论拜占廷文化在中世纪欧洲和东地中海文化发展中的地位和作用》，《历史教学》，1986 年第 8 期。
Chen Zhiqiang, Xu Jialing. "A Preliminary Discussion on the Role and Function of Byzantine Culture in Cultural Development in the Medieval Europe and Eastern Mediterranean Sea". *History Teaching and Study,* No. 8, 1986.

79. 李长林：《明末清初欧洲文艺复兴文化在中国的流传》，《湖南师范大学社会科学学报》，2002 年第 5 期。
Li Changlin. "Spread of Renaissance Culture in China during Late Ming Dynasty and Early Qing Dynasty". *Social Sciences Journal of Hunan Normal University*, No. 5, 2002.

80. 滨下武志：《近代中国的国际契机》，朱荫贵，等译，北京：中国社会科学出版社，1999 年。
Takeshi Hamashita. *International Opportunities in Modern China*. Trans. Zhu Yingui et al. Beijing: China Social Sciences Press, 1999.

81. 李长莉：《19 世纪中叶上海租界风尚与民间生活伦理》，《学术月刊》，1955 年第 2 期。
Li Changli. "Fashions and Folk Life's Ethics in Shanghai's Foreign Concessions during the Mid-19th Century". *The Scholarly Monthly*, No. 2, 1955.

82. 段光清：《镜湖自撰年谱》，北京：中华书局，1984 年。
Duan Guangqing. *Jinghu's Self-written Chronicle*. Beijing: Zhonghua Book Company, 1984.

83. 《郭嵩焘日记》，长沙：湖南人民出版社，1981 年。
Guo Songtao's Diary. Changsha: Hunan People's Publishing House, 1981.

84. 刘佛丁、王玉茹、于建玮：《近代中国的经济发展》，济南：山东人民出版社，1997 年。

Liu Foding, Wang Yuru, Yu Jianwei. *Economic Development in Modern China*. Jinan: Shandong People's Publishing House, 1997.

85. 严中平等：《中国近代经济史统计资料选辑》，北京：科学出版社，1955 年。

Yan Zhongping, et al. *Selected Archives of Statistical Materials on Modern Chinese Economic History*. Beijing: Science Publishing Company, 1955.

86. 许涤新、吴承明主编：《中国资本主义发展史》(第二卷、第三卷)，北京：人民出版社，1990 年，1993 年。

Xu Dixin, Wu Chengming. eds. *History of China's Capitalist Development (Volume II, Volume III)*. Beijing: People's Publishing House, 1990, 1993.

87. 刘佛丁主编：《中国近代经济发展史》，北京：高等教育出版社，1999 年。

Liu Foding. ed. *History of China's Economic Development in Modern Times*. Beijing: Higher Education Press, 1999.

88. 宁可主编：《中国经济发展史》(第四卷)，北京：中国经济出版社，1999 年。

Ning Ke. ed. *History of China's Economic Development (Volume IV)*. Beijing: Economy Publishing House, 1999.

89. 郑友揆：《中国的对外贸易和工业发展》，上海：上海社会科学出版社，1984 年。

Zheng Yougui. *China's Foreign Trade and Industrial Development*. Shanghai: Shanghai Social Sciences Publishing House, 1984.

90. 上海市粮食局、上海市工商行政管理局、上海市社科院经济所编：《中国近代面粉工业史》，北京：中华书局，1987 年。

Shanghai Municipal Foodstuff Bureau, Shanghai Administration of Industry and Commerce, Shanghai Municipal Academy of Social Sciences Economy Institute. *History of China's Modern Flour Industry*. Beijing: Zhonghua Book Company, 1987.

91. 熊月之：《中国近代民主思想史》，上海：上海人民出版社，1986 年。

Xiong Yuezhi. *History of Ideology in Modern China*. Shanghai: Shanghai People's Publishing House, 1986.

92.《严复集》，北京：中华书局，1986 年。

Collection of Yan Fu's Works. Beijing: Zhonghua Book Company, 1986.

93. 赖特：《中国经济和社会中的煤矿业》，北京：东方出版社，1991 年。

Lai Te. *Coal Industry in China's Economy and Society*. Beijing: Oriental Press, 1991.

94. 郝延平：《中国近代商业革命》，上海：上海人民出版社，1991 年。

Hao Yanping. *China's Modern Commercial Revolution*. Shanghai: Shanghai People's

Publishing House, 1991.

95. 梁廷枏：《粤海关志》（卷二三），广州：广东人民出版社，2002 年。

Liang Tingzhan. *History of the Cantonese Maritime Customs (Volume XXIII)*. Guangzhou: Guangdong People's Publishing House, 2002.

96.《清仁宗实录》（卷三二〇），北京：中华书局，1986 年。

Annals of the Period of Emperor Jiaqing (Volume CCCXX). Beijing: Zhonghua Book Company, 1986.

97. 许华著：《甲午海祭》，北京：华夏出版社，1996 年。

Xu Hua. *Sacrificial Offerings to Sea for the Sino-Japanese War of 1894-1895*. Beijing: Huaxia Publishing House, 1996.

98. 江华：《论全球化对中国文化的六大挑战》，《石油大学学报》，2002 年 3 月。

Jiang Hua. "On the Six Challenges of Globalization to China's Culture". *Journal of Petroleum University*, March, 2002.